The Assassination

OF JOSEPH
SMITH

RYAN C. JENKINS

The Assassination

OF JOSEPH
SMITH

INNOCENT BLOOD
— *on the* —
BANNER OF LIBERTY

CFI
An Imprint of Cedar Fort, Inc.
Springville, Utah

ISBN 13: 978-1-4621-1649-2

Published by CFI, an imprint of Cedar Fort, Inc.
2373 W. 700 S., Springville, UT 84663
Distributed by Cedar Fort, Inc., www.cedarfort.com

LIBRARY OF CONGRESS CATALOGING-IN-PUBLICATION DATA

Jenkins, Ryan C., 1972- author.
The assassination of Joseph Smith / Ryan C. Jenkins.
    pages cm
Includes bibliographical references.
ISBN 978-1-4621-1649-2 (alk. paper)
1. Smith, Joseph, Jr., 1805-1844--Assassination. 2. Mormon Church--History--19th century.
3. Church of Jesus Christ of Latter-day Saints--History--19th century. I. Title.

BX8695.S6J38 2015
289.3092--dc23

2015009553

Cover design by Shawnda T. Craig
Cover design © 2015 Lyle Mortimer
Edited and typeset by Jessica B. Ellingson

Printed in the United States of America

10 9 8 7 6 5 4 3 2 1

Printed on acid-free paper

If they don't hang me,
I don't care how they kill me.

—Joseph Smith

CONTENTS

CONTENTS

NOTE TO READERS

*T*HIS IS A story about events that led to the assassination of the first president and prophet of The Church of Jesus Christ of Latter-day Saints—Joseph Smith. There are no fictional characters placed into the narrative. I have tried to include observations of people, places, and proceedings that help tell the story of his assassination. Statements set apart with quotation marks designate words spoken by Joseph Smith, friends, and foes, and on occasion they represent modern-day observers of his life. The narrative is written in present tense and at a reading level for both youth and adults.

This is a not a comprehensive biography. The time period is the last five years and eight months of Joseph Smith's life. This is to establish context as the chase to kill him intensified. I have placed the events in sequential order. The chapters specify the days, months, or years of the story. Toward the end, the chapters identify the sequence of events in hours. To help me align the narrative with an acceptable timeline, I used the *Joseph Smith Papers* chronology online and "A Chronology of the Life of Joseph Smith," which identifies key events in his personal life, visions and revelations, writings, ecclesiastical duties, legal events, travels, and political events (see *BYU Studies*, Vol. 46, No. 4, 2007). I also used *History of the Church,* particularly volumes 3–6. I have included a bibliography of sources.

Additionally, I refer to Joseph Smith by his entire name and sometimes by Joseph. Likewise, I refer to members of The Church of Jesus Christ of Latter-day Saints as Latter-day Saints or as Mormons, a common name stemming from their belief in the Book of Mormon.

Ryan Jenkins

PROLOGUE

HE MAN YOU will read about in this book is heralded as a prophet by some and held in contempt by others. His name is had for both good and evil. Loyal members of the Church, varied historians, and his most passionate critics—then and now—can at least agree on one thing: Joseph Smith was murdered in cold blood.

Attempts on Joseph Smith's life started in his early teenage years. Not long before his first declared vision, a young Joseph was returning home from an errand. It was dark. As he entered his parents' property, some unidentified person (or persons) fired a gun at him. Immediately recognizing he was in danger, he sprang for the door and entered the home very much frightened. The next day the family identified that the shooter (or shooters) found seclusion under a wagon in the field. They found two bullets lodged into the neck and head of a cow that apparently had been in the trajectory. His mother never knew why some attempted to kill him. She said he was a "remarkably quiet, well-disposed child; we did not suppose that anyone had aught against him."

The day the contract for printing the Book of Mormon was signed, several men obscured themselves somewhere between Palmyra, New York, where the book was being printed, and Manchester, New York, where Joseph resided at the time. They hid themselves off the road to do harm to him and stop the printing of the Book of Mormon. Their plan was foiled. The Book of Mormon is still being printed today in over 115 languages. Well over a 150 million copies have been printed since the first copies were released in March of 1830.

In March of 1832, he was pulled from his home in Hiram, Ohio, in the middle of the night. He was stripped and then tarred and feathered. Members of the mob tried to put poison in his mouth, but he fought vigorously to stop them. Failing to get the poison into his mouth, they instead scratched and gnawed at his naked body, saying,

PROLOGUE

"This is the way the Holy Ghost falls on a man." Stunningly, he was able to preach the next morning. Three months later while staying in Greenville, Indiana, at a tavern to help a friend back to health, he was severely poisoned from food he was served. He vomited so violently that he dislocated his jaw and had to put it back into place himself.

He was often chased while en route for personal or Church business. He had constant threats on his life. Many times while in court, he had to be protected by friends and Divine Providence as unruly citizens and juries sought to overrun him. He had to flee Kirtland, Ohio, on the cold night of January 12, 1838, by horseback as his enemies were in pursuit to kill him. Fleeing from Ohio to Missouri did not stop the attempts on his life. The worst was still before him.

In June and July of 1838, Sidney Rigdon, a Mormon leader close to Joseph Smith, gave two fiery speeches that further agitated Mormon apostates and anti-Mormons in Missouri. Their agitation surfaced, and the Mormons were no longer welcome in Missouri. Hostilities against the Mormons began to escalate in 1838. By September and October, a small number of Mormons started fighting back, and both they and their enemies were guilty of "indiscriminate acts of intimidation and hostility." The "Mormon phobia," along with the Latter-day Saints' exasperation with being persecuted, led to lawlessness and what has been termed the Mormon War. The man in the center of it all was Joseph Smith.

This narrative begins with Joseph Smith in Northern Missouri. He is thirty-two years old and has less than six years to live.

Chapter 1

OCTOBER 31–NOVEMBER 2, 1838

Far West, Missouri

JOSEPH SMITH RESTLESSLY endures the last morning of October 1838. As the dew begins to dissipate, a flag of truce is seen approaching the Mormons' hastily established fortification in Far West Missouri. The mounting pressure of a bloody conflict is weakening the courage of some of the once loyal Mormons. George Hinkle acts as a colonel for the Mormons and with a few men meets the flag bearer in the open field.

Joseph Smith can see but not hear the exchange.

Mormon enemies tell Hinkle that the Mormon leaders need to be turned over to be tried and punished. They also demand property and weapons to be turned over for the appropriation to pay the debts of the assembling county militias. The militias, resembling more of a mob at this point, also request that all Latter-day Saints leave the state, echoing Governor Lilburn W. Boggs's strong statement penned a few days earlier. In bureaucratic language it is known as Executive Order No. 44. "The Mormons must be treated as enemies, and must be exterminated or driven from the state if necessary for the public peace—their outrages are beyond all description."

Fortunately for the mobocrats, they have a Judas Iscariot in the Mormon defenses.

1

George Hinkle capitulates. Operating under cowardice and treachery, he secretly arranges to meet the demands of the mob. Hinkle, most likely due to his lapse of loyalty and onslaught of shame, returns to the city of Far West in a roundabout way. Later in the day, Hinkle meets up with Joseph Smith and tells him the commanders of the militias would like him and other leaders to come to their camp and settle the disagreements peacefully. With the concern for the safety and security of the Latter-day Saints, Joseph readily agrees to go into their camp and give himself up that evening, even though he doesn't know entirely what good it would do. Four other prominent Mormon men go with him.

Bloodthirsty men in the mob impatiently await Joseph Smith's arrival, threatening to shoot him at first sight. As Joseph and his friends arrive, Hinkle stays close to the script of Judas: "These are the prisoners I agreed to deliver up." At this moment, the mob opens up a cheerful outburst. Joseph Smith and his friends instantly know they are betrayed.

There are no intentions of agreeing to terms of peace. The prisoners are removed to a nearby hollow. The presiding officer, Samuel Lucas, displays and waves his sword as if some brave thing has just been done. At this time the abductors continue to yell and holler "as bloodhounds let loose upon their prey."

The madness reaches the ears of the people in Far West. Joseph Smith's parents stand in the doorway of their home and "distinctly hear their horrid yellings." This is of great alarm because they cannot see what is taking place. The screaming is accompanied by five or six guns discharging. At this moment, Joseph's father (also named Joseph) folds his arms tightly across his chest and cries out, "Oh, my God! my God! They have killed my son! They have murdered him! And I must die, for I cannot live without him!"

Stricken herself, Joseph Smith's mother, Lucy, has no way to console her anguished husband. With assistance, Mother Smith is able to get her husband to his bed, where he falls back "helpless as a child." Unfortunately for these distressed parents, the shrieking continues, heightening the awful sensations in their ears and breasts. Relief is delayed; assurance of their son's safety won't come until the next day.

In the hollow, the five prisoners are put to the ground and told they "need never expect their liberties again." It starts to rain, and they are provided no shelter. They spend the night lying on their backs in the open air without a break in the rain. The guards keep up a heavy dose of mockery and jeering, demanding miracles, signs, and revelations. "Deliver yourselves, and then we will be Mormons," they taunt. Their language also boasts of Mormon homes they have broken into and the virgins and wives they have defiled. The prisoners pass the night under these conditions.

By most accounts, the Mormon leaders are doomed to oblivion. The dawn of November 1, 1838, is neither peaceful nor favorable for the prisoners. Joseph Smith asks some leading officers and guards why he and his friends are being held and treated in such an inhumane way. No answers; no immediate conversations. On this day, the Missouri militias also find Sampson Avard, a man who is secretly leading a band of vigilante Mormons. He has drawn attention to his movements. Avard himself is undermining Joseph's teachings and is disobedient to his counsel. Avard and his small following are stealing and destroying property. He believes the time for "forbearance [has] passed." However, when the Missourians find him, he changes his tone and his message. He tells his captors he is operating under the heads of the Church.

Avard's secret-oath movement, called the "Danites," takes their retaliations too far. When their disgraceful offenses had come to light, Joseph Smith rebuked them for not being law-abiding citizens. Joseph had not been "briefed on all of their plans and likely did not sanction the full range of their activities." Joseph calls Avard's group "secret combinations." When captured, Avard becomes a key witness and testifies against Joseph Smith. According to Joseph, Avard's unwieldy behavior and his defiant lying are to "make the Church a scape-goat for his sins." As Hinkle is a Judas Iscariot, Avard is a Benedict Arnold.

Another notable prisoner brought into the militia (mob) encampment this dreadful Thursday afternoon is Hyrum Smith, Joseph's older brother. Sometime by evening, Joseph draws conversation with General Robert Wilson of Randolph County, one of the three military leaders who want charge of the prisoners. He dislikes General

Samuel Lucas currently in command. Joseph asks Wilson why he is being treated in such a manner, telling him that he's not worthy of the affliction and that he has always been "a supporter of the Constitution and of democracy." Wilson ignorantly responds, "I know it, and that is the reason why I want to kill you, or have you killed." His response gives Joseph a glimpse of the mentality of his oppressors—not only godless, but lawless. Nonetheless, Robert Wilson becomes a US Senator in 1862.

Some sanity is beginning to rest upon the individuals under Lucas's orders. Alexander Doniphan, a leader in the Clay County militia and a friend and fellow attorney of David Atchison to Joseph Smith, sees the injustice unfolding. He wants nothing to do with the events transpiring. Samuel Lucas, a stranger to discernment, orders Doniphan, "You will take Joseph Smith and the other prisoners into the public square of Far West, and shoot them at 9 o'clock to-morrow morning."

Not fearing his military superior, Doniphan lays down the judgment and his intentions: "It is cold-blooded murder. I will not obey your order. My brigade shall march for Liberty [MO] tomorrow morning, at 8 o'clock; and if you execute these men, I will hold you responsible before an earthly tribunal, so help me God." The rebuke stuns and silences Lucas. Doniphan proves to be a major player in changing the attitude of some in the camp.

The next morning, good on his word, Doniphan approaches Joseph and Hyrum Smith. He shakes hands with them and tells them good-bye. "His first salutation is, 'You have been sentenced by the court-martial to be shot this morning; but I will be d———d if I will have any of the honor of it, or any disgrace of it; therefore I have ordered my brigade to take up the line of march, and to leave the camp, for I consider it to be cold-blooded murder, and I bid you farewell." This buckles the knees of those in the militia who hear the interchange. It causes "considerable excitement . . . and there [are] considerable whisperings among the officers."

Hyrum under oath states of this crucial moment, "We listened very attentively, and frequently heard it mentioned by the guard, the d———d 'Mormons' would not be shot this time. . . . For the movement of General Doniphan [has] frustrated the whole plan, and that the officers [have] called another court-martial, and [have] ordered us to be taken to Jackson county, and there to be executed."

Unfortunately, Doniphan's spirit doesn't reflect the current majority. As the Mormon prophet and his friends are being lawlessly treated, members of the pretended militia go into Far West. They plunder homes and "without any restraint . . . abuse the innocent and unoffending inhabitants." Their pillaging leaves many Latter-day Saints destitute. Joseph Smith's wife Emma and his father and mother are driven out of doors. Most of Joseph Smith's personal property is taken.

Before nightfall, some of the men acting like incarnate devils deprive women and then force Mormon men at point of bayonet to sign deeds of trust to their lands. They forbid Mormons to gather more than three in one place.

Near the hollow just outside of town, Joseph and Hyrum Smith watch two heavily fortified wagons approach. They are ordered to get in the wagons. As they enter the wagons, four or five men confront them. They "snap" their pistols in a rush attempt to kill them. The guns flash and snap but do not fire. Some right-minded fellows acting more like militia rather than mob arrest those who tried to shoot.

The prisoners return to Far West on the morning of November 2. Part of the court martial decision is fulfilled—they are brought to the public square. After a bullish parade, General Lucas allows Joseph and Hyrum to go to their homes with a strict guard around them. They are allowed to retrieve some clothing and see their suffering families. But painfully, they are not permitted to speak to anyone. If they do so, they are promised death. As they enter their homes, their wives and children cling to every part of them. "My father, my father, why can't you stay with us?" one of Joseph Smith's children asks. "O, my father, what are the men going to do with you?"

The boy's supplications seem to fall on deaf ears. No consolation or affection can be granted. Joseph Smith is hurried off by bayonet after a few personal items are obtained.

The shadow of death hovers as they are put back into the transportable cells. The sobbing of their family and friends is unbearable.

Seeing that their sons are alive, Father and Mother Smith revive. One man regains some tenderness and tells the parents that if they should ever see their sons alive again, they must go immediately to them in the wagons. For in a few minutes they would be on their way to Independence, Jackson County, and would never return alive. Lucy, along with one of her daughters, finds the physical grit to approach the wagons.

At a hundred yards from the wagon, they are abruptly stopped. The crowd of people, consisting of both Mormons and their enemies, hinders Lucy Smith from pushing on to her sons. She calls out in sheer desperation, "I am the mother of the Prophet—is there not a gentleman here, who will assist me to that wagon, that I may take a last look at my children, and speak to them once more before I die?"

An unknown gentleman steps forward and clears a path through the crowd. They are threatened the entire way. The man who leads them through the crowd calls out to Hyrum, telling him that his mother has come to see him. Hyrum puts his hand through the tightly bound canvas on the wagon and touches his mother's hand. This touch is short lived; Lucy and her daughter are ordered away by the mob. The gentleman leads them to the back part of the wagon. Here Joseph Smith sits in confinement. The gentleman says, "Mr. Smith, your mother and sister are here, and wish to shake hands with you." At this, the exiled prophet fights his hand through the tightly canvassed wagon. His mother catches hold of it and softly speaks: "Joseph, do speak to your poor mother once more—I cannot bear to go till I hear your voice." Her son quietly sobs out, "God bless you, Mother!"

Before the wagons are ordered off, his sister is able to press her brother's hand to her lips. The moment of mercy is gone. The prisoners will be taken twelve miles south before camping for the night.

The Smith home in Far West is filled with mourning. But again, the intervening power of God is manifest to Lucy Smith. As she stabilizes her senses, she is filled with the Spirit of God and receives what she terms a gift of prophecy: "Let your heart be comforted concerning your children, they shall not be harmed by their enemies; and, in less than four years, Joseph shall speak before the judges and great men of the land, for his voice shall be heard in their councils. And in five years from this time he will have power over all his enemies."

This relieves her mind and provides her strength to comfort her husband and children. The family members accept her manifestation and trust in God for its fulfillment.

Chapter 2
NOVEMBER 3–8, 1838
Far West, Missouri

GOVERNOR BOGGS NOW has his man in position. General John Bullock Clark boastfully arrives in Far West. The Latter-day Saints have already surrendered, and Joseph Smith and a few other prominent leaders are heading south to Jackson County under General Lucas's command. The "royal prisoners" are the prize money, and Lucas has them. Clark desires to round up some prisoners of his own.

Clark collects the names of prominent Mormon men still remaining in Far West. Fifty-six men are called out to form a line. They are kept under close guard but are never told for what reasons they are prisoners. No sheriff or legal process is present. Clark's ego gets in the way of justice. Heber C. Kimball, a Mormon Apostle, is one of the prisoners. He has just returned from a mission in England where about 1,500 people joined the Church in twelve months. Kimball is guilty because of proximity.

Kimball and fifty-five other men are ordered to sit in the public square. Though he is sitting, Kimball stands out. He is well known by Mormons and by apostate Mormons. Non-Mormon enemies may not know his person, but they have heard his name and know his allegiance to Joseph Smith. Kimball bravely looks at his guards and his traitorous friends and calmly bears the oaths and curses that his brains are about to be blown out. He and his fellow prisoners are armless, so their enemies' rants are not only strangely abusive but also entirely possible.

One William E. McLellin, who for eight years sustained Joseph Smith as a prophet and seer, now is shoulder to shoulder with some of Joseph's most vehement enemies. McLellin seeks out his once friend and fellow Latter-day Saint. "Brother Heber, what do you think of Joseph Smith, the fallen prophet, now? Has he not led you blindfolded long enough? Look and see yourself poor, your family stripped and robbed, and your brethren in the same fix. Are you not satisfied with Joseph?"

Kimball's response slashes McLellin to his hypocritical core: "Yes, I am more satisfied a hundred fold than I was before; for I see you in the very position that he [Smith] foretold you would be in—a Judas to betray your brethren, if you did not forsake your adultery, fornication, lying and abominations. Where are you? What are you about—you, and Hinkle, and scores of others? Have you not betrayed Joseph and his brethren into the hands of the mob, as Judas did Jesus? Yes, verily, you have! I tell you 'Mormonism' is true, and Joseph is a true Prophet of the living God, and you with all others that turn therefrom will be damned and go to hell, and Judas will rule over you!"

McLellin is silenced and withdraws.

General Clark deems it his personal duty to read the contents of the extermination order to the Mormon people in Far West. He outlines the terms of the treaty that General Lucas had previously negotiated, which strips the Saints of all their arms and property and requires them to leave the state immediately. In his "harangue," he allows all, except the prisoners, to go to their labors and provide for their families' immediate needs with the promise to "sign over [their] properties to defray the expenses of the war" and "leave the State forth with."

And then with some apparent show of austerity as a military officer speaking to the conquered, he says, "And whatever may be your feelings concerning this, or whatever your innocence, it is nothing to me." Ignoring all the atrocities of murder, rape, stealing property, and forcefully driving the Latter-day Saints from two counties in

Missouri, he states, "The character of this State has suffered almost beyond redemption, from the character, conduct and influence that you have exerted; and we deem it an act of justice to restore her character to its former standing among the States by every proper means."

This is an interesting statement from a man who is a slaveholder and will eventually choose secession over union in 1861. But he is not through yet; his speech is full of duplicity. "The orders of the governor to me were, that you should be exterminated, and not allowed to remain in the State. And had not your leaders been given up, and the terms of the treaty complied with, before this time you and your families would have been destroyed, and your houses in ashes. There is a discretionary power vested in my hands, which, considering your circumstances, I shall exercise for a season. You are indebted to me for this clemency."

He extends a short dose of mercy by allowing the Saints to stay for a time, as long as they don't think of putting in another season of crops. He finishes his abuse by saying, "As for your leaders, do not think, do not imagine for a moment, do not let it enter into your minds, that they will be delivered and restored to you again, for their fate is fixed, their die is cast, their doom is sealed." In this, Clark speaks hastily. And not knowing when to stop his contempt, Clark bashes religion and belief in God. "I am sorry, gentlemen, to see so many apparently intelligent men found in the situation that you are; and oh! if I could invoke that Great Spirit, THE UNKNOWN GOD, to rest upon and deliver you from that awful chain of superstition, and liberate you from those fetters of fanaticism with which you are bound—that you no longer do homage to a man. I would advise you to scatter abroad, and never again organize yourselves."

As Clark's time in Far West is unfolding, Lucas has been steadily moving Joseph Smith toward Jackson County, Missouri.

On the third morning of their imprisonment, Joseph Smith tells the other prisoners in a soft but optimistic voice, "Be of good cheer. The word of the Lord came to me last night that our lives should be given us, and that whatever we may suffer during this captivity, no one of your lives shall be taken."

Lucas is about to take the prisoners across the Missouri River into Jackson County. Joseph Smith hasn't been to Jackson County since 1832. They were told any Mormon returning after late 1833 would be shot.

As Lucas and his men, with their walking trophies, near Jackson County, Lucas receives a dispatch from General Clark ordering the prisoners to be sent to him in Richmond Missouri. There Clark will assimilate them with his prisoners. Clark and Lucas are fierce competitors. It is no secret they don't like each. They both desire the public attention of having in their possession the Mormon prophet. Lucas and his men want to parade Joseph and the others; Clark and his men want to hang them. In defiance, Lucas ignores Clark's directive and continues southward to Independence.

Robert Wilson, a cohort with Lucas, tells Parley Pratt that Clark is so "stuffed with lies and prejudice that [he and his men] would shoot you down in a moment." As of right now, the prisoners are in better hands.

While they make their way to Independence, local men and women desire to visit with the prisoners. An out spoken woman approaches and asks, "Which one is the Lord whom the Mormons worship?" A guard points to Joseph Smith and says, "This is he." Confronting Joseph Smith, the woman pressed her questions. "Do you profess to be the Lord and Savior?" To this Joseph says, "I profess to be nothing more than a man, a minister of salvation, sent by Jesus Christ to preach the Gospel."

The woman sought more information and inquired into the doctrine of the Mormons. She takes advantage of getting answers about Mormonism from a Mormon. At this point, Joseph Smith preaches a discourse to not only her but those with her.

The soldiers listen in.

Joseph sets forth the first principles of the gospel: faith in the Lord Jesus Christ, repentance, baptism by immersion for remission of sins, and conferral of the Holy Ghost by those authorized. He relies on Acts 2 to emphasize his points. When he finishes, the woman is satisfied at what she has heard. She leaves his presence calling upon God to deliver him from his predicament. His discourse fulfills a prophecy he had uttered publicly months prior when all attempts were being made to confine the Latter-day Saints to Caldwell County. He said, notwithstanding the hatred and evil threats of some of the Jacksonian residents, that an elder of the Church would stand upon the county soil and preach a sermon before the close of 1838.

Not only is the discourse preached, it is happily received. Many hearts are softened. By the time the prisoners make it to Independence, more Missouri spectators have gathered. The prisoners are taken to a vacant house. They spend the night on the floor and use blocks of wood for pillows.

In the morning they see the mood of their captors has changed. Courtesy and civility returns. They are permitted to speak to inquirers. This gives Joseph and the others a chance to explain their beliefs and religious practices. This "removed mountains of prejudice and enlisted the populace in our favor," Joseph states.

To further win the softening hearts of the militia officers, the prisoners prepare a statement of appreciation. The statement acknowledges the "kindness and civility shown to them after having been taken from Far West." Lucas and Wilson are so pleased with the statement they desire it to be printed in the newspaper.

After five days in Independence, Lucas now has to comply with Clark. General Clark has sent a colonel to Lucas ordering him to send the prisoners to Richmond immediately. His grandstanding is over. It took Lucas and several thousand men to pull Joseph Smith from among the people of Far West. Hundreds helped escort Joseph and the others to Jackson County. When Joseph Smith and the others are transported to Richmond, Missouri, on November 8, 1838, there are only three guards willing to transport them, and they could only be "obtained with great difficulty."

About a half-mile out of Jackson County and well short of Richmond, Ray County, Missouri, the three guards get drunk. Joseph Smith and the other prisoners get possession of their arms and their horses. Yet they make no effort to escape. They want their names, their people, their God, and their religion to be cleared of any wrongdoing. A painful decision in retrospect as the next five months will test their souls to the core.

Chapter 3

NOVEMBER 1838

Richmond, Missouri

OVER SIXTY MORMON prisoners converge at Richmond, the seat of Ray County, on November 9, 1838.

Joseph Smith and six other Mormon men are taken to an old log house located near Richmond's public square and courthouse. They are placed under ten testy guards, all having "a thumb upon the cock of their guns" while a man chains the prisoners together with hefty padlocks. The windows are nailed down and the exterior perimeter secured. Some prisoners are ill, like Sidney Rigdon, one of Joseph Smith's counselors in the Church's governing presidency. Rigdon's daughter is allowed in to care for her father. She is also the wife of George Robinson, one of the other prisoners. Her presence doesn't curtail the vileness spewing from the guards.

The prisoners are checked one more time. All of their pocket knives are taken away. The other prisoners removed from Far West are taken to the courthouse for holding.

Sometime later in the day, General John Clark comes to the jail and is introduced to Joseph Smith. But Clark's haughtiness on display at Far West has been subdued. He can't say much, or doesn't want to say much. The prisoners inquire why they were taken from their homes without cause and what exactly the charges against them are. In an awkward stumble of confidence, Clark said that "he was not then able to determine, but would be in a short time; and with very little more conversation withdrew."

Clark sheepishly hits the books. He doesn't know how to try them, by court martial or by civil court, or what to try them for. The prisoners sit in confinement while he figures it out. The next day, Clark makes his decision and sends Governor Boggs a letter: "I this day made out charges against the prisoners, and called on Judge [Austin] King to try them as a committing court; and I am now busily engaged in procuring witnesses and submitting facts." He apparently didn't collect and arrange those facts before he stripped people from their families and their homes.

"Most of the prisoners here," he writes the governor, "I consider guilty of treason; and I believe will be convicted." But there is a difficulty in the law and a questionable procedure. "Can they be tried in any county but Caldwell? If not, they cannot be there indicted, until a change of population (too many Mormons in Caldwell County). In the event the latter view is taken by the civil courts, I suggest the propriety of trying Jo Smith and those leaders taken by General Lucas, by a court martial, for mutiny."

Clark, who three days earlier stood strong and bold, now is quivering. "I would have taken this course with Smith at any rate; but it being doubtful whether a court martial has jurisdiction or not in the present case—that is, whether these people are to be treated as in time of war, and the mutineers as having mutinied in time of war— and I would here ask you to forward to me the attorney general's opinion on this point."

He wants someone else to make the decision. He is finding it difficult to call it a war when only one side—the state of Missouri, its ranking civic officers, and many of their widely known clergy— pushed aggression to a warlike stance. "It will not do," he argues in his letter, "to allow these leaders to return to their treasonable work again, on account of their not being indicted in Caldwell. They have committed treason, murder, arson, burglary, robbery, larceny, and perjury."

The prisoners sit in confinement for three days before being brought before a judge.

One night in their confinement, the prisoners digest the vulgarities of the guards. The guards brag of their hellish behaviors toward Mormons. They revel in their brutalities and injustice. It is a "tedious" night according to Parley P. Pratt, who is lying next to Joseph Smith quietly on the floor. Their taunting becomes more and more horrendous and insufferable. The prisoners' ears and hearts are pained.

"[We] listened for hours to the obscene jests, the horrid oaths, the dreadful blasphemies and filthy language of our guards," Pratt says. They "recounted to each other their deeds of rapine, murder, robbery, etc., which they had committed among the 'Mormons' while at Far West and vicinity." They "boast of defiling by force wives, daughters, and virgins, and of shooting or dashing out the brains of men, women, and children."

Pratt is speechless by what he hears. Yet courageous stamina is swelling inside him to arise and rebuke the guards. He hesitates, knowing Joseph Smith is awake and conscious to the situation. Pratt hears a rush, and "on a sudden," the Prophet Joseph Smith arises "to his feet, and [speaks] in a voice of thunder, or as the roaring lion." The direct reprimand rolls with power from his lips: "SILENCE, ye fiends of the infernal pit. In the name of Jesus Christ I rebuke you, and command you to be still; I will not live another minute and bear such language. Cease such talk, or you or I die THIS INSTANT!"

All vulgarities end instantly.

Joseph Smith ceases "to speak. He [stands] erect in terrible majesty. Chained, and without a weapon; calm, unruffled, and dignified as an angel, [he looks] upon the quailing guards, whose weapons [are] lowered or dropped to the ground. . . . [They beg] his pardon, and [remain] quiet till a change of guards."

Pratt is a well-traveled missionary for the Church on both sides of the Atlantic Ocean. He observes, "I have seen the ministers of justice, clothed in magisterial robes, and criminals arraigned before them, while life was suspended on a breath, in the Courts of England; I have witnessed a Congress in solemn session to give laws to nations; I have tried to conceive of kings, of royal courts, of thrones and crowns; and of emperors assembled to decide the fate of kingdoms;

but dignity and majesty have I seen but once, as it stood in chains, at midnight, in a dungeon in an obscure village of Missouri."

Twelve days after having been ripped from their families and their homes, the prisoners are brought before a judge. Their day in court was a preliminary hearing to determine if they should stand trial.

Someone appoints Thomas Burch and William Wood as prosecutors. The prisoners are fortunate to have Alexander Doniphan and Amos Rees. Doniphan is trying to sway the scales of justice for his Mormon friends. He is willing to stand for the Mormons when it was precariously unpopular and potentially damaging to his personal, professional, and political well-being.

But Joseph Smith has an even more intimate friend at this time, his wife Emma. He sends her a letter on the opening day of the hearing. "We are prisoners in chains, and under strong guards, for Christ's sake and for no other cause, although there has been things that were unbeknown to us, and altogether beyond our control, that might seem, to the mob to be a pretext, for them to persecute us, but on examination, I think that the authorities, will discover our innocence, and set us free, but if this blessing cannot be obtained, I have this consolation that I am an innocent man, let what will befall me."

Emma reads his words under great stress. In her own way, she is in prison. She is still in Far West, and itinerate mobs constantly hound her and her fellow Mormon friends. Amid her loneliness of being separated from her husband and the responsibility of caring for her four children with little means, his next words in the letter bring her some momentary relief: "Oh God grant that I may have the privilege of seeing once more my lovely Family, in the enjoyment, of the sweets of liberty, and social life, to press them to my bosom and kissing their lovely cheeks would fill my heart with unspeakable great gratitude. . . . Oh my affectionate Emma, I want you to remember that I am a true and faithful friend, to you and the children, forever."

That joy of pressing his wife and children to his bosom is delayed. Day after day the evidence is presented against them. But the truth of the evidence falls short of reality. So another day yields more fabricated evidence, and the prosecutors stumble in their illegitimate proceedings. They threaten some of those detained. Chandler Holbrook, who was arrested in Far West, refuses to testify in behalf of the state, stating, "I will stay in this dungeon until the worms carry me out the keyhole, and then I won't [testify]."

For the next eighteen days (until November 29), inquiry is made and witnesses are rounded up. When the witnesses are favorable to the Mormons and the justice due them, the witnesses are either arrested and detained or chased off by verbal and physical threats. According to Parley P. Pratt, at one point they had a favorable witness for their behalf. The following occurred:

> A member of the Church, named Allen, was just then seen to pass the window. The prisoners requested that he might be introduced and sworn. He was immediately called in and sworn. He began to give his testimony, which went to establish the innocence of the prisoners, and to show the murders, robberies, etc., committed by their accusers. But he was suddenly interrupted and cut short by cries of 'Put him out;' 'Kick him out;' 'G—d d—n him, shoot him;' 'Kill him, d—n him, kill him;' 'He's a d—d Mormon.' The Court then ordered the guard to put him out, which was done amid the yells, threats, insults, and violence of the mob who thronged in and around the courthouse. He barely escaped with his life.

Doniphan advises his clients to hold their tongues and call no witnesses. "Though a legion of angels from the opening heavens should declare your innocence, the Court and populace have decreed your destruction," he sadly declares. He, like Joseph Smith, has the good sense and remarkable faith to the leave the event with God.

With not much to go on, Judge King and the attorneys bring into question the doctrine of The Church of Jesus Christ of Latter-day Saints. They "inquired diligently into our belief of the seventh chapter of Daniel concerning the kingdom of God, which should subdue all other kingdoms and stand forever. And when told that we believed in that prophecy, the Court turned to the clerk and said: 'Write that down; it is a strong point for treason.' Our lawyer observed as follows: 'Judge, you had better make the Bible treason.' The Court made no reply."

The court then challenged the "missionary operations" of the Church going to Europe as another argument of treason, holding that this was their attempt to build up a "temporal kingdom" to rise up against Missouri, and possibly the United States.

Judge Austin King, who is presiding over the hearings, incriminates himself. In stunning audacity, he declares, "If the members of the Church remained on their lands to put in another crop they should be destroyed indiscriminately, and their bones be left to bleach on the plains without a burial." The Mormons had every right to plant crops unmolested. They held legal rights to the land "issued by the United States land office, and signed by the President of the Republic."

Apostle Parley P. Pratt is livid. He pens a few months later, "Judge Austin A. King, in open court, pronounced a capital offence, for which a whole community were prejudged and sentenced to death. While those who should be the instruments to execute this sentence were called by the dignified name of citizens, and these good citizens afterwards elected that same Judge for Governor of the State."

The court proceedings are rough for the defendants. And it gets extremely coarser when the judge and jury are drunk.

After each day of the legal nonsense being suspended, Joseph and Hyrum Smith and five fellow prisoners are directed back to the log house for the night. The other prisoners remain confined to the courthouse, which is not entirely finished and is susceptible to the unfavorable weather. There are up to sixty-four prisoners. As November rolls along, Judge King reaches a conclusion that there is enough evidence to continue to contain thirty-five of the Mormon men. The other twenty-nine are to be released and told leave the state at once.

Parley P. Pratt and four others are charged with the murder of Moses Rowland, who was killed at the battle of Crooked River. It's a "non-bailable" offense. Parley P. Pratt was there trying to free three prisoners whom Moses Rowland and his cohorts had taken without cause. No one is charged for the kidnappings or murders of three Mormon men in the same battle. King will order Pratt be held in the Richmond jail until March of 1839.

After days of spending their free time in chains, Joseph Smith, his brother, and the others are charged with treason, the other "non-bailable" offense. This gives the frontier ruffians a chance to strangle all the Mormons in the state into submission to leave while their key leaders are defenseless and helpless. Their trial is also set for March of 1839. Joseph Smith and five others are ordered to be locked up, ironically in a jail in the town of Liberty.

The snow and bitter cold have already arrived. It is going to be a dreary winter. The emotional, physical, mental, and spiritual faculties of these men will be challenged and tested to the utmost boundary of personal survival.

LIBERTY JAIL HAS a 14 × 14–foot floor plan. There are two levels, with the jail quarters below and partially underground. The ceiling of the lower dungeon is barely over six feet high. There is no door to the outside from the lower dungeon. Prisoners come and go through a door in the floor of the top level. The walls are four feet thick. The outer wall is masonry, and the inner wall oak logs, with about a foot of space between the two walls. Sand and rock fill the core of the wall between the masonry and the oak logs.

Two small barred windows, two feet wide and six inches high, offer very little light and allow too much cold to enter. At these windows, people come to mock and insult the prisoners. From these windows, the prisoners reach for food and other items from the hands of Latter-day Saints willing to offer comfort at the peril of their own lives. At first Joseph Smith doesn't even have a blanket as he beds down on a filthy straw floor. Buckets are provided for bodily waste. The food is scanty and insufficient for good health. Occasionally, the prisoners eat poisoned food, unknowingly or out of cringing hunger. The poison causes the prisoners to vomit violently.

Notwithstanding the conditions of his environment, Joseph pens a letter to his wife: "My dear Emma, I very well know your toils and sympathize with you. If God will spare my life once more to have the privilege of taking care of you, I will ease your care and endeavor to comfort your heart. . . . I want you to try to gain time and write to me a long letter and tell me all you can . . . and what those little prattlers say that cling around your neck. . . . Tell them I am in prison that their lives might be saved."

The separation from his family is extremely difficult. In a subsequent letter, he conveys, "My dear Emma, I think of you and the children continually. . . . I want to see little Frederick, Joseph, Julia, and Alexander, Johanna [an orphan who was living with the Smiths], and old Major [the family dog]. And as to yourself, if you want to know how much I want to see you, examine your feelings, how much you want to see me, and judge for yourself. I would gladly walk from here to you barefoot and bareheaded and half-naked to see you and think it great pleasure, and never count it toil."

To help relieve her husband's anxiety and loneliness, Emma visits her husband at least three times between December 1838 and January 1839.

In one letter, Joseph Smith concludes to his wife, "I bear with fortitude all my oppression; so do those that are with me. Not one of us has flinched yet."

The "yet" refers Sidney Rigdon, the Prophet's close confidant. He is breaking down spiritually, emotionally, and mentally. Joseph recognizes this. Somehow Rigdon finds legal favor and gets out of Liberty Jail two months before the others. He suffered greatly, and his spiritual trouble for the cause of Christ is deep. But he left the jail "muttering that 'the sufferings of Jesus Christ were . . . fool[ish compared] to his.'" A poor miscue in judgment, and arguably the decline of Rigdon's role and station among the Latter-day Saints.

On the other hand, Hyrum Smith, Joseph's older brother, is amazingly resilient as the cold winter months pass along. His wife Jerusha had died a year earlier, leaving him with five children, the oldest only being eleven years old. He married a convert from Canada named Mary Fielding. Notwithstanding the persecution Hyrum and his wife had been under since their marriage, affection and love somehow found their moments. Mary Fielding gives birth to their first child (Hyrum's sixth) while Hyrum is in prison. For several months, Mary can't even a pen a letter to Hyrum to tell him she is sick, let alone bear the travel to visit him. This brings him great anguish and worry. When she is well enough to travel, it is February and bitterly cold.

The visits from their wives leave Joseph and Hyrum with greater ability to endure. Any visits from friends and fellow Saints resuscitates their joy and hope. "Those who have not been enclosed in the walls of a prison without cause or provocation, can have but little idea how sweet the voice of a friend is; one token of friendship from any source whatever awakens and calls into action every sympathetic feeling," Joseph declares.

In these difficult days of confinement, Joseph writes that the "things of God are of great import; and time, and experience, and careful and ponderous and solemn thoughts can only find them out. . . . [One] must commune with God." Such reflection and acquaintance with God allows Joseph Smith to prepare a lengthy two-part letter to the Church near the end of his four-month confinement.

Joseph isn't ignorant to the fact that Saints don't always act like Saints or talk like Saints. "We would suggest," he conveys in letter, "the propriety of being aware of an aspiring spirit, which spirit has often times urged men forward to make foul speeches, and influence the Church to reject milder counsels." He also adds, "How vain and trifling have been our spirits, our conferences, our councils, our meetings, our private as well as public conversations—too low, too mean, too vulgar, too condescending for the dignified characters of the called and chosen of God."

And so, the Latter-day Saints are driven from Missouri. Emma makes her unavoidable exodus across northeastern Missouri in February 1839. Important Church documents are spread amongst the Saints with careful attention in attempt to elude enemies who are burning anything tied to the records of the Church.

The night Emma Smith flees Far West, she has an impromptu visit from a Miss Ann Scott. Ann is carrying with her important Church documents given to her from James Mulholland, a scribe for Joseph Smith. She feels some security in passing them off to Emma. Mulholland requested that Ann take charge of the papers and important documents in part because she was a woman and was less likely to be searched by the mob. As soon as she takes "possession of the papers, [she makes] two cotton bags of sufficient size to contain them, sewing a band around the top ends of sufficient length to button around [her] waist." She wore this contraption in the day and slept with the belongings under her pillow at night until giving both cotton bags and the documents to Emma, who then carries them into Illinois.

Emma finds temporary refuge for her family in Quincy, Illinois.

While Joseph Smith is bearing his imprisonment, Brigham Young is bearing the load of the Church. He spends February urging Saints to provide necessary means for the poor of their people to be removed from Missouri. Brigham Young proposes a covenant that the Saints "stand by and assist each other to the utmost of our abilities in removing from this state, and that we will never desert the poor who are worthy, till they shall be out of the reach of the exterminating order." The experience prepares Brigham Young for another exodus about seven years later.

Many honor the covenant. Having been driven from New York, Ohio, and now Missouri, the Latter-day Saints turn to Illinois. A new Church headquarters is about to be born. Joseph Smith has about six more difficult weeks in Liberty Jail.

Chapter 5

APRIL 4–22, 1839

Missouri

$\mathscr{I}$N LATE MARCH 1839, two men who are loyal to Joseph Smith visit Judge Austin King. Heber C. Kimball and Theodore Turley are looking for the mittimus, or court order, explaining the holding of the prisoners. Neither the governor nor local officials can produce a court order. They "confess they had none." Judge King in some rude and hurried matter makes up a fake order to keep the prisoners confined to jail.

Kimball and Turley go to Jefferson City, Missouri, and present their friends' cases to state officials. For some unknown reason, Governor Boggs is absent. However, the secretary of state treats "them very kindly." When he reviews the papers made up on the whim by Judge King, he can "hardly believe those were all the documents by which the prisoners were held in custody." The secretary knows they are made on impulse and completely illegal. Kimball and Turley are treated with respect from the civil officers of the state but cannot get them to commit to see the justice through.

By April 4, Judge King finds out about Kimball and Turely's visit to the capital. He is enraged, stating, "I could have done all the business for you properly, if you had come to me; and I would have signed the petition for all except Joe, and he is not fit to live." King operates in blindness and ignorance because of his hatred for Joseph Smith. He wants "Joe" dead but isn't willing to kill him himself.

About this time, Joseph Smith tells his fellow prisoners that he feels they will be delivered. His optimism rejuvenates them.

On April 6, 1839, the prisoners are removed from Liberty Jail. Judge King is nervous about his questionable judicial behavior being more and more exposed. The prisoners' rights to go before a jury and have their day in court are shedding a dark shadow on his already shady character. He has them removed to Daviess County near the town of Gallatin, just north of Far West. After four months in the dungeon, the prisoners make a wearisome two-day journey with weak legs. They are free from a difficult confinement but now face brutal threats in the open. Three days before their arrival in Gallatin, a group of fifty men in the town swear "that they [will] not eat or drink, until they had murdered 'Joe Smith.'"

A mile from Gallatin, Joseph Smith and his fellow prisoners are turned over to the sheriff of Daviess County, William Morgan, and his guards. The next day, the prisoners finally get their day in court. They sit patiently before Austin King and the grand jury. King and the jury are drunk. Their deportment and the fabricated scene of justice makes the day long. The defendants bear out the rambling proceedings and then return to prison walls. Two friends cheer up their spirits this night. Stephen Markham, a devout Mormon, arrives with a hundred dollars for them, which eases their destitute situation. Also, a non-Mormon judge, Josiah Morin from Millport, Missouri—a town near Gallatin—arrives to witness the trial. He is friendly to the Mormon leaders and desires to see them escape their unjustified persecution.

Morin stays with the prisoners that night. They enjoy his pleasant company and begin to feel deliverance is soon at hand.

On April 10, witnesses for the defendants are not allowed to take the stand. The prisoners have sat confined for over five months without having an honest day in court. And when they do get a day, their enemies control the proceedings, are drunk, and won't allow witnesses for the defendants to testify. Finally on April 11, Stephen Markham gives his testimony, which reaches some of the hearts of those present. When Markham leaves the witness stand, one of the guards by the name of Blakely follows him out and says, "I'll kill you." He attempts to strike Markham with his fist but isn't successful. This doesn't satisfy Blakely, who then reaches for a club and attempts to strike Markham. This isn't successful either. Markham is able to take the club from him and throw it over a fence. At least ten mobbers advance on Markham, but they stop at his word that he can "kill the whole of them at one blow apiece." Miraculously, Markham single-handedly drives them off.

Joseph Smith sits bewildered at the scene not because of Markham, but because the judge and the jury see the whole interchange unfold. They hear Blakely and others threaten Markham's life, yet they do nothing about it. Things quiet down for a bit. The ten mobbers run home to get their guns so they can shoot Markham. Stephen Markham survives and will be positioned again five years later to defend his friend Joseph Smith.

The fiasco in Gallatin ends on April 15. The prisoners are granted a change of venue to Boone County. By nightfall the guards taking them to Boone County are drunk. Joseph Smith and the others agree that this is a favorable situation to escape. He states, "It was necessary for us, inasmuch as we loved our lives, and did not wish to die by the hand of murderers and assassins; and inasmuch as we loved our families and friends, to deliver ourselves from our enemies, and from that land of tyranny and oppression, and again take our stand among a people in whose bosoms dwell those feelings of republicanism and liberty which gave rise to our nation."

According to Hyrum Smith, the guards are careless and irresponsible for a reason. They want the prisoners to escape. The injustice had been going on far too long. The guards take them via Judge Morin's home. He graciously accepts them and feeds them. Here the prisoners buy a jug of whiskey and treat the guards. By now there are only five guards for five prisoners, and Morin sides with the Mormons.

William Morgan, the sheriff over their transport, says, "I shall take a good drink of grog, and go to bed, and you may do as you have a mind to." The whiskey, sweetened with honey, puts four of the five guards to sleep quickly. The sober guard puts up no resistance to the prisoners' escape. In fact, he goes along with them, helping to saddle the two horses. Three of the men escape by walking; two escape on the horses. The moon lights their path. Sheriff Morgan will go back to Gallatin and be ridden on a rail and dragged by the hair across the town square for allowing the Mormon leaders to escape.

Daylight to freedom has come, but the prisoners have to keep moving and keep secluded as they make their way to Illinois. It takes Joseph and the others about eight days to get to the Mississippi. Crossing the Mississippi is going to be risky. They are hardly recognizable, and they don't dare make their presence entirely known, not even to loyal followers and kind acquaintances. They can't draw attention to themselves until they are more securely out of the reach of their Missouri enemies.

At the same time the prisoners are fleeing, the last few Latter-day Saints are fleeing Far West. By mid-April, most of the Mormon settlers have left Far West. Some of them are forced out at gun point. Mobbers shoot cows while young Mormon girls are milking them. Property is constantly being destroyed, and men are beaten. By this time, the Saints hear rumors that the Prophet and the others have made their escape. It is time to leave and put Missouri behind them.

As Joseph Smith and his fellows approach the Mississippi River, they see the true condition of the Saints. Many of them strewn up and down both banks. They have minimal shelter. With poles and sheets, they try to block the winds. An extended winter is still producing snow. Meager fires can do little to warm them. Great effort is being made to get into Quincy, Illinois, and other towns nearby. Those on the west bank of the Mississippi River are delayed a few days because of floating ice.

The inhabitants of Quincy are stirred into action. They call a meeting for the purpose of relieving the Latter-day Saints' most pressing needs. Donations come in freely. Some of the local merchants compete to see who can donate more liberally. Their charitable competition yields a handsome supply of food, which includes "flour, pork, coffee, sugar, boots, shoes, and clothing, everything these poor outcasts so much need." Civility has resurfaced in Illinois.

After safely crossing the Mississippi River, Joseph Smith will never return to the state of Missouri. He leaves on record, "Missouri officials [have] purged the state of American citizens whose forbears bore scars evidencing their patriotic sacrifice for free institutions."

Emma Smith is living three miles from Quincy at the Cleveland family farm. Joseph's trek must continue. Joseph is a grisly sight. He is "ragged, dirty, and emaciated." Notwithstanding his physical condition, Emma Smith recognizes him approaching and runs to her husband, who has just walked through the front gate of the farm. He doesn't even make it halfway to the house before she can throw her arms around him. Hugs and kisses come from other family members and friends as well. The children are excited but slightly nervous at the sight of the man before them.

Emma gets a few days with her husband, the man more and more people are calling a modern-day prophet of God.

Brigham Young's committee of removal has been busy, and they welcome the counsel and guidance of Joseph Smith. There are several Church decisions to be made. While their prophet was in jail, the Saints were busy doing two things: preparing an investigation into the wrongs against them in Missouri, and identifying and purchasing land for homeless and migrating members of the Church. They will cautiously gather once again.

David Rice Atchison was a lawyer, judge, agriculturist, politician, and farmer. In September 1838, Joseph Smith employed him as legal counsel. Atchison refused to carry out the extermination order by Governor Boggs. Atchison chose secession in 1861 and served as a general in the Missouri State guard for one year. He moved to Texas in 1862 and waited out the Civil War in seclusion. He moved back to Missouri after the war. Unfortunately, his private library burned down during his retirement years. All documentation, letters, and others items detailing his involvement in the Mormon War in Missouri are no longer extant.

Alexander W. Doniphan rejected General Samuel Lucas's order to shoot Joseph and Hyrum Smith in the public square. Knowing of the illegality and injustice of General Lucas's actions, Doniphan confronted his superior and said, "It is cold-blooded murder. I will not obey your order . . . and if you execute these men, I will hold you responsible before an earthly tribunal, so help me God." Before his death in 1887, Doniphan visited Salt Lake City and was warmly welcomed.

Lilburn W. Boggs was the governor of Missouri from 1836 to 1841. He gave his consent to drive all Mormons from the state in 1838–1839. In 1846, he left Missouri for California, where he died in 1860.

Robert Wilson was a brigadier general in the Missouri militia during the Mormon War in 1838. Joseph Smith told Wilson that he had always been "a supporter of the Constitution and of democracy." Wilson ignorantly responded, "I know it, and that is the reason why I want to kill you, or have you killed." After parading Joseph Smith in Independence, Jackson County, Missouri, Wilson lost interest in killing Joseph Smith.

John B. Clark was appointed by Governor Boggs to carry out the extermination order. He arrived in Far West and gave the Latter-day Saints an arrogant lecture. He told the Latter-day Saints they would never see the faces of their leaders again. "For their fate is fixed—their die is cast—their doom is sealed." He served as a US congressman from 1857 to 1861. He chose the Confederacy when the Civil War broke out and served as a brigadier general.

Austin King presided at the hearings in Richmond and Gallatin, Missouri. During the Richmond hearings, he declared, "If the members of the Church remained on their lands to put in another crop they should be destroyed indiscriminately, and their bones be left to bleach on the plains without a burial." Within ten years, he became the governor of Missouri.

Heber C. Kimball was a member of the Church's Quorum of the Twelve Apostles. He had just returned from a mission in England when the troubles at Far West broke out. He was unflinchingly loyal to Joseph Smith. Kimball heard Clark's speech in Far West. He said of John B. Clark, "I can truly say that he is a liar and the truth is not in him." He played a significant role in helping Brigham Young get the Latter-day Saints West.

Joseph (right) and Hyrum (left). Many accounts confirm Joseph was at least six feet tall, well built, strong, and active. Josiah Quincy, a politician from Boston, said, "A fine looking man is what the passer-by would instinctively have murmured upon meeting the remarkable individual." He had a fair complexion, light hair, and blue eyes. Rachel Grant said he was a "fine, noble-looking man, always so neat." But she also cautioned, "There are some of the pictures that do not look a particle like him." Joseph Smith did claim to be a modern-day prophet and seer, yet he reasoned, "Although I do wrong, I do not the wrongs that I am charged with doing: the wrong that I do is through the frailty of human nature, like other men. No man lives without fault. Do you think that even Jesus, if He

were here, would be without fault in your eyes? His enemies said all manner of evil against Him—they all watched for iniquity in Him." Near the end of his life, he told recent converts, "I was but a man, and they must not expect me to be perfect; if they expected perfection from me, I should expect it from them; but if they would bear with my infirmities and the infirmities of the brethren, I would likewise bear with their infirmities."

Chapter 6

SPRING—EARLY FALL 1839

Western Illinois

AT PRESENT, THE Iowa Territory and the mighty Mississippi River act as a natural buffer for the Missourians and the Mormons.

The Mormons once again put their persistence and industry in motion. One of their main objectives was to obtain land. What at first appears to be an unbearable swamp catches their attention. It is not all swamp, and there is a town called Commerce that occupies the land the Mormons are interested in. It is on a large bend of the Mississippi River. Three land owners have rights to the bend. Part of the bend is owned by a Mr. Hugh White. Initially, the price is favorable, but the destitute Saints have no means collectively to make the purchase and pay full costs.

Mr. White is more than willing to sell some land, but he is anxious and increases the price. He first asks for "twenty-five hundred dollars, five hundred dollars of the amount to be paid down," with the balance due within the next year.

As Joseph and some other Mormon men discuss the price, someone sours the discussion by blurting out, "We can't buy it, for we lack the money." To illustrate his faith and assurance they are doing the right thing, "Joseph [takes] out his purse and, emptying out its contents, offered a half dollar" to one of those present. The man declines the half dollar. Joseph presses him to take it. He then kindly offers each man present a half dollar. When he is done giving out half dollars, he is left without any. At this point, Joseph jovially says, "Now you all have money, and I have none; but the time will come when I will have money and you will have none!"

Turning to Vinson Knight—a bishop in the Church—Joseph directly commands, "You go back and buy the farm!" Brother Knight immediately goes to White. When he arrives, White has raised the price one hundred dollars. Dejectedly, Bishop Knight returns without making an agreement. When Joseph learns of his hesitancy, he becomes even more adamant: "Go purchase that land." White, feeling confident in his potential buyers, raises the price another hundred dollars. The bishop refuses to make a deal. Upon returning, Knight has to confront Joseph Smith in his failure to purchase the land. For the third time, and somewhat irritated, Joseph tells Bishop Knight "to go and buy the farm" and "charges him not to come back till he had done so."

Not surprisingly, White is now up to twenty-eight hundred dollars. Bishop Knight, although out an additional three hundred dollars, accepts an agreement. Half relieved and half embarrassed for causing the price to go up, Knight tells Joseph of the deal. The money to be laid down is not yet forthcoming. No one knows how they can possibly make the payment of five hundred dollars. The next morning, Joseph and several others meet with Mr. White to make the first payment on the land.

A table is brought out with the papers upon it. Joseph quietly signs them and then moves back from the table with his head down, as if in thought for a moment. Just then a man drives up in a carriage and asks if Mr. Smith is there. Joseph, hearing the man's question, gets up and goes to the door. "The man said, 'Good morning, Mr. Smith; I am on a speculation today. I want to buy some land, and thought I would come and see you.' Joseph then points around where his land lay he had just signed on, but the man said: 'I can't go with you today to see the land. Do you want any money this morning?'"

All eyes and ears await Joseph Smith's response. "Joseph replies that he would like some," and the stranger asks, "How much?" Joseph Smith says, "Five hundred dollars." Without any hesitation

"The man walk[s] into the house with Joseph, emptie[s] a small sack of gold on the table, and count[s] out that amount. He then hand[s] to Joseph another hundred dollars, saying: 'Mr. Smith, I make you a present of this!'" Everyone stands mesmerized at the seeming divine intervention. "After this transpire[s], Joseph laughed at the brethren and says: 'You trusted in money; but I trusted in God. Now I have money and you have none.'"

ONE OF THE other landowners, Isaac Galland, has been in the region of Western Illinois and the Iowa Territory for about six years before the Mormons arrive. He is familiar with the land and owns thousands of acres. He is living in Commerce when migrating Saints start arriving. Galland sells land to Mormons in Commerce, as well as 19,000 acres across the Mississippi River in the Iowa Territory. His affinity for the people and interest in what they are all about increases. He chooses to be baptized. Joseph Smith will personally ordain him an elder in the Church. Galland is asked by the Church to help with land transactions with incoming Saints. He accepts.

There are at least two other land purchases that occur. This allows the Latter-day Saints to have a significant staying power on the beautiful bend of the Mississippi River. The first name early settlers had given to this unique place on the Mississippi was Venus, a reference to a Roman goddess of love and beauty. The only substantial building besides a few homes is a post office. To satisfy their secular ambitions, settlers before the Saints change the name to Commerce. But they have a hard time surviving. Many die and leave a few vacant homes.

According to Benjamin Brown, "It was a common saying among the inhabitants of the surrounding country, that, if the 'Mormons' could live here, they could live anywhere. It truly was a most unhealthy spot, filled with ponds and stagnant waters, left by the overflowing of the Mississippi River, afflicting all the neighborhood with fevers and agues. From this condition I saw the city become, through the industry of the Saints, a healthy and prosperous place, being drained of these swamps."

Joseph Smith changes the name to Nauvoo, a Hebrew term meaning "a beautiful location or place of rest." This will be their home for nearly seven years. However, only about two of those years will be a time of rest. Interruption from their enemies will again press down upon them. Devout Mormons, politicians, and retches of all kinds will come and go. Joseph Smith attracts all of their attention.

The city is instantly put on the map. The Saints spread into surrounding counties, start settlements, and purchase homes and farms in existing towns both in Illinois and in the Iowa Territory. Church leaders agree initially that they should spread out to avoid the problems that had followed them in other states. Perhaps by blending into the population they will not bring the attention they had received when they were concentrated more heavily in one place. At least seventeen Mormon communities are established throughout Western Illinois. Nauvoo is the hub, and Joseph Smith's family makes Nauvoo their residence on May 10, 1839.

Though temporarily free from their enemies in Missouri and with a new spot to call home, the Latter-day Saints face another enemy that strikes fast: malaria. This "sickly season" peaks in midsummer and causes much heartache through autumn. The "shakes" and the "chills" weaken individuals, and many lie sick throughout the community. On Sunday, July 21, no Church meetings are held. The sick are too numerous, and rain has moved in.

The following Monday and Tuesday, there is a report of the sick being "administered unto with great success." The infirm lie "along the bank of the river; Joseph arises from his sick bed and attends" to many of the Saints' needs. Several miracles are performed, and many individuals are healed, according to a number of personal accounts. While in the home of "Joseph Bates Noble, who lay very sick," Joseph Smith, under a voice of God, heals him. "After Noble [is] healed, all [kneel] down to pray." A brother named Elijah Fordham, who had been healed earlier in the day, offers the prayer. However, "while praying he [falls] to the floor. The Prophet [arises], and on looking around he [sees] quite a number of unbelievers in the house, whom he [orders] out. When the room is cleared, Brother Fordham arises and finishes his prayer."

Sickness starts to subside by early September, and the Saints are meeting regularly in Sunday worship services. They hold a semi-annual general conference of the Church in October and accept their lot in Western Illinois as a new gathering place for believers. Before the conference adjourns, three men are appointed to go to Washington, DC, and present the Saints' troubles and loss of property to the heads of government. Joseph Smith, Sidney Rigdon, and Elias Higbee are designated. His mother's impression in Far West of Joseph speaking before judges and great men of America is beginning to come to pass.

Notwithstanding his absence and the enormous task of building a city, Joseph Smith sends the Church's Quorum of the Twelve Apostles on missions to the British Isles. Nine will fulfill their missions. Orson Hyde will go as far as Israel. His purpose is to dedicate the land of Israel for the preaching of the gospel and the gathering of Jews. The Apostles' labors will bring not only new converts to the faith but new converts with skills and trades that will accelerate and magnify Nauvoo's growth and industry.

*N*OT QUITE THIRTY-FOUR years old, Joseph Smith sets off to the East with a few companions to meet with government officials. The well-spoken Sidney Rigdon joins him. Rigdon is twelve years older than Joseph. Elias Higbee—a Caldwell County, Missouri, judge near Rigdon's age—is also in the company. For security, a fourth person is part of the entourage—Orrin Porter Rockwell. He is only twenty-six years old. Joseph and Orrin developed a unique friendship in upper state New York during their childhood. Rockwell was privy to Joseph Smith's earliest religious experiences regarding his visitations and his bringing forth the Book of Mormon. Rockwell is also aware of the tribulation and mob spirit that started immediately following Joseph's claims.

Their travel to Washington, DC, is slow. They go one hundred miles before having to stop for assistance in Springfield, the recently chosen capital of Illinois. Rigdon failed to leave his malaria in Nauvoo. He is too ill to continue. His health hinders their prospects. However, they become acquainted with Robert D. Foster, a physician in his late twenties who has recently joined Church. He helps Rigdon's recuperation. Foster's willingness to join them and his kindness is welcomed. They want to make speed to the nation's capital. Little do they know of the duplicity dormant in Robert Foster.

Their course east takes them through Indiana and right to the heart of Ohio. Sidney Rigdon is again too ill to push forward. Joseph Smith's urgency separates the group. He, Elias Higbee, and the ever-vigilant Porter Rockwell continue to push forward. They travel many miles by stage coach. On one segment of their travels, the passengers of the stage include a woman with a small child and two US elected officials. The stage is driven by a man who loves to hold a "glass of spirits." He is constantly drunk, and the patience of the passengers is wearing thin. At one pit stop, even the horses are bothered with the driver. They run away unexpectedly, with the coach attached, and show no sign of stopping. They make a fretful run for a solid three miles.

The horses defer no respect to the occupants inside the coach. They keep a good pace, and passengers start to jump from the coach. Joseph tells the woman not to throw her baby from the coach. "Sit down," he tells her. "Not a hair of [your] head or any one on the coach [shall] be hurt." Joseph Smith climbs out of the coach and gets a hold of the reigns. When the speed has been reduced, Elias Higbee leaps from the coach in an attempt to help calm the horses. Joseph and Elias bring the horses to a stop. Not one passenger is injured, the horses regain their composure, and the drunk driver is behind them, aloof to the fiasco and removed from his duties.

They safely arrive in Washington, DC, on November 28, 1839. They check into an inexpensive boarding house just west of the US Capitol building. Nothing in the nation's capital is very comfortable in the late 1830s. The boarding house, as fate would have it, is on the corner of Missouri and Third streets. Washington, DC, is not a welcoming city. It is dirty and not well-maintained. Joseph is not there on vacation. He wants a visit with the president, Martin Van Buren.

Joseph Smith's endorsements from a variety of letters sustain that he is "a very important character in Illinois." He has only been a resident of Illinois for a few months. US congressman John Reynolds from Illinois urges his colleagues to "give [Joseph Smith] the civilities and attention that [is] due him." The next day Joseph and Higbee get an interview with the president. Congressman Reynolds walks the American-born prophet before the president. As they enter, Joseph tells Reynolds, "Introduce me as a Latter-day Saint."

Reynolds thinks his request is strange and nonsense. Joseph again insists on being introduced as a Latter-day Saint. Reynolds grants his request. The introduction makes President Martin Van Buren "smile."

President Van Buren is twenty-three years older than Joseph Smith, but Joseph isn't deterred by his age or his position. He instantly presents the president with letters of introduction and the calamities the Saints suffered at the hands of Missourians. After reading one letter, the rather plump Van Buren looks up at Smith and Higbee. With a "half frown," he says, "What can I do for you? I can do nothing for you; if I do anything, I shall come in contact with the whole State of Missouri." The *I* dripping from Van Buren's statement reveals he is more concerned with his political career than justice.

In 1839, Van Buren is dealing with a host of issues: the aftermath of the financial panic of 1837, the removal of Cherokee Indians from Georgia, the beginnings of the underground railroad, troubles with Great Britain, and his own re-election.

If he sympathizes with the Mormons, it will cost Van Buren the state of Missouri, a state he needs for re-election. He sees no political advantage in helping the Mormons. Nonetheless, Higbee refuses to be intimidated and demands a hearing for their constitutional rights. Joseph likewise presses him, and he does promise to reconsider what he has said, a shallow promise that Higbee detects. Higbee later writes that he and Joseph Smith were "eyewitnesses of his majesty," a jab mocking Van Buren. The president's performance of nobility doesn't impress the two Mormons. Van Buren attempts to change the discussion by interrogating them about "wherein [they] differed in [their] religion from the other religions of the day." Joseph declares they differ in mode of baptism and the gift of the Holy Ghost by the laying on of hands. But Van Buren is wanting to know more about political positioning than understanding religious doctrine.

Their visit with the president ends.

For a few weeks, Joseph Smith and Elias Higbee present their troubles in Missouri to the Illinois delegation and Congress. Higbee specifically goes before the Senate Judiciary committee. Joseph is also able to meet with Senator John C. Calhoun of South Carolina. But Calhoun is unwilling to show Joseph any pleasantries.

As they mingle with national legislators and labor to gain support for their situation, a newspaper prints their purpose in Washington and the atrocities committed against them in Missouri. Affidavit after affidavit is being presented to the leaders of the nation from the exiled Latter-day Saints of Missouri. The newspaper editors have enough sympathy to print the atrocities, but hearts are not moved into action.

Congressmen John Reynolds recognizes Joseph Smith as someone who has "applied himself, with much industry, to the acquisition of knowledge." Reynolds and other Washingtonian observers of Joseph Smith quickly learn that "although his diction is inaccurate, and his selection of words not always in good taste, he converses very fluently on the subject nearest to his heart, and whatever may be thought of the correctness of his opinions, no one who talks with him can doubt that his convictions of their truth are sincere and settled. His eye betokens a resolute spirit, and he would doubtless go to the stake to attest his firmness and devotion, with as little hesitation as did any of the leaders of the olden time."

Joseph leaves Higbee in the nation's capital for a few weeks while he visits Saints in Pennsylvania and New Jersey. This gives him further opportunities to preach the gospel. While in Philadelphia, the Wilkinson family asks him to write his autograph in their family album. He consents. They later join the Church.

When Joseph Smith returns, he visits Higbee and reviews the work among the elected officials. No one is willing to flex their political muscle in behalf of the alarming injustices the Mormons have suffered in Missouri. Rather they wish to grandstand. In a letter to his brother Hyrum, Joseph Smith also observes, "There is such an itching disposition to display their oratory on the most trivial occasions, and so much etiquette, bowing and scraping, twisting and turning, to make a display of their witticism, that it seems to us rather a display of folly and show, more than substance and gravity, such as becomes a great nation like ours." But he also tells Hyrum, "There are some exceptions."

Joseph Smith and others most likely visited the president one more time. But in the end, the visits to the president leave a bad taste in Joseph Smith's mouth. On his return trip home to Illinois, he writes "I did not fail to proclaim the iniquity and insolence of Martin Van Buren, toward myself and an injured people . . . and may he never be elected again to any office of trust or power." Here, again, Joseph Smith proves prophetic. Van Buren will lose the election of 1840 to William Henry Harrison.

The trip to Washington, DC, isn't an entire failure. Joseph Smith is able to preach often in the city. He is able to put forth his convictions, his revelations, and his teachings before a variety of influential people. Congressman Reynolds and other leading men gain a familiarity with him as he spends many days in and around the capital city. Reynolds remarks of the pleasant Mormon and the religion he introduced, "He did not appear to possess any harshness or barbarity in his composition, nor did he appear to possess that great talent and boundless mind that would enable him to accomplish the wonders he performed. No one can for tell the destiny of this sect, and it would be blasphemy, at this day, to compare its founder to the Saviour, but, nevertheless it may become veritable history, in a thousand years, that the standing and character of Joseph Smith, as a prophet, may rank equal to any of the prophets who have preceded him."

Congressman Reynolds's brother Thomas doesn't feel the same way. Thomas is running for governor of Missouri. He will replace Lilburn Boggs. He is quite aware of Boggs's order of extermination against the Mormons. He doesn't rescind it. Instead he seeks to put the pressure on Joseph Smith's freedom. Efforts are being made to extradite Joseph back to Missouri for alleged crimes.

Joseph Smith leaves Washington in February of 1840 with Porter Rockwell and Robert Foster. He arrives in Nauvoo by March 4. Rockwell proves faithful in providing security to the prophet, while Foster fails in keeping up with the pen. "I depended on Dr. Foster to keep my daily journal during this journey, but he has failed me," Joseph writes in his history.

It won't be the last time Foster fails him.

Chapter 8
SPRING 1840—SPRING 1842
Nauvoo, Illinois

EMMA SMITH IS delighted to see her husband. For sixteen months she has shouldered the persecutions of Missouri and regrouped her family in Illinois. She has done a marvelous job establishing a new home in what may be considered initially the least of places. She graciously looks after her husband's parents and other destitute Latter-day Saints. Of the past sixteen months, Joseph and Emma have only been together six. Shortly before Joseph Smith goes to Washington, DC, Emma conceives her seventh child.

Unfortunately, upon his return from the East Coast, Joseph can't promise Emma and the Saints any compensation for their losses or any justice for their enemies. He declares of his Washington experience, "I witnessed many vexatious movements in government officers, whose sole object should be the peace and prosperity and happiness of the whole people; but instead of this, I discovered that popular clamor and personal aggrandizement were the ruling principles of those in authority; and my heart faints within me when I see, by the visions of the Almighty, the end of this nation, if she continues to disregard the cries and petitions of her virtuous citizens, as she has done, and is now doing." But he says that they will "continue pleading like the Widow at the feet of the unjust judge."

For two years Joseph Smith, his family, and the Latter-day Saints will enjoy a respite from their enemies. This interval isn't entirely free from lawsuits and persecution, but the threats on his person can easily be kept in check by a loyal security band of Mormons. Extradition attempts to haul him back to Missouri fall short. During this respite, a once significant member who apostatized in Missouri and joined the enemy's ranks is seeking fellowship again among Saints.

William W. Phelps has many gifts, but during the Missouri persecutions, he allowed bitterness and fear to take him another direction. He bore a false testimony against Joseph Smith. By June 1840, Phelps is writing to Smith, pleading for forgiveness. Joseph Smith replies, "I must say that it is with no ordinary feelings I endeavor to write a few lines to you; . . . at the same time I am rejoiced at the privilege granted me. You may in some measure realize what my feelings, as well as Elder Rigdon's and Brother Hyrum's were, when we read your letter. . . . I feel a disposition to act on your case in a manner that will meet the approbation of Jehovah, (whose servant I am)." Without any bitterness, Joseph conveys further, "It is true, that we have suffered much in consequence of your behavior. . . . However, the cup has been drunk, the will of our Father has been done, and we are yet alive, for which we thank the Lord."

And then Joseph concludes his letter to Phelps by extending the olive leaf: "Believing your confession to be real, and your repentance genuine, I shall be happy once again to give you the right hand of fellowship, and rejoice over the returning prodigal. . . . Come on, dear brother, since the war is past, For friends at first, are friends again at last.'"

With prodigals returning and converts streaming in, Nauvoo is starting to flourish. Many hands are doing a great work fast. They divert the waters rolling off the bluff. This dries out the flats between the bluff and the Mississippi River. Streets and homes are quickly taking shape. Farms are showing great promise, and sickness is not so prevalent. Joseph Smith is satisfied with the rapid improvements. He has more time to give to the Church and his family. He gives discourses, writes letters, holds conferences, receives what he terms *revelations*, and organizes building projects.

During this respite from his enemies, Joseph also shoulders the loss of a dear loved one. His Father, worn out from his persecutions in Missouri, succumbs to death. It was his father who seventeen years earlier listened rationally to his son's religious experiences. Joseph Smith Jr. had approached his father and told him what had transpired during a particular evening: a resurrected personage who lived in the fourth century visited him. His father counseled, "My son, these things are of God; take heed that you proceed in all holiness to do His will." A messenger coming to his son must have resonated with him of the messenger in his own inspired dreams. Prior to his son's divine experiences, Joseph Smith Sr. had at least seven dreams that he concluded to be of God and were telling of forthcoming events in his life. Through his son's experiences, he saw the fulfillment of his dreams.

In attempt to distinguish objective and loyal voices, Joseph prints an "extensive list of books, pamphlets, and letters published for and against, the Latter-day Saints during the past year" by the end of 1840. This wins some of the general public hearts and minds to the Mormon cause. He also continues to prepare his personal history "to disabuse the public mind, and put all inquirers after truth in possession of the facts."

Joseph Smith wants all to know that the honest and good people of the earth are welcome in Nauvoo. Early in 1841, he presents a bill to the Nauvoo City Council asking that an ordinance be agreed upon for "free toleration and equal privileges" to all sects and religious persuasions. Joseph Smith is in no way exclusive in the preaching of religion. He has had a constant flow of religious leaders visit him. They were given a chance to address the Saints if they so desired.

During this respite, one central building project to the city is announced and started: the building of another temple. They have already built one in Kirtland, Ohio, that they had to abandon because of enemies. They tried to build one in Missouri but were hindered.

A beautiful spot on the bluff of the peninsula is chosen for the temple. It will face west, towering over the constant Mississippi River. The temple lot is noticeable from the plateau in Illinois and strikingly placed for anyone standing in Iowa looking east. Joseph will introduce what he calls ordinances of exaltation for both the living and the dead in the temple.

NOT ONLY IS Joseph Smith's religious muscle improving, so is his political muscle.

One year after Joseph gets the snub from Van Buren, he gets a gracious nod by the Illinois State Legislature. Illinoisans were in large number surprised at the brutal way the Saints were treated in Missouri. To provide greater aid, the legislature grants greater power to this gathering people by guaranteeing them legal safeguards in a city charter. On December 16, 1840, legislation is signed into law designating Nauvoo as a city with a generous charter; "only Alton, Chicago, Galena, Quincy, and Springfield shared such distinctive legal status" at the time.

"Encouraged by state political leaders, the Saints believe that a city charter will guarantee them a kind of security they had never yet enjoyed. Even State Supreme Court Justice Stephen A. Douglas, despite prior judicial decisions to the contrary, opined that a corporate charter was irrevocable and perpetual." This is the legal ground Joseph and his followers need.

The Nauvoo Charter not only designates municipal purposes, it also grants a charter for a university and another charter for a militia. When a few politically and economically driven Illinoisans in nearby towns learn of the generous charter, they turn vehemently jealous. Nauvoo has the exploding population and work force to become the dominant economic force on the mid-section of the Mississippi. A handful of envious Warsaw settlers twenty miles south do not like the legal status Nauvoo is obtaining. They will use their press to make it known.

Joseph Smith is not the first mayor of Nauvoo, but he does take the reins of the independent militia as Lieutenant General of the Nauvoo Legion. "In granting the charter, some legislators may have hoped to protect Latter-day Saints from persecution." But the political tide will turn, and the compassion for the Latter-day Saints will subside.

The charter's importance is quickly tested. On the day of his father's funeral, Joseph Smith learns that the unpleasant harassment from Lilburn W. Boggs, now former governor of Missouri, won't go away. Boggs demands the extradition of Joseph Smith Jr. as a fugitive from justice. Within a few months, Governor Thomas Carlin of Illinois issues a warrant for the Prophet's arrest, and a Sheriff King takes him into custody. Joseph obtains a writ of habeas corpus in Nauvoo. A few days later, Stephen A. Douglas dismisses the extradition.

In this two-year respite, Joseph Smith, with the help of rapidly increasing converts, is able to put Nauvoo on the economic and political map of Illinois and the surrounding regions. The growth of this people and their industry bewilder many Illinoisans. Joseph Smith is also putting "Mormonism" on the world religious map by sending missionaries and the Church's Apostles to the nations of the earth and encouraging full speed on building a temple.

Joseph also empowers women of the Church and organizes them into a "Relief Society." The Relief Society members are to take care of the poor and extend a helping hand to the afflicted. They will also play an essential role in the temple ceremonies revealed by Joseph Smith in early May. The society instantly becomes a pillar in what Joseph calls the "Kingdom of God on Earth." This gives Mormon women a vital position in the dominating male culture of the nineteenth century. Joseph observed these organizing women as "a select Society separate from all the evils of the world, choice, virtuous, and holy."

Nauvoo for the time being is a safe haven for the Mormon prophet. But he still is susceptible to mortal blows. He and Emma lose their ninth child, fourteen-month-old Don Carlos, leaving them with only four living children. Enemies and death are constantly at their door. He is also susceptible to the entrapments of deceivers.

DURING THIS TWO-YEAR period, Joseph Smith puts an enormous amount of trust in a new convert named John C. Bennett. This man will be the epitome of a wolf in sheep's clothing. Joseph Smith initially misjudges Bennett's character, and it will cause terrible ramifications the remaining years of his life.

An abusive Bennett, who is on the run from a wife and children in another state, hides his identity when he joins the Latter-day Saints. His rise to influential positions within the Church is perplexing. His deceit and powerful personality help draft and secure the Nauvoo Charter. Because of his ability to see the city charter through the Illinois legislature, the Latter-day Saints obviously see his talent in their collective favor. They give him a pedestal prematurely, making him the first mayor of Nauvoo. But Bennett loves women and power more than God. His employ of physician is a charade for his lusts of the flesh. His pretense also has a persuasive power among the men of the Nauvoo militia. They elect him major general and inspector general.

In late summer of 1840, Joseph Smith starts to receive reports from reputable individuals in Ohio concerning Bennett's true character. The reports confirm Bennett is not a bachelor. This is troubling to Joseph because Bennett is courting a "young lady" of Nauvoo. Joseph Smith tells Bennett he will take his promiscuity public if he doesn't end his current courtship. Bennett continues to deny his true identity. He turns on Joseph Smith when his lustful persuasions lose their spark on Mormon women. Having been privy to inner Church leadership for nearly a year, he begins to tell women the leadership of the Church favor promiscuity and they themselves practice it. Bennett reintroduces a term from another generation called "spiritual wifery" (free and communal love by preferential assignment of a religious authority).

Bennett tries to continue his immorality by teaching that when people divinely meet and share a mutual affection for each other, they can share that affection through physical intimacy, regardless of who they are or what their social status is.

In the summer of 1841, more reports come in that Bennett is a fake. One report comes from Joseph Smith's brother Hyrum. At this point, Bennett is backed up to the hypocritical wall. He confesses his misdeeds. Disgusted himself with his shallow and shady character, Bennett tries to commit suicide by taking poison. He is spared by antidote, but his life continues to spiral out of control. He is angry and bitter at being exposed. Sadly, a few other men join Bennett in his seduction and lewdness practices.

As the evidences pile up against Bennett, Church leaders begin to take action. He is dropped from Church membership on May 11, 1842, for immoral behavior. One of the women he has seduced is Sarah Pratt, wife of the Mormon Apostle Orson Pratt. Orson is in Europe on a mission in 1841. Their illicit relationship caused quite a stir in Nauvoo, and when Bennett is excommunicated, he quickly publishes a book describing Joseph Smith as the one who seduced Sarah Pratt. When Orson returns from his mission, he initially believes Bennett and his wife, who wasn't entirely forthcoming.

However, truth prevails. Orson's brother Parley P. Pratt said, "Bro. Orson Pratt is in the Church and always has been and has the confidence of Joseph Smith and all good men who know him. . . . As to Bennett or his book [*The History of the Saints, 1842*] I consider it a little stooping to mention it. It is beneath contempt and would disgrace the society of hell and the Devil. . . . His object was vengeance on those who exposed his iniquity." Orson himself comes to peace with the truth and the intentions of Bennett. As an addition to his brother's letter, he writes, "J. C. Bennett has published lies concerning myself and family and the people with which I am connected."

Orson Pratt stays faithful and retains his Church membership and place as an Apostle.

When Bennett is first excommunicated, he pleads for mercy, promising to change his ways. It is short lived. Within a week, Hyrum Smith learns that Bennett has "promised to give his victims medicine to produce abortions, providing they should become pregnant." Hyrum desires to prosecute Bennett. But once again, Bennett's persuasiveness stays justice. In granting him mercy, Joseph Smith demands Bennett make a "sworn deposition to the effect that he, Bennett, had never known Joseph to teach or practice anything contrary to the highest standards of virtue." Bennett immediately repairs to city alderman Daniel H. Wells, where in the presence of William Clayton and Hyrum Smith, he "[stands] at the desk" and writes that he "has never heard anything in the least contrary to the strictest principles of the Gospel, or of virtue, or of the laws of God, or man, under any occasion either directly or indirectly, in word or deed, by Joseph Smith; and that he never knew the said Smith to countenance any improper conduct whatever, either in public or private;" and that Joseph had never taught him or anyone else that illicit relationships were, "under any circumstances, justifiable."

Joseph Smith is pacified. But his adulterous and fornicating enemies are not, especially Bennett. His remorse is short lived. Bennett resigns as mayor and puts on a short parade of penitence and sorrow before turning even more vicious. To fill the void, Joseph Smith is appointed mayor. News of Bennett being expelled from an Ohio Masonic lodge for misconduct confirms that Church leadership made the right decision. Non-Mormons send letters stating Bennett is a controversial man.

Like most exposed adulterers, Bennett knows he is no longer welcome. He skips town suddenly and then turns to inciting surrounding communities about the awful nature of the Latter-day Saints. At first, Joseph Smith turns his cheek and ignores Bennett's lies. But in the end, he is compelled to address Bennett's claims. For another dishonorable twelve years, Bennett will wander, being rejected from other communities. He will die in Iowa in 1856. But his words of disdain from 1842 to 1844 add to the pile of persecution Joseph Smith will suffer.

BENNETT IS TWISTING Joseph Smith's initiation of plural marriage for his own selfish purposes. As far back as 1831, while Joseph Smith was working on what he called an inspired translation of the Old Testament, he read about some of the ancient prophets practicing plural marriage, such as the account of Abram and Sarai and Hagar (see Genesis 16:1–3). Joseph Smith was reluctant to begin the practice of plural marriage. He did not openly teach it to the Saints at the time, although he received divine instruction concerning the practice. He begins teaching the practice of plural marriage (not spiritual wifery) while in Nauvoo.

It isn't entirely clear when he begins living the ancient law of plural marriage. However, evidence suggests that by 1841 the Prophet has entered into an additional marriage. Over the next three years, he takes additional wives. Some other Mormon men do likewise. Although some select men and women called to live this principle under the direction of Joseph Smith initially experience hesitancy and frustration, they receive individual confirmations. Many record open visions and miraculous experiences from angels.

Rumors begin to surface and contribute to the increased persecution against the Saints. To curtail the rumors and keep the practice quiet, the Nauvoo City Council passes an ordinance in February 1842 allowing "all marriages to occur without licenses or public notice."

Under these circumstances and a thousand rumors, Bennett is able to operate his immoral desires and manipulate those willing to listen to him. But by May 6, 1842, as Bennett is being cut off from the Church, another accusation unrelated to plural marriage is about to press down upon Joseph Smith.

Chapter 9

MAY 6, 1842

Independence, Jackson County, Missouri

𝒜 SIX-YEAR-OLD GIRL GENTLY rocks her infant sister in a cradle. Next to the cradle sits the father of the young girls, Lilburn W. Boggs. He is no longer governor of Missouri but a candidate for the state senate. He has his political enemies. He also has the disdain of nearly every Mormon.

Boggs peruses the paper in the family room. It has been over three years since the Mormons left the state. His extermination order has not been rescinded. The Mormons are not welcome in Missouri, and their return for business or family matters is at their own peril.

LATTER-DAY SAINTS ARRIVED on the western frontier and wasted no time exerting their industry. It only took two years for the other residents to fret about their growing economic and political power. Governor Boggs was initially friendly to the Mormons. They were arriving in large numbers and were an active voting bloc. Boggs even hired Mormon tailors to make him look respectable in public. But when he saw that he couldn't leverage the Mormon voting bloc, he turned against them.

In 1833, as Lieutenant Governor, Boggs was a silent assailant sitting on horseback, watching when a Mormon press was destroyed and two men of the faith were tarred and feathered in the town square of Independence. He did nothing to stop persecution that day. And in the days following, he saw nothing wrong with Mormons being driven from their homes and property in Jackson County just before harvest time in 1833. Boggs, his political hacks, and accompanying blacklegs enjoyed Mormon spoils. They drove Latter-day Saints from three counties, and eventually the state, all within a decade.

BOGGS IS ROCKING in a chair in his Independence, Jackson County, home—a home built by a Mormon family. It is a small house on South Spring Street, a few blocks from a site where the Mormons intend to build a temple one day. On this night dark, clouds have moved in and a consistent rain pounds the frontier home. Other members of his family are in an adjacent room finishing a meal. Between the rain and the noise of a large family, no one is suspicious or aware of an attacker who has made his way onto the property. This brazen foe stands just outside the window where Boggs rocks in his chair, newspaper in hand.

It was immediate. At least three shots were fired at close range. Boggs falls unconscious instantly. One of his boys quickly finds him, "in his chair, with his jaw fallen down, and his head leant back." As the boy discovers his father's severe wounds, he gives an alarm. When the rush of other family and neighbors gather, the perpetrator has already fled and the ghastly site of Boggs is before them. Doctors find serious head and neck wounds. He is bleeding copiously, and everyone present thinks death is imminent. While doctors and a few family members attend to him, others turn to the identity and flight of the assailant.

Foot tracks are seen in the garden and below the window, and an overloaded pistol that had been thrown by the assailant is located. The three shots found place in Boggs's body; one going through his mouth, one into the brain, and another probably in or near the brain, all entering through the back part of the head and neck.

Amazingly, Boggs continues to breathe. He makes it through the night.

Meanwhile, Joseph Smith is in Nauvoo, 225 miles as the crow flies from Boggs. He is preparing to entertain an Illinois circuit judge by the name of Stephen A. Douglas. Douglas will be a reputable alibi for accusations and affidavits that are about to be poured out upon Joseph. Douglas is in Nauvoo on May 7, 1842, to watch the Nauvoo Legion parade and perform a sham battle.

But Joseph Smith's childhood friend and self-acclaimed body-guard Orrin Porter Rockwell will not have such an alibi. As fate has it, he is in Independence incognito, safely leading his wife, who is pregnant, to her family's home.

Missourians know he is "a fiercely loyal acolyte" to Joseph Smith, according to a newspaper editor accusing Rockwell. Rockwell has pseudonyms for his travels in and around Missouri. He has no interest being in the region, but he yields respect to his wife's wishes to be with family for the delivery of their child.

As soon as he hears of the assassination attempt on Boggs, Rockwell starts for Nauvoo with all the physical stamina he can muster. He knows he is guilty by proximity in the eyes of some Missourians. He also knows that his uncompromising loyalty for Joseph Smith irks the Missourians.

Chapter 10
MAY 7–8, 1842
Nauvoo, Illinois

*N*EWS OF THE attempt on Boggs life doesn't travel far beyond the Missouri River on the night of May 6. Joseph Smith wakes up on May 7 in Nauvoo, Illinois, unaware of what has befallen the Mormon foe.

The Nauvoo Legion sham battle scheduled late in the morning continues. The military exercise is a forum for public entertainment. The Mormon prophet is surrounded by local and state dignitaries. The dignitaries have a great interest in the events of the day. As the events begin to unfold, there is harmony and order. Drunkards and noise makers stay away, and the people enjoy the festivities. Many, like Stephen A. Douglas, express satisfaction with the military exercise.

However, on this day, John C. Bennett seals his excommunication from the Church. Notwithstanding the nature of his immoral character, which had for weeks been coming to light, he still holds reputable rank in the Nauvoo Legion. Some of Bennett's followers are members of the legion and easily camouflage themselves in the sham battle. They have real bullets. To hide the deed, Bennett tries persuading Joseph Smith to occupy certain positions during the sham battle. He asks Joseph to take command of the "first cohort." Discerning Bennett's purposes, Joseph Smith declines. Bennett then

Lieutenant General **Joseph Smith**, Staff, Guard and Ladies on Horseback

---

Band of Music

Major General J. C. Bennett and Staff

Brigadier General Charles C. Rich and Staff 2nd Cohort Cavalry

Brigadier General W. Law and Staff 1st Cohort Cavalry

Artillery

suggests the Prophet and general take a position behind the artillery, "without his staff."

Bennett's hidden purpose and pathetic suggestions are coming to light. The suggestion to take a position behind the artillery is met with a stiff rebuke from A. P. Rockwood, acting commander of Smith's bodyguards. Bennett's planned assassination is crumbling. Joseph Smith chooses his own position. Wisely he views the battle from the position as diagramed. (See *History of the Church*, 5:5 for diagram.)

Considering Bennett's suggested positions for Joseph Smith, he must have at least one accomplice in the second cohort. Most likely, the fellow fiend or fiends are parading near the right side of the second cohort, near the artillery. As the pretended battle unfolded, it would have been difficult to identify any coconspirators aligned with Bennett.

Joseph Smith surmises Bennett's treachery at the sham battle by recording, "If General Bennett's true feelings toward me are not made manifest to the world in a very short time, then it may be possible that the gentle breathings of that Spirit which whispered to me on parade, that there was mischief concealed in that sham battle, were false; a short time will determine the point. Let John C. Bennett answer at the day of judgment: Why did you request me to command one of the cohorts, and also to take my position without my staff, during the sham battle, on the 7th of May, 1842, where my life might have been the forfeit, and no man have known who did the deed?"

His life being spared, Joseph Smith spends the next day, a Sabbath, hearing a sermon from Sidney Rigdon. Afterward, he witnesses the baptisms of converts in the font located in the unfinished temple, and in the Mississippi River. The coming week he will spend with his family and in addressing temporal matters, a normal quiet week. But the uproar and accusations from Missouri are approaching.

ORTER ROCKWELL ARRIVES in Nauvoo by steamboat from St. Louis eight days after Boggs was shot. For the most part, his route back to Illinois is by waterways. The Missouri and Mississippi Rivers provided Rockwell with an advantage. However, he must have been just hours, perhaps even only one, ahead of those seeking to stop all fleeing suspects.

According to John C. Bennett, Rockwell arrives in Nauvoo on Saturday, May 14. Joseph Smith records in his history that on this day he receives reports that Boggs has been shot. Rockwell, a few days ahead of the newspapers, assures Joseph Smith of the attempt on the ex-governor's life. Other reports also reach Nauvoo that night and early the next morning. Confident in the reports arriving, Joseph Smith thinks it expedient to announce the news in a public service. "An audible gasp which escaped the gathering was interpreted by some as a cheer; certainly a majority of the Mormons suppressed an urge to celebrate openly." The man who had ordered their expulsion and extermination is dead. So they think.

Though miserably uncomfortable, Boggs still has life.

Just prior to the accusations of Joseph Smith being involved in Boggs murder attempt, Bennett offers his sworn statement that Joseph Smith has been "in public and in private . . . strictly virtuous."

But Bennett is all façade and now has pulled other conniving men into his ranks. They welcome the accusations that Joseph Smith and Orrin Rockwell are the attempted murderers of Boggs. The news helps deflect the public pressure mounting against Bennett's disgraceful behavior.

On May 22, after a busy week meeting the demands of private and Church business, Joseph Smith spends the day reading the recent newspaper reports of the Boggs assassination attempt. The *Quincy Whig* (an Illinois paper fifty miles south of Nauvoo) reports that an "unknown hand" had done the deed. Yet the article fuels the assumption that the Mormons are behind it: "There are several rumors in circulation in regard to the horrid affair; one of which throws the crime upon the Mormons, from the fact, we suppose, that Mr. Boggs was governor at the time, and in no small degree instrumental in driving them from the state. Smith, too, the Mormon Prophet, as we understand, prophesied, a year or so ago, his death by violent means. Hence, there is plenty of foundation for rumor."

Bennett plants the false prophecy rumor and the idea that Porter Rockwell was sent by Joseph Smith to fulfill the prophecy. It is proven to be a lie but is easily believable at the time. Bennett was "a man of great talents according to the Gentiles," Joseph Hovey observes. "He . . . went into the other cities and states and tried to bring persecution upon us by telling that we believed in more than one wife and having all things in common; in fact, everything the devil could do to destroy our Prophet Joseph. The newspapers were filled with the most vile and audacious calumnies that could be invented by the enemies of all good."

The Mormons feel the article by the editors of the *Quincy Whig* is escalating all rumors. "We suppose" and "as we understand" reveal that the editors of the paper didn't check all the sources.

But the Latter-day Saints have their means to publish words. By the end of the day, Joseph Smith is standing in the editor's office of the *Wasp*, a newspaper printed in Nauvoo. "Mr. Bartlett," Smith addresses the editor of the Whig. "Dear Sir. . . . You have done me manifest injustice in ascribing to me a prediction of the demise of Lilburn W. Boggs, Esq., ex-governor of Missouri, by violent hands. Boggs was a candidate for the state senate, and, I presume, fell by the hand of a political opponent, with 'his hands and face yet dripping with the blood of murder;' but he died not through my instrumentality. My hands are clean, and my heart pure, from the blood of all men. I am tired of the misrepresentation, calumny and detraction, heaped upon me by wicked men; and desire and claim, only those principles guaranteed to all men by the Constitution and laws of the United States and of Illinois. Will you do me the justice to publish this communication?"

Amidst the Bennett scandal and the assassination attempt on Boggs bearing down on him, Joseph is able to keep a remarkable mental, emotional, spiritual, and physical stamina. He is having a good week. He is appointed mayor to fill the void of Bennett. He immediately holds a city council meeting and passes ordinances banning brothels and punishing adulterers.

At this same council meeting, Joseph speaks "at some length concerning the evil reports which were abroad in the city" concerning him. To counter the evil reports and the forthcoming threats from Missouri, he establishes, with the council's blessing, a "night watch." He will have around-the-clock protection nearly every day for the remaining two years of his life. Before the meeting ends, Joseph Smith turns to John C. Bennett, who for unknown reasons is still present. "Do you have anything ought against me, Dr. Bennett?" Joseph asks the pretended doctor. "Before the council and a house filled with spectators," Bennett declares, "I have no difficulty with the heads of the Church." Yet he tried to murder the head leader a few days prior.

He then emphatically declares, "I publicly avow that anyone who has said that I have stated that General Joseph Smith has given me authority to hold illicit intercourse with women is a liar in the face of God. Those who have said it are damned liars; they are infernal liars. He never either in public or private gave me any such authority or license." A safe distance from Nauvoo and with the aid of willing publishers, Bennett changes his story and his tone. Bennett is a twisted man and distorted in his words. His lies adapt to his audience.

Notwithstanding the outside pressures building against the Latter-day Saints, Joseph is able to press through the week. He publishes a translation of an ancient text he calls the book of Abraham. He also addresses and resolves several business transactions and spends time with his family.

Chapter 12

LATE MAY 1842

Nauvoo, Illinois

THE SIFTING INTENSIFIES. On the heels of Bennett, other questionable souls are being exposed. A man by the name of Chauncey Higbee is cut off from the Church for following the mold of Bennett: "Unchaste and unvirtuous conduct toward certain females" is right if "kept secret," Higbee holds. He doesn't have good judgment when it comes to friends. He joins a circle of influence that causes him to stray from the body of the Church. He confesses his misdeeds and is dropped from the Church. But he doesn't go away like Bennett. Higbee will stay on the scene for more than two years and will recruit others into his hatred for Joseph Smith.

These two public cases of immoral men preying on Latter-day Saint women cause Joseph Smith to spend a whole day with Mormon bishops. Nauvoo has ten geographical wards. Each ward is presided over by a bishop. With the bishops, Joseph talks of the right way of exposing iniquity and bringing the guilty into judgment to answer and repent of their behaviors. The following day, he meets with the women of the Relief Society and teaches them how to expose iniquity justly. According to Eliza R. Snow, Joseph explains "the guilty should not be told openly, strange as this may seem. . . . We must use precaution in bringing sinners to justice, lest in exposing these heinous sins we draw the indignation of a Gentile world upon us. It is necessary to hold an influence in the world, and thus spare our-selves an extermination. . . . All things contrary to the will of God, should be cast from us, but don't do more hurt than good, with your tongues—be pure in heart."

Bennett's own words suggest that he admits he operates with a mind of lust and seduction. Attempts had been made repeatedly to correct him privately. Bennett was no doubt hearing that Joseph Smith had entered into plural marriage. Having already left a wife and children in Ohio, Bennett wanted none of that arrangement or responsibility He preferred loose women for a few minutes and, in some situations, for a few dollars.

With the private judgment and correction of Bennett and Higbee now over, Joseph Smith spends a day in late May 1842 near the rising walls of the unfinished temple. He addresses citizens of Nauvoo, members of the Church, and friends. He calls into ques-tion the practices and motives of the Whig and Democratic tickets surfacing for the next election: "I [do] not intend to vote the Whig or Democratic ticket as such, but would go for those who would sup-port good order." Apparently no one on either ticket is satisfying. At this meeting, the people nominate candidates for the varied offices in the coming election.

Those nominated speak out and close the meeting by expressing "disapprobation of the *Quincy Whig*, relative to [Joseph's] being con-cerned against Governor Boggs." They know the pressure is build-ing. The Missourians want the man responsible for the assassination attempt on Boggs. Joseph Smith and Orrin Porter Rockwell know this; so do Boggs's political enemies.

Joseph Smith finishes this difficult month by suffering a bil-ious attack. Not knowing what is entirely wrong with his digestion dilemma, he takes some medicine and spends the next four days close to home.

Chapter 13

JUNE 1842

Nauvoo, Illinois

*N*OT ONLY DOES the thirty-six-year-old rising prophet have to keep his enemies at bay, he has to welcome a flood of converts from Europe who are constantly arriving in Nauvoo. Many of them are hard workers but are only familiar with work in factories and of spinning and weaving. Factories are something Nauvoo is short of. To alleviate the curse of idleness, city and Church council meetings are devoted to determining "ways and means to furnish the poor with labor."

At this time, Apostle Parley P. Pratt is presiding at a conference of the Church in Manchester, England, where eight thousand Latter-day Saints, many recent converts, are gathered. The flood of Mormon converts arriving to Western Illinois continues to put the Latter-day Saints in an influential civic and economic role. This gives Joseph Smith greater comfort to say what he said a few weeks back: "I don't intend to vote Whig or Democrat." Politicians in Illinois don't like to hear that.

Dissenters from the Church and a handful of non-Mormon neighbors begin a constant stir of agitation and lies upon Joseph Smith and his followers. The positive public sentiment toward the Latter-day Saints is weaning. Even once neutral heads in political positions are easily persuaded by the rhetoric and see the powerful dominance the Latter-day Saints are becoming.

Arguably contrary to his message to the bishops and Relief Society women the previous month, Joseph preaches a hearty sermon in early June comparing the modern-day kingdoms of the world to that of Pharaoh of Egypt. "If the nations now rolling in splendor over the globe," he boldly asserts, "do not repent . . . they shall go down to the pit also and be rejoiced over, and ruled over by old Pharaoh, king devil of the mobocrats, miracle-rejecters, Saint-killers, hypocritical priests, and all other fit subjects to fester in their own infamy."

Joseph's enemies, and perhaps even neutral political leaders, feel a rising threat. Some of his enemies want a fight, and tough language like being compared to "old Pharaoh, king devil" doesn't settle well with them.

Joseph Smith also preaches other sermons this month, but his enemies don't find any fodder in his words to justify their actions. He writes and speaks to Church membership about the Holy Ghost operating upon the minds and hearts of mankind as a still, small voice. In a more private setting, he preaches to the women of the Relief Society, urging them to be quick to extend charity and mercy. "The power and glory of godliness is spread out on a broad principle. . . . God does not look on sin with allowance, but when men have sinned, there must be allowance made for them." Joseph Smith often errs on the side of mercy, perhaps to his mortal detriment, but perhaps also to his eternal favor. Repentant souls are always welcome in his presence and within the Church.

But such mercy doesn't win over his enemies.

John C. Bennett is growing angrier for being exposed. Joseph is forced to publish a message in the paper and send private letters to Masonic lodges who may inadvertently harbor Bennett on his next stage of deception. Non-Mormons aware of Bennett's true character are also warning about his track record. Yet in Bennett's eyes, it is the Mormons who are vile and lacking virtue, especially those at the head. His rhetoric is able to sway public opinion.

But his fabricated moral campaign calling into question the character of the Mormon leaders meets resistance. One Mormon by the name of William Law publishes a defense of the Latter-day

Saints. Law joined Mormonism in 1836 while living in Ontario, Canada. He presided over a branch of the Church there before moving to Nauvoo in 1839. He is a man of great talent. His words and demeanor win the hearts of many, including Joseph Smith. By 1841, Law is sitting with Joseph and Rigdon in the First Presidency of the Church.

Law uses his power of language and persuasion to defend the Saints. "What have Mormons done to Illinois?" he asks. "We say their faults are few compared to the population." At this time, some are agitating Illinoisans with lies and rumors of Mormons being constant lawbreakers. "Where is there a record of murder committed by any of our people? None in the State. Where is there a record against any of our people for a penitentiary crime?—Not in the State. Where is there a record of fine or county imprisonment (for any breach of law) against any of the Latter-day Saints? I know of none in the State. If, then, they have broken no law, they consequently have taken away no man's rights—they have infringed upon no man's liberties."

William Law keeps the pen rolling: "We have been three years in this State, and have not asked for any county or state office. Laws have been administered by those not of our persuasion; administered rigorously, even against the appearance of crime, and yet there has been no conviction of which I have heard. Where is there another community in any state, against none of whom there is a record of conviction for crime in any court during the space of three years? And yet there are those who cry out treason! murder! bigamy! burglary! arson! and everything that is evil, without being able to refer to a single case that has ever been proved against the Mormons."

William Law continues his defense of the Saints by stating why people in the state are becoming unsettled with the Mormon presence in Western Illinois:

> This, then, must be the "head and front of our offending," that by industry in both spiritual and temporal things, we are becoming a great and numerous people; we convert our thousands and tens of thousands yearly to the light of truth—to the glorious liberty of the Gospel of Christ; we bring thousands from foreign lands, from under the yoke of oppression and the iron hand of poverty, and we place them in a situation where they can sustain themselves, which is

the highest act of charity toward the poor. We dry the widow's tear, we fill the orphan's hand with bread, and clothe the naked; we teach them principles of morality and righteousness, and they rejoice in the God of Abraham and in the Holy One of Israel, and are happy.

Nauvoo city leaders passed ordinances against houses of ill repute, against the distribution of spirituous liquors, and against vagrants and disorderly persons. This "morality and righteousness" is apparently offensive to some. William Law acknowledges why the enemies of Joseph Smith act like they do: "When the wicked creep in amongst us for evil, to trample upon the most holy and virtuous precepts, and find our moral and religious laws too strict for them, they cry out, 'Delusion, false prophets, speculation, oppression, illegal ordinances, usurpation of power, treason against the government. . . . You must have your charters taken away.'"

The city is flourishing under the principles being taught by Joseph Smith. Nauvoo is gaining greater and greater promise by denying practices that have for thousands of years ruined other communities and nations. But strict laws against practices that lead to ruin don't sit well with false priests, speculators, and selfish and aspiring politicians.

William Law concludes his defense by arguing how the Saints have brought industry, thousands of tax dollars, and immense sums of gold and silver from other countries, and have established the best produce market in the West, not to mention the manufacturing was starting to bud and would soon be a blossom. Yet the moral laws were too strict for some: no alcohol to be sold, no immorality winked at, no indolent person given a free pass. "As to the city ordinances we have passed," Law ends his letter, "all such as we deemed necessary for the peace, welfare and happiness of the inhabitants, whether Jew or Greek, Mohammedan, Roman Catholic, Latter-day Saint or any other; that they all worship God according to their own conscience, and enjoy the rights of American freemen."

This defense from William Law deepens the affection of the Latter-day Saints toward him. He has an honorable reputation among them—at least for another year and half.

During June of 1842, Joseph Smith has to pick up the pen as well. He puts forth the Bennett scandal to the Saints and presents part of the details he would rather not. He also writes to Governor Thomas Carlin of Illinois, who is hearing much about Joseph Smith, Nauvoo, and the great success of the community. He is also hearing about John C. Bennett. Because of Bennett's standing in the Nauvoo Legion (a state militia), Joseph, as a major general, sees fit to explain why Bennett was excused from duty and left Nauvoo.

Bennett is an "adulterer of the worst kind," Joseph conveys to Governor Carlin. "He brings disgrace upon a whole community." Joseph then tells the governor of the affidavit in his possession where Bennett confesses his wrongdoings and states the innocence of Joseph Smith, acknowledging that his (Bennett's) behavior was out of a selfish passion and not influenced by the words or practices of the Mormon prophet. Joseph is under the impression that Bennett resigned his commission as major general. He asks the governor for clarification on this matter. Resignation or no resignation, Joseph states, "It can be proven by hundreds of witnesses that he is one of the basest of liars."

Before sealing the letter and sending it to the governor, Joseph Smith adds, "I have . . . heard that you have entertained of late very unfavorable feelings towards us as a people, and especially so with regard to myself, and that you have said that I ought to be shot. . . . If this be true, I should be pleased to know from yourself the reason of such hostile feelings, for I know of no cause which can possibly exist that might produce such feelings in your breast."

Six days later, on June 30, 1842, Governor Carlin responds. He acknowledges that disapproving reports of Bennett's true identity and character have been sent to his desk for two years. "I have desired to have as little intercourse with him as possible," Carlin writes to Joseph Smith. Bennett has not sent a resignation either, Carlin reports. The two leaders agree on Bennett—he is wretched man.

Carlin then addresses Joseph Smith's concern about his unfavorable feelings toward him. The governor is forthright: "I can in truth say that I do not entertain or cherish hostile or revengeful feelings towards any man or set of men on earth; but that I may have used strong expressions in reference to yourself, at times when my indignation has been somewhat aroused by repeated admonitions of my friends (both before and since the attempt to assassinate

Ex-Governor Boggs) to be upon my guard; that you had prophesied that Boggs should die a violent death, and that I should die in a ditch." Governor Carlin implies neutrality in his letter. He acknowledges that he read Joseph's denial published in the *Wasp*. He also warns the Mormon prophet that some of his followers are certifying he did predict the death of Boggs and how he should die, but he provides no names of those followers.

Carlin closes his reply to Joseph by conveying he has every right as an American citizen to "resort to the first law of nature, namely to defend your own rights." Joseph had told him of mob rule and kidnappers who lay in wait to come upon the Mormons. Carlin tells Joseph to act in "a quiet submission," yet don't "fold your arms, and silently look on." Carlin has no knowledge of threat or mob action against the Mormons. If he did, "[he] should feel it [his] duty to endeavor to arrest [the mob]."

Joseph Smith is reluctantly pacified with the governor's comments. He has other personal matters to draw his attention. One is to meet with Francis Higbee, who, like Bennett, is upset that his adultery has been exposed. Joseph meets with him one on one and assures Higbee that he spoke of him in self-defense. Higbee shows signs of repentance and promises to reform.

A second personal matter occurs near the last day of June. Joseph Smith marries Eliza R. Snow as a plural wife. Whereas adultery is lustful behavior that rudely ignores the marriage covenant and the responsibility a man and woman are to share in union, in plural marriage, the union is sacred. Nonetheless, the restoration of the biblical practice was "entirely foreign" to the Latter-day Saints.

Eliza is a talented woman blessed with the gift of expression. She writes poetry, keeps a good personal history, and isn't reluctant to address the principles and doctrine in the scriptures. She is outspoken for her day and in no way manipulated or coerced into her marriage relationship. She obtains her own witness of plural marriage, and much like her husband knows, she has the Christian world staring her in the face. Eliza Snow feels her witness cannot be denied. She and her husband view their relationship with the backdrop of eternity, notwithstanding the Christian world still staring them in the face.

Chapter 14

JULY 3–5, 1842

Nauvoo, Illinois

ON SUNDAY, JULY 3, Joseph Smith stands before eight thousand Latter-day Saints. They are gathered in a grove most likely just west of their rising temple. The grove is located on a slope just off the bluff the temple stands on. It is Mother Nature's best offering for some shade and sound quality as speakers use every capacity of their lungs. In this setting Joseph Smith holds his own. "He possesse[s] a noble boldness . . . his language abounding in original eloquence peculiar to himself—not polished—not studied—not smoothed and softened by education and refined by art, but flowing forth in its own native simplicity," Parley P. Pratt records. Most reports say Joseph Smith has a high pitched tenor voice, with a whistle, because of a tooth that had been broken when enemies attempted to force-fully poison him in March of 1832.

On this day, Joseph Smith took up the subject of Daniel's prophecy. Daniel prophesied to a mighty king of Babylon named Nebuchadnezzar that in the last days "the God of heaven [shall] set up a kingdom, which shall never be destroyed." Joseph assures the gathering Saints in the grove that The Church of Jesus Christ of Latter-day Saints is that kingdom—preparing the earth for an assimilation with the kingdom of heaven when the Savior returns in His glory. He reminds his listeners that this drives and motivates their practices, their gatherings, and their missionary labors throughout the earth.

The following day, the subject matter turns to security and patriotism. John C. Bennett's replacement, Wilson Law, has the Nauvoo Legion on parade. Three steamboats from neighboring towns carry several passengers. They all want to see for themselves the active and swelling community of Nauvoo. They also want to catch a glimpse of the American-born prophet. With other spectators gathering on land, the legion has a captive and rather large audience for their display. The visitors are able to see not only the commanding officers of the legion but their companions as well. Emma Smith is on horseback next to her husband. She is darker in hair color and skin. Joseph is fair, with light brown hair. The contrast highlights their "beautiful riding-habits" and their distinctiveness as a couple. They are an "imposing sight."

Joseph and Emma dismount. Her husband once again has a speaking arrangement. He stands and "illustrate[s] the design of the organization of the Legion . . . to yield obedience to the institutions of our country." Joseph Smith loves America. He loves the Constitution—a "part of his religion." He speaks of it often "in the highest terms." One reason is that he and his followers are a "cried down people and misrepresented" as not being part of the American fabric. Nothing is further from the truth in Joseph Smith's eyes.

With growing interest in his person, Joseph Smith writes a letter to the residents of Hancock County. Political anti-Mormon meetings are being held where candidates promise to distance themselves from Mormons and attempt to exclude them from representative democracy. "As a people, The Church of Jesus Christ of Latter-day Saints are found 'more sinned against than sinning,'" he writes. "In political affairs we are ever ready to yield to our fellow citizens of the county equal participation in the selection of candidates for office. We have been disappointed in our hopes of being met with the same disposition on the part of some of the old citizens of the county— they indeed seem to manifest a spirit of intolerance and exclusion incompatible with the liberal doctrines of true republicanism."

It is a letter expressing the true condition but also calling into question the hearts and behaviors of the "old citizens." Though Joseph tries to be pleasant and forthright, he has to call out their character and their motives as being anti-American. Many are offended.

To prepare for the retaliation, the city council of Nauvoo meets to pass an ordinance. The ordinance is in relation to writ of habeas corpus. "No citizen of this city shall be taken out of the city by any writs without the privilege of investigation before the municipal court, and the benefit of a writ of habeas corpus, as granted in the 17th section of the Charter of this city. Be it understood that this ordinance is enacted for the protection of the citizens of this city, that they may in all cases have the right of trial in this city, and not be subjected to illegal process by their enemies."

In other words, if people try to detain or arrest Joseph Smith, they must come before a Nauvoo court first. That court determines if he is detained and arrested legally and if it is for good reasons. If anyone is being unlawfully detained, he is set free from law enforcement from outside jurisdictions. This ordinance is perfect timing for what is right around the corner. The ordinance will extend Joseph Smith's life another two years.

EAST OF NAUVOO the Latter-day Saints establish many farms. They are on lovely ground and the farms are high yielding. Joseph Smith has a farm a few miles from Nauvoo. He frequents it regularly. Cornelius P. Lott is an assigned farmer for Joseph's affairs. During the heat of July, Joseph hoes potatoes with Lott.

Joseph is not opposed to putting his hands in the soil or playing a variety of games with children for physical exercise. Some people question his behavior at times because it doesn't fit their mold of how a prophet should act, or in some cases speak. Pulling sticks, wrestling, snowball fights, playing ball, swimming, and hunting are part of his disposition.

To answer the criticism, Joseph tells "a parable about a prophet and a hunter"—clearly explaining his own philosophy about the relationship of play to work. As the story goes, a certain prophet sat under a tree "amusing himself in some way." Along came a hunter and reproved him. The prophet asked the hunter if he always kept his hunting bow strung up. "Oh no," said the hunter.

"Why not?"

"Because it would lose its elasticity."

"It is just so with my mind," stated Joseph. "I do not want it strung up all the time."

With the pressing responsibilities and the relentless whereabouts and motives of his enemies, Joseph Smith has to find time for amusement. He is jovial and loves to promote merriment, perhaps giving him a high dose of optimism. He tells his cousin, "I should never get discouraged, whatever difficulties should surround me, if I was sunk in the lowest pit of Nova Scotia and all the Rocky Mountains piled on top of me, I ought not to be discouraged but hang on, exercise faith and keep up good courage and I should come out on the top of the heap."

He needs all the amusement and optimism he can muster, because on July 20, 1842, former Governor Lilburn Boggs is well enough to sit before Samuel Weston, a justice of the peace in Independence, Jackson County, and swear an affidavit that Porter Rockwell, who Boggs sees as a the puppet of the Mormon prophet, is the "one who shot him."

John C. Bennett is full steam ahead in his falsehoods against Joseph Smith and other Nauvoo residents. A resolution is passed in a general meeting of the citizens of Nauvoo that Joseph is a "good, moral, virtuous, peaceable and patriotic man." Eight hundred men sign the resolution and present it to Governor Carlin of Illinois.

Not to be outdone, a thousand women of the Relief Society also draw up a petition in behalf of Joseph Smith defending his virtue, philanthropy, and benevolence. They ask Governor Carlin that "their families might have the privilege of enjoying their peaceable rights."

John C. Bennett is no longer acknowledging his own impropriety and wickedness. He is constantly publishing accusations against Joseph to defer the letters and complaints about him from both Mormon and non-Mormon sources.

Joseph Smith is establishing plural marriages in the presence of witnesses. Witnesses are something Bennett has come to loathe. All of his attempts and successes of illicit affairs are accomplished secretly and void of commitment and responsibility. Nonetheless he argues Joseph Smith is promoting promiscuous polygamy.

Daniel H. Wells of Nauvoo writes in the Mormon periodical *Times and Seasons*, "John C. Bennett . . . professed the greatest fidelity, and eternal friendship, yet was he an adder in the path, and a viper in the bosom. He . . . introduced infamy into families, reveled in voluptuousness and crime and led the youth that he had influence over to tread in his unhallowed steps; he professed to fear God, yet did he desecrate His name, and prostitute his authority to the most unhallowed and diabolical purposes . . . defiling of his neighbors' bed."

Strikingly, when Wells pens this, he isn't even a member of the Church (he joins two years after Smith's murder). He is a city council member and judge in Nauvoo. Wells's acceptance in Nauvoo is a testimony that non-Mormons are included in society. Wells is a "Jack Mormon," a label for those who defend or are friendly to the Mormon cause. Wells has a good read on Bennett. He continues to observe Bennett's character by writing, "He professed indignation against Missouri, saying, 'My hand shall avenge the blood of the innocent.' Yet now he calls upon Missouri to come out against the Saints, and he 'will lead them on to glory and to victory.'"

On top of Bennett's accusations and Boggs's sworn affidavit, Joseph learns that Governor Thomas Reynolds, Boggs's successor, has issued a demand to Illinois Governor Carlin for the extradition of Joseph Smith and Orrin Porter Rockwell. Before Reynolds's demand reaches Governor Carlin, Joseph corresponds with his governor. "I shall consider myself and our citizens secure from harm under the broad canopy of the law under your administration. . . . Any service we can do the state at any time will be cheerfully done, for our ambition is to be serviceable to our country. With sentiments of respect and esteem, I remain your humble servant."

Carlin remains neutral. He doesn't send a state bodyguard to protect Joseph Smith. The Mormon leader has to rely on his own men to keep ahead of his enemies now crossing the Mississippi River and coming in all directions by a variety of disguises and with an assortment of schemes. Joseph's public appearances are about to be limited. Far too many enemies are lurking in and around Nauvoo to drag him back to Missouri.

Chapter 16

AUGUST 1–8, 1842

Montrose, Iowa, and Nauvoo, Illinois

*A*S AUGUST ROLLS around, Joseph Smith interrupts one day of his pressing schedule to join about fifteen other men of the Nauvoo Legion in sword maneuvers conducted by a Colonel Brewer. He is cautious not to lose his elasticity. He needs some recreation time as his mental and emotional faculties are being stretched. He finds exercise and sport rejuvenating.

On August 6, Joseph Smith crosses the Mississippi River into Iowa. Here he witnesses the "installation of the officers" for a lodge of Masons. Leaving the proceedings of the meeting, Joseph gathers with several men in the shade of the building. He rehearses the persecutions Mormons suffered in Missouri and the "constant annoyance" they are suffering since being driven from the state.

Anson Call stands nearby and hears the conversation. Joseph speaks of "things that should transpire in the mountains." Those familiar with Illinois and Iowa know there are no mountains—perhaps some rolling hills, but no mountains.

JOSEPH SMITH KNOWS that Nauvoo is only a temporary place for the Latter-day Saints. The premonition is not widely known among the members of the faith, though some are aware of a statement by one of the Apostles of the Church, Heber C. Kimball. In May of 1839, when the Saints arrived on the peninsula, Kimball declared: "It is a very pretty place, but not a long abiding home for the Saints." Sidney Rigdon took offense and didn't want to hear it: "I should suppose that Elder Kimball had passed through sufferings and privations and mobbings and drivings enough, to learn to prophesy good concerning Israel."

"With a mixture of meekness and humor, Heber replied: 'President Rigdon, I'll prophesy good concerning you all the time—if you can get it.' The retort amused Joseph, who laughed heartily with the brethren, and Elder Rigdon yielded the point." Rigdon, as well as others, didn't like to hear those premonitions. As it became more obvious that state officers and citizens were turning their backs on the Saints, Joseph Smith once again broached the subject of moving to a new home.

"Mountains" had reference to the Rocky Mountains. Joseph Smith's vision is westward.

As THE MEN continue their conversation, they gather around a barrel of water. After drinking some water from the barrel, Anson Call hears Joseph prophesy. "Brethren, this water tastes much like the crystal streams that are running in the Rocky Mountains. . . . There are some of those standing here that will perform a great work in that land." Anson is attentive. He has suffered through the persecution and fatigues the Saints experienced in Ohio and Missouri.

"There is Anson," Joseph continues. "He shall go and shall assist in building cities from one end of the country to the other, and you shall perform as great a work as has ever been done by man, so that the nations of the earth shall be astonished, and many of them will be gathered in that land, assisting in building cities and temples, and Israel shall be made to rejoice." Anson will settle communities on the westside of the Rockies in at least seven different counties in what will become three different states. He will start settlements with new converts from Europe. His posterity will be numerous and honored in many communities. Before he dies in 1890, the Latter-day Saints will build four temples in that region.

But Joseph's prophecy isn't ignorant of the trials Call and many other Mormons will have to tread through. "But before you see this day, you (speaking to Call and the others gathered) will pass through scenes that are but little understood by you. This people will be made to mourn, multitudes will die, and many will apostatize, but the priesthood shall prevail over all its enemies, triumph over the devil, and be established upon the earth, never more to be thrown down."

The moment is permanently fixed in Anson Call's memory.

Two days after this prophecy, Joseph Smith is back on the Illinois side of the Mississippi River. The relentless attempts to extradite him back to Missouri begin. Thomas King, a sheriff from Adams County, just south of Nauvoo, arrives in the morning with two assistants. They have a warrant issued by Governor Carlin. Carlin's neutrality has wavered. Missourians can come and get Joseph Smith and Porter Rockwell.

"I have yet to learn by what rule of right I was arrested to be transported to Missouri for a trial," Joseph Smith writes in his history. "An accessory to an assault with intent to kill does not come under the provision of the fugitive act"—an act that could go after someone fleeing justice from another state. In his affidavit, ex-Governor Boggs says "nothing about Joseph having fled from justice . . . and the constitution only authorizes the delivery up of a 'fugitive from Justice to the Executive authority of the State from which he fled.'" Boggs can only say Joseph is "an accessory . . . with intent to kill."

Nonetheless, he is arrested by the sheriff from Adams County, but it has no staying power. The Nauvoo municipal court intervenes. The court issues a writ of habeas corpus, and Joseph is placed under the watch of the city marshal, Henry G. Sherwood, a friend and fellow Mormon. Sheriff King from Adams County and his two assistants angrily leave. The city council of Nauvoo meets before the day is through and reiterates the ordinance on habeas corpus procedures. "All cases where any person or persons, shall at any time hereafter, be arrested or under arrest in this city, under any writ or process, and shall be brought before the municipal court of this city, by virtue of a writ of habeas corpus."

Even with the strengthening of the ordinances and the powers vested in the Nauvoo Charter, Joseph takes all precautions. He sees being kidnapped more probable than being taken by the law.

After dark he goes into hiding and will move his whereabouts frequently for the next few months. Joseph refuses to go back to Missouri to sit in judgment by his enemies. There is much more to teach and instruct the Latter-day Saints before he chooses death.

Chapter 11

AUGUST 9–14, 1842

Around Nauvoo, Illinois

JOSEPH HAS NON-MORMON friends. A state senator named James Harvey Ralston comes to his aid. Ralston is from Quincy and was a circuit judge before becoming an Illinois state senator. Joseph refers to him as Judge Ralston. He also finds some confidence in Stephen Powers, an attorney from Keokuk, Iowa. Somewhere in or around Nauvoo, most likely across the river in Iowa, Joseph Smith meets with the both of them. They prepare a stratagem for Sheriff King's return.

Thomas King reappears in Nauvoo on August 10. Joseph Smith and Porter Rockwell avoid his apprehension. Plenty of Latter-day Saints are willing to throw decoys and false whereabouts to protect their prophet. King threatens some, particularly Emma Smith, Joseph's wife. His threats fall flat. Emma is composed. She has seen plenty of officers come and arrest her husband before.

"AMONG HIS OTHER tribulations," Joseph Smith's ministry is "shadowed by many persistent legal prosecutions." The lawsuits are "all-consuming" and "demand [his] time, assets, body and mind." From 1827 until 1842, Joseph Smith has been involved in nearly "two hundred total suits . . . whether as a defendant, plaintiff, witness or judge. . . . That makes an average of about fourteen cases per year."

He was not convicted in any of the lawsuits.

EMMA FACES THE sheriff with calmness and courage, deflecting her husband's whereabouts. Once again she has to fall asleep without her husband by her side.

On the morning of August 11, William Law has cornered Thomas King before breakfast. At this time, Law is unquestionably a friend of Joseph. Law brings attention to the illegality in attempting to arrest Joseph Smith. King can't muster an argument. He tells Law he knows Joseph Smith is an innocent man and that "Governor Carlin's course . . . was unjustifiable and illegal." Meanwhile, Joseph Smith is at breakfast across the river in Iowa, hunkered down in a Mormon community called Zarahemla (a town named after a city in the Book of Mormon).

One advantage Joseph holds is his alert and dutiful friends. He sends a message to his wife that he wishes to see her. He arranges a meeting place on a small island in the Mississippi River. The meeting place buffers him from anyone pursuing to arrest him. Emma is being watched and tracked herself. She has to be creative in her comings and goings. She has the help of several friends. After dark, she meets her husband's brother Hyrum and several other men near the banks of the Mississippi River. They retrieve a skiff just behind Smith's red brick store and make their way to the island.

Emma and her bodyguards arrive first.

After a short wait, Emma sees an approaching skiff. She is much relieved when she sees her husband step out onto the island. Joseph is accompanied by a few men; still in tow are Judge Ralston and his legal counsel, Powers. Another man, Erastus Derby has just returned from Missouri, where he personally asked Governor Reynolds to revoke the arrest warrant for his friend and prophet. His plea falls on deaf ears.

The island may be the only neutral ground for Joseph Smith. He now is hearing reports that the territorial governor of Iowa has issued a warrant for arrest. If true, Joseph has two sheriffs looking for him on both sides of the river. Joseph tells his wife and friends, "It is absolutely certain that the whole business is another glaring instance of the effects of prejudice against me as a religious teacher, and that it proceeds from a persecuting spirit, the parties have signified their determination to have me taken to Missouri."

He refuses to be taken.

The decision by those gathered on the island is to take him up river, just north of Nauvoo's city limits. He will go into solitude at the home of Edward Sayers. Sayers is not a member of the faith, but his wife is. A man is assigned to go by land up the bank of the river and light two fires marking the spot they should come ashore. Once back in Illinois, Joseph and Erastus Derby make their way through some timber and arrive undetected at Sayers's home, where they are treated hospitably.

The following morning, William Walker takes Joseph Smith's horse in broad daylight across the river into Iowa. This is a planned distraction to get the sheriffs and even a majority of the Mormons to believe that Joseph is on the Iowa side of the river.

Joseph Smith's secretary, William Clayton, is able to visit him after dark. He finds Joseph in an optimistic spirit. Joseph desires Emma to come and see him. His wife Emma likewise wants to be with her husband. When her carriage is being prepared, the sheriff notices. To avoid being followed in the carriage, Emma walks to a friend's home and there awaits the carriage.

In an open prairie four miles north of Nauvoo, Emma gets out of the carriage and walks the remaining way. The carriage and its driver return to Nauvoo. Joseph is overjoyed at his wife's arrival. They will have a night and a day to spend with each other. They get some private time. The distraction of sending Walker over to Iowa on Smith's horse is working. Men gathered to apprehend Joseph are searching fervently in Keokuk, Montrose, and Nashville, three Iowa communities.

In the morning, Joseph and Emma spend time reading and correcting Joseph's personal history. The eighteen-hour reunion revives their spirits and union. Love finds a way, even in stressful times. Sometime just before or during this rendezvous, Emma Smith becomes pregnant with their eighth child. Unfortunately, the child will be stillborn in late December.

To reenter Nauvoo city limits, Emma is taken across the river to Iowa, where she makes a public appearance and then is put on a skiff and taken over to Nauvoo, being seen by several crossing the river. The decoy continues to work. It is a roundabout way and a dangerously windy day on the river to go home this way. Emma passes the trouble courageously.

A rumor also brings Joseph more time in his hiding place. There is a report flooding wider than the Mississippi river: Joseph has been commissioned by the United States to go to Indian land and negotiate a large piece of land for the Mormons to settle on. Even Mr. Powers, Joseph Smith's legal counsel, thinks the report is probable.

Chapter 18
AUGUST 15—END OF NOVEMBER, 1842
In and Around Nauvoo, Illinois

THOUGH IN HIDING, Joseph Smith has a steady flow of visitors. These visits are usually after dark. He has learned that the officers of the law are getting agitated and are willing to bring in additional forces to search every house in Nauvoo. Those bearing the reports to Joseph are themselves becoming agitated at what they are hearing. He counsels his visitors to "maintain an even, undaunted mind." "God Almighty is my shield; and what can man do if God is my friend? I shall not be sacrificed until my time comes; then I shall be offered freely." Like prophets and saints in ancient days, he has to remind his followers, "All that will live godly in Christ Jesus shall suffer persecution."

Two faithful Apostles and friends of the Joseph Smith, John Taylor and Wilford Woodruff, publish an article while he is in hiding: "Ever since the formation of The Church of Jesus Christ of Latter-day Saints, calumny, reproach and persecution have flown plentifully into their lap. . . . Missouri, frantic with rage, and not yet filled with blood, wishes now to follow her bleeding victims to their exile, and satiate herself with blood. And not satisfied with staining her own escutcheon, she wishes to decoy the noble, generous and patriotic sons of Illinois—to deceive them with appearances—to draw them into her snare, that they may be sharer in her crimes, and participate in her guilt and stamp with eternal infamy their character."

When Joseph reads these words, he slaps the editorial as a sign he is in total agreement.

Emma makes another short visit to her husband. In his letters to her, he conveys his gratitude for her tender kindness and encouraging visits. On August 18, a week after arriving at the Sayers home, Emma encourages Joseph to change his location. She helps him move to Carlos Granger's home on the outskirts of Nauvoo. Granger is a non-Mormon who has not been blinded by the atrocities of many Missourians and the current injustices piling against Joseph Smith. Granger extends the hand of friendship and secrecy to his whereabouts.

As August comes to a close, the Illinois authorities, being pressured and persuaded via the Missouri mob, can't apprehend Joseph Smith. Governor Carlin writes to Emma to assure her that he is compelled to act "by a strict sense of duty." He tries to persuade Emma that if her husband is "innocent of any crime, and the proceedings are illegal, it would be the more easy for him procure an acquittal."

Emma replies with a poignant question: "If the law was made for the lawless and disobedient, and punishment instituted for the guilty, why not execute the law upon those that have transgressed it, and punish those who have committed crime, and grant encouragement to the innocent, and liberality to the industrious and peaceable?"

On August 28, Joseph Smith cautiously returns home. The next day he is able to stand before a large gathering of Latter-day Saints. He had been in hiding for three weeks. When he is recognized at the stand, it causes a "great animation and cheerfulness." He wasn't among the Indians; he wasn't in Washington or Europe, as additional rumors proposed. He is before his people, and all felt to rejoice.

For the next three months, Joseph is in and out of Nauvoo. At one moment he is hiding, and the next he is standing in a public setting giving discourses and instructions to the Latter-day Saints. He also wastes no time when in hiding; he writes a few letters in his exile that eventually the Mormons will canonize. One subject occupying his mind is that of baptisms for the dead. "It seems to occupy my mind, and press itself upon my feelings the strongest," he conveys, "since [being] pursued by my enemies." He reintroduces what the ancient Apostles practiced and the Apostle Paul sanctioned: the idea that those who have died without essential gospel ordinances, such as baptism, might have those ordinances performed for them (1 Corinthians 15:29). These ordinances, he tells the Latter-day Saints, must be performed in temples, one of which he is trying to finish before his death.

One morning in September, Joseph feels safe to be at home. Shortly after lunch, another sheriff, James Pitman of Quincy, approaches the residence with two other men. Well-armed they abruptly enter the home and one of Joseph's secretaries immediately greets them. "Where is Mr. Smith?" The secretary says he hasn't seen him since the morning and doesn't know where he is. Joseph Smith is in the next room eating with his family and hears the conversation. He arises and calmly slips out the back door and through his corn, which is fully grown. He makes it unnoticed to a Mormon bishop's house. He finds respite in the bishop's upstairs room.

Emma confronts Pitman and demands the warrant. He admits he has no warrant to search the house. Knowing her husband is free from the property, she allows Pitman to search the home. This close call with his enemies puts Joseph back into hiding for a few days. He writes more instructions concerning baptisms for the dead, declares his testimony in writing to some friends, and conducts business affairs of the Church with a pen.

Joseph is becoming a well-known American through the missionary labors of his followers and also through the newspapers of his day. Editors are taking interest. People want to see and read about him. He is becoming increasingly well-known. David Rogers of New York arrives in Nauvoo and would like to paint a portrait of the man more and more are calling a prophet. Joseph gratifies the request and comes out of hiding in the middle of September to sit for an oil portrait. It takes Rogers two non-consecutive days to complete the portrait.

A painter finds an audience with Joseph, but the law enforcement of Illinois cannot. Governor Carlin is growing more embarrassed that Joseph Smith is not in custody. He offers a two-hundred-dollar reward for him. With some physical and mental stamina, Joseph stands for two hours and addresses the topic of persecution. He has a solid bodyguard around him and other alert men on the peripheral, which allows him to remain in the public eye for the discourse. When in his private home, he has vigilant men watching the residence continually. This gives him an opportunity to nurse his wife who is sick.

Governor Reynolds adds to Carlin's offer by a hundred dollars. He will also give three hundred dollars for Orrin Porter Rockwell. How much time Joseph and Rockwell are spending together is unknown. Rockwell's physical appearance is conspicuous, and Joseph's is easily disguised. By October, Joseph and Emma are both sick. Tired of going in and out of hiding, Joseph prays that he might "guide [Almighty Jehovah's] people in righteousness, until my head is white with old age."

His hair will go a bit gray but never reach white.

Some honest men of law try helping Joseph Smith reach old age. Justin Butterfield, who is a district attorney, comes to the Saints' defense arguing that he along with others, including the state supreme court, see the folly in the extradition attempt. They know Joseph has not and cannot justifiably be charged; therefore, he is in no way a fugitive of justice. If he was guilty, the Constitution would hold him accountable and Joseph would honor it. Butterfield emphatically states the requisition made by the governor of Missouri and upheld by Governor Carlin has no substance. Butterfield is sure Joseph Smith will be granted a discharge given the legal rights and procedures of habeas corpus.

The letter Butterfield sends to the Latter-day Saints impresses Joseph Smith. He says that his opinion "accords with the opinions of every intelligent man. The opinions of ex-Governor Boggs, Governor Reynolds of Missouri, and Governor Carlin, to the contrary, notwithstanding."

Enemies are still lurking, looking for any possible moment to bear Joseph off to Missouri. Notwithstanding, he devotes some attention to the construction of the temple. A temporary floor is in place by mid-October, and Joseph approves of meetings being held there. One day at the end of October, Joseph rides his horse to the bluff and views the temple rising over the Mississippi River. He is pleased with the progress of what he calls a "sacred edifice."

While dodging his enemies, Joseph is also continuously greeting immigrating and migrating converts. Near the banks of the river, he tells a group of converts that he is "but a man, and they must not expect me to be perfect; if they expected perfection from me, I should expect it from them; but if they would bear with my infirmities and the infirmities of the brethren, I would likewise bear with their infirmities." He tells the newcomers that he will most likely have to "again hide up in the woods." He bids them a temporary good-bye.

November passes with some normalcy. Joseph spends time with his children and takes them on outings. One day, he and three of his children are thrown from their carriage, which is overturned. They all walk away. Unhurt, Joseph chops wood for the winter, receives visitors constantly, and visits friends.

In late November, Brigham Young is taken sick with apoplexy, a disease where internal bleeding causes neurological problems. Most die in a short amount of time. Joseph Smith arrives to bless and comfort Young. Young said of this visit, "The Prophet prophesied that I should live and recover from my sickness. He sat by me for six hours, and directed my attendants what to do for me." Brigham Young fights the sickness for eighteen days. Joseph checks on him constantly. To his delight, Brigham is restored to health. Joseph Smith recognizes Brigham's greatness and gifts. Young has unique discernment and keen judgment to recognize when Joseph Smith is granted God's grace as a prophet and when he is merely speaking as a man.

Another man who had unique discernment and keen judgment was Joseph's brother Hyrum. Joseph says of him, "Brother Hyrum, what a faithful heart you have got! Oh may the Eternal Jehovah crown eternal blessings upon your head, as a reward for the care you have had for my soul! O how many are the sorrows we have shared together; and again we find ourselves shackled with the unrelenting hand of oppression. Hyrum, thy name shall be written in the book of the law of the Lord, for those who come after thee to look upon, that they may pattern after thy works."

RYAN C. JENKINS

In less than two years, Joseph's name will be laid on the altar of the souls of those who were slain for the word of God.

Chapter 19

DECEMBER 1842

Nauvoo and Springfield, Illinois

GOVERNOR CARLIN HAS a few days left in office. Thomas Ford has been elected. Joseph Smith sends a group of men to Ford before he even takes the oath of office. They want to get a read on his feelings regarding the warrants out for Joseph Smith. The Mormon men make an affidavit that Joseph Smith was in Illinois on May 6 when someone tried to assassinate Boggs. Stephen Douglas is also able to state that Joseph didn't flee any crime that day either, because he was with him the day following.

On December 9, while Ford embarks on his first day as governor, Joseph is two-hundred miles away in Nauvoo chopping wood. In his inaugural address Ford acknowledges that citizens of his state are objecting to the Nauvoo Charter and the powers granted. He hints that the charter should be modified. This is a blow to the Mormons. A representative from Bond County puts forth a resolution that the charter of Nauvoo be repealed. Another representative wants the state arms given to the Nauvoo Legion to be recalled and put back into state custody. The state had issued the Mormons three canons, muskets, swords, and pistols. Besides drills and parading, the guns haven't been used. This follows a pattern that proceeded the shedding of Mormon blood in Missouri. Take their weapons and then move in.

One of Joseph Smith's younger brothers—William—is at the state house watching and listening to the inauguration. A year earlier, William had won the seat from Hancock County. Sometime after Ford's address and the representatives' request to clamp down on the Nauvoo Charter, William asks the speaker of the House for the floor.

William argues that few in the House understand what privileges are even granted in the charter; therefore, how can they wisely, or even ignorantly, make a judgment? But more important, he doesn't understand why some are trying to strip a freedom-loving, law-abiding citizenry from their rights, which they have never abused. "The rights of the people of Nauvoo are just as sacred as those of any other people. The people that live there should have just the same privileges extended to them as are awarded the Springfield, Chicago, Quincy, or any other city in the state," he argues.

William's remarks stay the tide—for the time being.

After a week of being in office, Ford writes to Joseph Smith asking him to come to Springfield to have his case heard. He offers Joseph protection while he travels to and from his trial. Hesitant at first, Joseph agrees when he secures Justin Butterfield's promise to represent him. "I will stand by you, and see you safely delivered from your arrest," Butterfield conveys.

Even Joseph's loyal friends say the time is right to clear his name. As a formality he is arrested by Wilson Law, major general in the Nauvoo Legion. Two men visit Carthage and obtain a writ of habeas corpus for Joseph to be taken to Springfield. In the early evening, Emma delivers a stillborn child. With another blow and difficult heartache of not being able to be with his grieving wife, Joseph leaves the next morning for Springfield.

They travel to Plymouth in severe snow and cold and lodge at Samuel Smith's home, a younger brother of Joseph. Here Joseph also meets up with his other brother, William, who defended their cause in the state house of representatives. With Hyrum there as well, they enjoy some family time. Joseph sleeps this night on the floor on top of a buffalo skin. He dreams this night that he "was by a beautiful stream of water and saw a noble fish, which I threw out. Soon after, I saw a number more, and threw them out. I afterwards saw a multitude of fish, and threw out a great abundance, and sent for salt and salted them." He gives no interpretation.

As they continue their travels, Joseph has at least fifteen men and at least two women following him to Springfield. In a tavern for some entertainment, the group wants to mark the height of Joseph and Hyrum. According to that night's measurements, both come in at six feet. Additional reports suggest Hyrum was a bit taller. The next day the group travels thirty-two miles in extremely cold weather.

By December 30, Joseph has been introduced to Justin Butterfield. He spends time with Butterfield reviewing the Latter-day Saints' persecutions in Missouri. Joseph and many of his friends stay at the home of Judge James Adams, a Mormon convert of more than two years.

On the last day of 1842, Joseph Smith is arrested in front of his attorney, Justin Butterfield, who immediately appeals for a writ of habeas corpus to be heard. Before noon, Joseph is before Judge Pope. A writ is "granted, returned, and served in one minute." The courtroom is crowded with eager residents to see the Mormon prophet. "There goes Smith the Prophet and a good looking man he is," one shouts out.

Another not so kind yells, "And a damned rascal as ever lived."

Hyrum Smith with a smile defends his brother by stating to the one who made the comment, "And a good many ditto." Irked even more, the antagonist says to Hyrum, "Yes, ditto, ditto, G—d— you; and everyone that takes his part is as damned a rascal as he is." William Law also jumps in to confront the man. "I am the man, and I'll take his part." The antagonist whirls on Law, "You are a damned rascal too." Law rebuffs, "You are a lying scoundrel." Strangely, the man confronting them begins to take off his clothes as he makes a run for the street. This he did cursing and swearing. It was evident by all what spirit operated upon him.

Joseph takes his last dinner of 1842 with Butterfield and others at the American House, where Governor Ford is staying, a place familiar to Abraham and Mary Lincoln. After dinner a team of horses runs away "and [goes] past the state house, when the hue-and-cry [is] raised, 'Joe Smith is running away!' which produced a great excitement and a sudden adjournment of the House of Representatives."

Joseph Smith enjoys a laugh.

Chapter 20

JANUARY 1–6, 1843

Springfield, Illinois

THE YEAR 1843 begins on a Sabbath. No court proceedings will be held on this day. Instead the speaker of the House of Representatives offers the hall for preaching by the Latter-day Saints. Eager ears, many for the first time, want to hear the Mormons. The people also have "anxiety to see the Prophet." They have heard all kinds of reports and read various accounts about Joseph Smith and his people.

IN SPRINGFIELD, ILLINOIS, two men of great American significance are in close proximity. At this point in American history, the stage belongs to Joseph Smith, not Abraham Lincoln. Lincoln is aware of Joseph Smith. In 1840, he acknowledged that Joseph passed through Springfield on his return to Nauvoo from Washington, DC. He is following reports and reading newspapers on what the Mormons are doing and how rapidly they are establishing themselves in Western Illinois. These two men lived in the same state for five years, and given the legal battles Joseph Smith faced, Lincoln was no doubt privy to his successes and his troubles. Lincoln was a member of the Illinois state legislature in 1839, at the time Mormons were being driven from Missouri to Illinois and seeking a city charter for their gathering place. Lincoln noted that a "strange new sect" was moving into the state.

In all probability, Lincoln is an interested legal observer as he watches and hears of the events of Joseph Smith's trial. Both men have a burdensome mortal path ahead of them. Joseph Smith has only one and half years to live, Lincoln more than twenty. Historian Richard Bushman observed: "They both died significantly. Neither passed from this life by natural causes. Their deaths by assassins' bullets were a culmination, a punctuation mark, on their lives and accomplishments. Lincoln died for breaching the South's slave system, Joseph for claiming divine authority. Their deaths were seen as sacrifices for the causes they lived for, testaments of their works. The form of their deaths hallowed the memory of their lives."

Lincoln will revisit this "strange new sect" and the works of Joseph Smith in November of 1861. He will check out a copy of the Book of Mormon, which he himself will sign for. He will return the Book of Mormon in July of 1862.

BEFORE GOING TO the representatives' hall, Joseph Smith sits down for an interview with several people, including Butterfield—his legal counsel—and Judge Stephen Douglas. Putting the forthcoming trial aside, Butterfield inquires about the differences between Latter-day Saints and the other sectarians of the day. Joseph Smith explains that the most significant distinction is that the sectarians "were all circumscribed by some peculiar creed, which deprived its members the privilege of believing anything not contained" in their limited and often false creeds. "Whereas," Joseph Smith continues to explain, "the Latter-day Saints have no creed, but are ready to believe all true principles that exist, as they are made manifest from time to time."

"What is the nature of a prophet?" someone from the gathering asks. He is asked this in many settings and often says, "Noah came before the flood, I have come before the fire." On this occasion, he answers his inquirers, "If any person should ask me if I were a prophet, I should not deny it, as that would give me the lie; for, according to John, the testimony of Jesus is the spirit of prophecy; therefore if I profess to be a witness or teacher, and have not the spirit of prophecy, which is the testimony of Jesus, I must be a false witness; but if I be a true teacher and witness, I must possess the spirit of prophecy, and that constitutes a prophet; and any man who says he is a teacher or preacher of righteousness, and denies the spirit of prophecy, is a liar, and the truth is not in him; and by this key false teachers and imposters may be detected."

Just before noon, Joseph Smith and those in his immediate company remove to the representatives' hall, "where most of the members of the Legislature and the various departments of the state are in attendance." Joseph enters the hall as a celebrated guest. The past several months Joseph has had to bow out of public appearances to avoid his enemies. Now he finds himself before crowds of people and "respectable congregations."

Latter-day Saints fortunate to occupy a portion of the chamber and sing "The Spirit of God like a Fire is Burning." Joseph Smith deflects the attention modestly. He calls on other Mormons to speak. Mormon Apostle Orson Hyde addresses the congregation. He gives a discourse on Malachi 3, where the ancient prophet describes how the Lord will send messengers to prepare the way for the Second Coming. Arguably, Hyde is setting forth that Joseph Smith was such a messenger. Joseph Smith and his Apostles are teaching individuals about preparing for the Second Coming of the Savior.

Hyde takes the majority of the meeting with his discourse. Joseph doesn't speak. Adjourning for dinner, Joseph takes company with Judge James Adams.

ADAMS SOUGHT JOSEPH Smith out when he passed through Springfield in 1839 on his way to Washington, DC, and the two of them spent a few days and considerable time at Adams's residence. James Adams is a prominent county official and an active politician and mason. Joseph Smith put on record that in 1839 Adams took him in and "treated [him] like a father." Joseph couldn't delay his commitment to address the Missouri sufferings in Washington. So he left Adams in the hands of a Mormon elder who baptized Judge Adams under secrecy. Adams felt he could help the Mormon people in greater measure if "those in the political arena remained unaware of his religious affiliation." His loyalty and frequent visits to Nauvoo probably "tipped his hand."

In the 1830s, Abraham Lincoln challenged the character of James Adams for a friend who was running against him for probate justice of the peace. Lincoln's vilification of Adams didn't work to help his friend win the election, but it probably did work in tempering Lincoln's approach to politics. He initially accused Adams of being a "forger, a whiner, a fool, and a liar." Joseph Smith sees Adam's as a "pillar of society." Lincoln seems to have wanted to bury his "character assassination" on Adams. "His motive in this instance appears less than noble." By the time Joseph Smith's habeas corpus hearing rolls around in January 1843, Adams is still one of the prominent men in the community and held in high respect by the citizens, some even who know of his membership in the Mormon Church.

IN THE LATE afternoon, another respectable gathering fills the representatives' hall. They listen to another Mormon Apostle, John Taylor. He preaches on Revelations 14, setting forth that the gospel of Jesus Christ would be restored in the last days by angelic ministry. According to John Taylor, "All leading characters mentioned in the scriptures, who operated in the various dispensations, came and conferred upon Joseph the various keys, rights, privileges and immunities which they enjoyed in their time." Taylor points the crowd's attention to the important ministry of Joseph Smith, who had the responsibility in establishing the preaching of the gospel to the whole earth, as instructed by these heavenly messengers.

Strangely, Joseph doesn't give a public address on this day. He has an impending trial first thing in the morning. He visits with gathering Latter-day Saints and retires at Judge Adams's home for the night. An optimistic spirit rests upon him when he arises. After breakfast and before leaving for his trial, Joseph Smith prophesies to a handful of men in his presence: "In the name of the Lord," he will not go to Missouri "dead or alive."

Joseph arrives at the court hearing thirty minutes early. He sits in quiet contemplation as the courtroom anxiously fills to capacity. Extra chairs are brought in. At ten o'clock, Judge Nathaniel Pope enters with several prominent Springfield women following him. Among them is Mary Todd Lincoln. She and the others take seats before the court. Whether her husband is in the room is not known.

Pope has been the US District Judge for Illinois for nearly twenty-four years. The case before him ranks as one of the most well-known. However, there is not much excitement in the courtroom this day. The prosecuting attorney wants the trial to be delayed a day or two. Joseph Smith's attorney sets forth some objections "referred to in the habeas corpus." Within thirty minutes, Joseph leaves the room and gathers in the Senate chamber to converse with "several gentlemen." Public sentiment toward Joseph Smith is softening some hearts. A man from St. Louis, Missouri, with ill feelings toward him quietly observes Joseph the first few days he is in Springfield. He confesses to Wilson Law that his "general impression [is] that Smith [is] innocent" and that it would be murder if he were killed. Not entirely walking in justice, the man adds, "He ought to be whipped a little and let go."

With court proceedings put on hold for a day, Joseph is constantly responding to people who seek an interview with him. The marshal gets his ear and tells him that it was "the first time during his administration that the ladies had attended court on trial." The marshal is pleasant and desires Joseph to come to dinner when he *is* freed.

ON THE MORNING of January 3, Joseph visits a woman and her newborn baby. He blesses the baby, who has been named Joseph Smith Crane. He then spends some considerable time with Butterfield, Judge Pope, and others discussing his case. In the evening, they enjoy a "very social manner" with several people. At this social, Joseph states another prophecy that "no formidable opposition would be raised at [his] trial on the morrow." Confident among those friends and legal authorities at Springfield, he sleeps soundly.

At nine o'clock, Judge Pope enters the courtroom. Before taking his seat, he gently bows to the ten women who have followed him into the room and who occupy seats to his side.

Attorney general for the state of Illinois, J. Lamborn, proceeds to excuse the US Constitution by saying the state or federal government doesn't have any "authority or jurisdiction to enquire into any facts behind the writ." He argues that Governor Reynolds's request to extradite Joseph Smith be granted.

Butterfield arises and presents the court "evidence, affidavits, and several persons" testifying Joseph Smith was in Nauvoo when Boggs was shot. Butterfield then argues "that an attempt . . . to deliver up a man who has never been out of the state, strikes at all the liberty of our institutions. His fate today may be yours tomorrow."

Striking at the personal liberty of all, Butterfield wins many hearts and minds. He concludes by declaring that if Joseph Smith goes to Missouri, "it is only to be murdered, and he had better be sent to the gallows. He is an innocent and unoffending man. If there is a difference between him and other men, it is that this people believe in prophecy, and others do not."

Joseph is pleased at Butterfield's words, even noting that his manner allows the "utmost decorum and good feeling" to prevail, "and much prejudice was allayed." Joseph has no hard feelings toward the attorney general, who excused the Constitution, knowing he was "saying little more than his relation to the case demanded."

Judge Pope adjourns the court proceedings until the next day. He isn't conflicted about the verdict he will render the next day. He spends the evening with Joseph Smith, along with a host of others, with "many interesting anecdotes, and everything to render the [meal] and visit agreeable." Joseph retires near midnight at Judge Adams's, knowing one prophecy was fulfilled and the other is soon to be fulfilled.

The next day, the courtroom, for the third day in a row, is filled beyond capacity with many "spectators anxious to behold the prophet." Honorable women of the community are once again granted premier seating. Judge Pope gives a lengthy decision. But the simple part of his decision is that Boggs's affidavit is a farce. He swears that he *believes* Joseph Smith was accessory to the facts in relation to the assassination attempt. "Is the Constitution satisfied with a charge upon suspicion?" Pope asks. The judge then provides three reasons why Boggs's affidavit is insufficient: It is not positive. It charges no crime. It charges no crime in the state of Missouri.

Boggs can't extradite someone just because he *believes* he did it. "The proceedings of this affair, from the affidavit to the arrest, afford a lesson to governors and judges whose action may hereafter be invoked in cases of this character." Pope calls into question the shallowness of those involved and believes this case is a precedent. Boggs's affidavit has "no legal existence." Governor Reynolds's requisition and warrant "cannot be received as evidence to deprive a citizen of his liberty and transport him to a foreign state for trial. For these reasons Smith must be discharged."

Pope finishes, and a feeling of relief enters the room. Joseph Smith feels to rejoice and is anxious to return to Nauvoo, where he doesn't have to go into hiding to avoid Missouri officials. To show his pleasure in the verdict, he stands and bows to the court. Pope requests to see him in the judges' chamber. Butterfield follows. For an hour they converse. Joseph declares to his friends of civil law, "I [do] not profess to be a prophet any more than every man ought to who professes to be a preacher of righteousness; and that the testimony Jesus is the spirit of prophecy." Butterfield presses Joseph to "prophesy how many inhabitants would come to Nauvoo."

Joseph Smith smiles and says, "I will not tell how many inhabitants will come to Nauvoo; but when I went to Commerce [now Nauvoo], I told the people I would build up a city, and the old inhabitants replied 'We will be damned if you can.' So I prophesied that I would build up a city, and the inhabitants prophesied that I could not; and we have now about 12,000 inhabitants. I will prophesy that we will build up a great city; for we have the stakes and have only to fill up the [space]." More than eight thousand more would come in the next fourteen months, trumping Springfield and equaling Chicago. Nauvoo is well on its way to becoming a great city.

January 5 will bring closure to five months of Joseph Smith being hounded by Missouri extradition attempts.

On his last day in Springfield, Joseph settles with Butterfield for his services, to the sum of 230 dollars. He meets also with Governor Ford, who recently replaced Carlin. Ford offers some advice, "Refrain from all political electioneering." Ford doesn't like the Mormon power. Pope's family doesn't mind it. Pope's son tells Joseph that he hopes he will not be persecuted anymore. Joseph blesses him. Butterfield sees the significance of the week and the work he has done. He asks Joseph Smith to place all the papers of the trial "in the archives of the Temple when it is completed."

As January 6, 1843, comes to a close, Joseph Smith receives "many invitations to visit distinguished gentlemen in Springfield." Did Lincoln want to have a private interview with him? It wouldn't have mattered because Smith doesn't have time to comply with the requests.

He leaves Springfield early the next morning to return to Nauvoo.

Chapter 21

REMAINDER OF JANUARY 1843

Nauvoo, Illinois

JOSEPH SMITH RETURNS home to Nauvoo and enjoys the company of family and Church members. He spends nearly a week free from the passion of enemies. However, by January 16, he has to answer a letter from John C. Bennett. The letter was sent to Sidney Rigdon and Orson Pratt, one of the Apostles whose wife Bennett had seduced. Pratt has no patience with Bennett's words. Immediately he shows the letter to Joseph. Pratt's immediacy in making the content of the letter known replenishes Joseph Smith's confidence in Pratt but diminishes his confidence in Rigdon. Sidney Rigdon sought to keep the contents secret and to hide that he is holding "a private correspondence with Bennett."

Bennett confides to Rigdon and Pratt, "New proceedings have been gotten up on the old charges, and no habeas corpus can then save [him]. We shall try Smith on the Boggs case, when we get him into Missouri. The war goes bravely on; and, although Smith thinks he is now safe, the enemy is near, even at the door. He has awoke the wrong passenger. The governor will relinquish Joe up at once on the new requisition. There is but one opinion on the case, and that is, nothing can save Joe on a new requisition and demand predicated on the old charges on the institution of new writs. He must go to Missouri; but he shall not be harmed, if he is not guilty: but he is a murderer, and must suffer the penalty of the law. Enough on this subject."

Bennett sneaks into Springfield a few days after Joseph Smith and his party left. It seems reasonable that Bennett would have presented his case a few days earlier when Joseph was there and brought the whole of the matter before the people. Bennett admits to Governor Ford he is one of the calloused foes of the Mormon prophet. He is angry, but it has nothing to do with Boggs and the Missourians. He wants to cut the throats of those who brought to light his immorality and exposed his carnal character.

Joseph Smith sends Jacob Backenstos, a non-Mormon willing to defend the rights of the Latter-day Saints, to Governor Ford. He tells Ford that before Joseph will "be troubled any more by Missouri, [Smith] would fight." Joseph has grown impatient with Bennett.

Even though Bennett is out on the perimeter lurking and seizing others with his reasoning, Joseph Smith's person isn't immediately threatened. He can enjoy his home and his family. He takes some time to push the political hounds back and follow Ford's advice of refraining from all political electioneering. In a short note he publishes: "I have of late had repeated solicitations to have something to do in relation to the political farce about dividing the county; but as my feelings revolt at the idea of having anything to do with politics, I have declined, in every instance, having anything to do on the subject. I think it would be well for politicians to regulate their own affairs. I wish to be let alone, that I may attend strictly to the spiritual welfare of the Church."

This seems to have been an olive branch to Ford in order to stay in his favor. The reality is, Joseph Smith will have a lot to do with politics and will have his views and policies published in just over a year.

Joseph has greater interest in the spiritual welfare of the Church. He continues to hold public meetings in the dead of winter. They are attended by large crowds. He speaks on the kingdom of God being restored to the earth. "Whenever there has been a righteous man on earth unto whom God revealed His word and gave power and authority to administer in His name, and where there is a priest of God—a minister who has power and authority from God to administer in the ordinances of the gospel and officiate in the priesthood of God, there is the kingdom of God," he sets forth. "In consequence of rejecting the Gospel of Jesus Christ and the Prophets whom God hath sent, the judgments of God have rested upon people, cities, and nations, in various ages of the world."

Joseph Smith is claiming in his discourse that he has the authority to administer in the ancient priesthood because he received the charge by those who held the priesthood anciently. This claim irks some, especially his enemies.

"Whenever men can find out the will of God and find an administrator legally authorized from God, there is the kingdom of God; but where these are not, the kingdom of God is not," Joseph continues to teach. "All the ordinances, systems, and administrations on the earth are of no use to the children of men, unless they are ordained and authorized of God; for nothing will save a man but a legal administrator; for none others will be acknowledged either by God or angels."

In this particular sermon, Joseph is speaking in a confident nature. "I know what I say; I understand my mission and business. God Almighty is my shield; and what can man do if God is my friend? I shall not be sacrificed until my time comes; then I shall be offered freely." He knows what is in his mortal forecast. Even though he was freed from the extradition attempt, the dark clouds are clearly on the horizon. Knowing God is his friend bolsters his conviction. "All flesh is as grass, and a governor is no better than other men; when he dies he is but a bag of dust. I thank God for preserving me from my enemies; I have no enemies but for the truth's sake. I have no desire but to do all men good. I feel to pray for all men. We don't ask any people to throw away any good they have got; we only ask them to come and get more. What if all the world should embrace this Gospel? They would then see eye to eye, and the blessings of God would be poured out upon the people, which is the desire of my whole soul."

He finishes with a loud *amen* and sits down. He is ready to face the troubling days ahead. A severe snowstorm and extreme cold settle down upon Nauvoo in late January.

Chapter 22

FEBRUARY–MARCH 1843

*Nauvoo, Illinois, and
Surrounding Communities*

URING THE COLD days of early February, Joseph Smith is unanimously reelected mayor of Nauvoo. He also spends one afternoon with his nearly seven-year-old son Frederick sliding on the ice, "exercising [himself]." This kind of behavior is bothersome to some. Just before sliding on the ice with young Frederick, Joseph entertains a couple from Michigan who desire to meet and speak with him. They told him that "a prophet is always a prophet." Joseph promptly sets his opinion forth: "A prophet was a prophet only when he was acting as such."

In the past thirteen years, Joseph Smith has produced many writings, translated ancient records, preached many of sermons, gathered many converts, and built a temple. But he has also participated in snowball fights, wrestling matches, stick-pulling, and playing ball with the boys. He has attended dances and other social parties. Joseph doesn't take himself too seriously and in no way does he feel these activities distort his calling as Prophet. He is at times demanding as a religious leader and forward in his statements.

He writes a parable that is printed in mid-February asking, "Why, then, the rage against me." He goes forth like "a young fawn," he writes. The political heads of the states surrounding him, along with the major editors of the community newspapers, are often against him, like "lions of the forest." Such lions he proposes in his parable begin to roar and run around telling everyone in the forest that this "fawn will be metamorphosed into a lion—will devour all the beasts of the field, destroy all the trees of the forest, and tread under foot all the rest of the lions."

Joseph marvels at the vehement public attention he and his people are receiving. They are trying to prosper on American soil on while being forced to stay off the lions of jealousy and bigotry. "I am innocent of the things whereof you accuse me," he tells the lions of the press. "I have not been guilty of violating your laws, nor of trespassing upon your rights. My hands are clean from the blood of all men, and I am at the defiance of the world to substantiate the crimes whereof I am accused."

In his parable, he calls out the press for ignorantly accepting the reports of John C. Bennett. "It is true that I once suffered an ass to feed in my pasture. He ate at my crib and drank at my waters; but possessing the true nature of an ass, he began to foul the water with his feet, and to trample underfoot the green grass and destroy it. I therefore put him out of my pasture, and he began to bray. Many of the lions in the adjoining jungles, mistaking the braying for the roaring of a lion, commenced roaring. When I proclaimed this abroad many of the lions began to enquire into the matter. A few, possessing a more noble nature than many of their fellows, drew near, and viewing the animal found that he was nothing more than a decrepit, broken down, worn out ass, that had scarcely anything left but his ears and voice."

Another who is about to begin braying is Wilson Law, brother of William Law. In February, Wilson Law is in a land dispute with a man named Nickerson. Joseph and the city council hear the disputes and reports of both men. After their testimonies, Joseph Smith explains the laws, which favor Nickerson as having the "oldest claim and best right" to the disputed property. Though both men shake hands "in token of a settlement of all difficulties," Wilson Law's allegiance to Joseph is waning.

While the city council is in session the following day, Joseph glances out the window and sees two boys fighting. He immediately leaves the council room and runs across the way to stop the boys, who by this time have taken to using clubs in their fight. He grabs one boy and then the other. The boys, recognizing who is intervening, quickly contain their anger. Joseph gives the "bystanders a lecture for not interfering in such cases, and told them to quell all disturbances in the street at the first onset." He returns to the council room and in a good-humored manner tells the assembled men "that nobody [is] allowed to fight in Nauvoo but myself."

Plenty of bigger of fights are coming.

One fight is extremely personal. From the early days of the Church (1830), Sidney Rigdon has been close to Joseph. The two have experienced intimate spiritual outpourings together, which Rigdon will never deny. They have suffered under the hands of perse-cutors together. They have preached to large congregations together. But Rigdon continues to align with conspirators, both inside and outside the Church.

Joseph writes to Rigdon, accusing him of "practicing deception and wickedness against" him and The Church of Jesus Christ of Lat-ter-day Saints. He is also accused of being in connection with John C. Bennett and others to destroy Joseph as the leader of the Saints. Rigdon controls the Nauvoo post office business as postmaster. It's a perfect position to hide deceit and to be privy to the Prophet's affairs and the communications he's having. Joseph Smith questions Rig-don's appointment to the postmaster position as being instigated and supported by Bennett's assistance and interest.

Rigdon immediately returns a reply to Joseph Smith denying any secret allegiance with Bennett. Nonetheless, Rigdon remains aloof and negligent in duties as a high officer in the Church. He gives more time to personal matters and his own business affairs. The relationship is strained and arguably fading fast.

After reading Rigdon's reply, Joseph returns home hoping to enjoy a carefree night from instigators and apostates. But before supper, a Josiah Butterfield—no relation to the Butterfield who helped him in Springfield—comes to his home and for some reason insults him so "outrageously" that Joseph "kicks him out of the house, across the yard, and into the street." Two young witnesses, one the Prophet's own boy Alexander and the other his nephew Joseph F. Smith, are playing marbles. "All of a sudden the door flew open and I looked," his nephew later recalls, "and there came a great, big man right off the end of Joseph Smith's foot, and he lit on the sidewalk just by the gate. Since I grew to be a man, I learned that this man was there insulting . . . and abusing him in his own house."

Butterfield is the stepfather of two daughters, Maria and Sarah Lawrence. They don't hold the same feelings toward Joseph Smith that their stepfather does. They will enter into plural marriage with Joseph, with Emma Smith's approval, two months after this incident.

The first punch in another fight is also thrown in March. A state senator moves that the Nauvoo Charter be repealed. Fortunately for Joseph Smith and the Latter-day Saints, the senate refuses to repeal it. But the charter's days are numbered.

With the charter backed for another season, the Latter-day Saints busily move ahead in civic and religious matters. While in a small company at dinner in early March, Joseph Smith says that "for a man to be great, he must not dwell on small things, though he may enjoy them." The proverb resonates with his scribes. They are busily and faithfully attempting to keep up with him. He has a resilient and productive mind that does not dwell on small things. He has a gift to keep people moving economically, physically, and spiritually.

On March 4, Joseph learns that Porter Rockwell is apprehended in St. Louis and put in jail. Rockwell was bravely venturing into Missouri to see family. This time he gets caught. The Missourians now have half of their claim in the Boggs assassination attempt. Taking a few days to reflect on his dear friend's situation, Joseph Smith utters a prophecy: "In the name of the Lord Jesus Christ . . . Orrin Porter Rockwell [will] get away honorably from the Missourians"—a brave statement given the situation.

Joseph remains cheerful and optimistic. One morning after conversation with friends, he lies down on the table in a room. It is large enough and sturdy enough to carry his six-foot frame. He uses as his pillow a pile of law books. He tells his scribes: "Write and tell the world I acknowledge myself a very great lawyer; I am going to study law, and this is the way I study it."

He falls asleep.

In March during one of his quiet slumbers, Joseph Smith dreams that he is "swimming in a river of pure water, clear as crystal, over a shoal of fish of the largest size I ever saw. They were directly under my belly. I was astonished, and felt afraid that they might drown me or do me injury."

Another impression of what is coming.

Chapter 23

APRIL–MAY 1843

Nauvoo, Illinois, and Surrounding Communities

*A*T THIS TIME in America, two other men are grabbing religious headlines. One is close in Illinois. Hyrum Redding of Ogle County claimed to have seen early one beautiful morning this spring "the sign of the Son of Man as foretold in the 24th chapter of Matthew." Editors of some of the newspapers pit him against Joseph, claiming "that Joe Smith has his match at last."

Joseph Smith responds to the editors.

He writes in an editorial without running from his professed role as a prophet of God. "Mr. Redding may have seen a wonderful appearance in the clouds one morning about sunrise (which is nothing very uncommon in the winter season,) he has not seen the sign of the Son of Man, as foretold by Jesus; neither has any man, nor will any man, until after the sun shall have been darkened and the moon bathed in blood; for the Lord hath not shown me any such sign; and as the prophet saith, so it must be—'Surely the Lord God will do nothing, but He revealeth His secret unto His servants the prophets.'" Even that statement isn't enough to make his point about Redding and himself. Joseph concludes his response to the paper: "Therefore hear this, O earth: The Lord will not come to reign over the righteous, in this world, in 1843, nor until everything for the Bridegroom is ready."

William Miller has also stirred a following in 1843. Miller is adamant that the time of the Savior's Second Coming was revealed through a close examination of biblical prophecy. He targets dates in 1843 and 1844. His biblical math is messy and complicated. One of the days he predicts is April 3, 1843. Joseph Smith is visiting the beautiful farmlands in Ramus, Illinois, on April 3. He and others are holding Church meetings. Miller's prediction has even worked the emotion of some of the Latter-day Saints. Mormon Apostle Orson Hyde on April 2, 1843, preaches a fiery sermon about the coming of the Savior. Hyde says that when the Lord appears, He will be "on a white horse as a warrior. . . . Our God is a warrior" and "it is our privilege to have the Father and Son dwelling in our hearts." According to Joseph, his sermon misses the mark and comes across with Redding's and Miller's tone.

Joseph Smith corrects him in a smaller gathering at dinner. Hyde welcomes the correction. Joseph says, "When the Savior shall appear, we shall see Him as He is. We shall see that He is a man like ourselves, and that the same sociality which exists among us here will exist among us there, only it will be coupled with eternal glory, which glory we do not now enjoy." And then addressing the verse (John 14:23) Hyde alluded to in his sermon, Joseph teaches, "The appearing of the Father and the Son, in that verse, is a personal appearance; and the idea that the Father and the Son dwell in a man's heart is an old sectarian notion, and is false."

Joseph Smith goes to bed with no worries that the Savior is coming the next day, according to Miller's statement. He is confident April 3, 1843, will pass like thousands before it. He declares before breakfast, "Miller's day of judgment has arrived, but it is too pleasant for false prophets."

At the dinner gathering the day before, Joseph had spoken like a true prophet who foresaw a future event and declared it. He prophesied that the "commencement of the difficulties which will cause much bloodshed previous to the coming of the Son of Man will be in South Carolina."

Some hold Joseph Smith in contempt for what may have at times come across as arrogance. But he is right in so many instances. This aggravates the priests of his day, who in turn speak ill against him to their congregants. Joseph's teachings on the character of God and His communication with His children challenge their beliefs and traditions. "The burdens which roll upon me are very great," Joseph declares. "My persecutors allow me no rest, and I find that in the midst of business and care the spirit is willing, but the flesh is weak. Although I was called of my Heavenly Father to lay the foundation of this great work and kingdom in this dispensation, and testify of His revealed will to scattered Israel, I am subject to like passions as other men, like the prophets of olden times."

One who gets to see and hear the dual role of Joseph Smith's intrinsic gifts firsthand is Stephen A. Douglas. He is on recess from Congress. He is only one month into his term in the US House of Representatives for Illinois's fifth district. He is starting to step onto the public stage and realizes the political expediency in courting Joseph. They have dinner in Carthage, Illinois, on May 18, 1843. Like many political heads have done in recent years, Douglas requests Joseph Smith to recite the Missouri persecutions. He is aware of the habeas corpus trial a few months back in Springfield.

For three hours, Joseph Smith talks to Douglas, adding details about his trip to Washington in the winter of 1839–40. Douglas listens with "the greatest attention and [speaks] warmly in depreciation of the conduct of Governor Boggs and the authorities of the Missouri," saying that "the mobs of Missouri . . . ought to be brought to judgment; they ought to be punished."

Though Douglas is a US representative, Joseph addresses him from his past post: "Judge, you will aspire to the presidency of the United States; and if you ever turn your hand against me or the Latter-day Saints, you will feel the weight of the hand of the Almighty upon you; and you will live to see and know that I have testified the truth to you; for the conversation of this day will stick to you through life." Feeling no threat, Douglas maintains a spirit of friendliness and acknowledges the "truth and propriety of President Smith's remarks."

By 1852, Douglas is a reputable leader among Democrats nation-wide. He will seek the presidency in 1852, 1856, and of course his most famous run in 1860 against Lincoln and others.

He is friendly to the Saints until Joseph Smith's death and the Saints' exodus from Illinois. In 1846, westward-moving Latter-day Saints no longer held political advantage to him. He will publicly ridicule the Saints, and particularly Brigham Young in an 1857 political speech. When the 1860 election is over, Douglas will carry only one state—ironically—Missouri. Douglas will die of typhoid fever shortly after Lincoln's inauguration in 1861. His political career and his life will come to an abrupt end four years after he turns his hand against the Saints and nearly eighteen years after having dinner with Joseph Smith.

Leaving Douglas in Carthage, Joseph Smith returns to Nauvoo. Upon his return, he explains the meaning of *Mormon*. Someone tries to denote the word as being Greek, *mormo*. "That is not the case," Joseph explains. "There was no Greek or Latin upon the plates from which I, through the grace of the Lord, translated the Book of Mormon. Let the language speak for itself." He informs his broadening audience that the characters on the plates he translated were reformed Egyptian. He states matter-of-factly that "the word Mormon, means literally, more good."

Chapter 24

JUNE–AUGUST 1843

Nauvoo, Illinois

THE MISSISSIPPI HAS risen above the high watermark, a dreadful sign of the flood coming upon Joseph Smith.

As Joseph continues to organize the ordinances and covenants with the rising temple he is having built, he does so with the implications of plural marriage, politics, and persecution.

In the summer of 1843, Joseph has committed to paper a revelation on plural marriage. A few men and women in the Church have already entered into its practice. About this time, Joseph broaches the subject at a public meeting. Joseph Robinson said after the public address, "The prophet went to his dinner . . . [and] several of the first women of the Church collected at the prophet's house with his wife and said . . . 'Oh Mr. Smith, you have done it now, it will never do for it is all but blasphemy. You must take back what you have said today. It is outrageous. It would ruin us as a people.' The prophet knew it would not avail anything to contend with the sisters. Said he, 'I will have to take that saying back and leave it as though there had been nothing said.' For he was aware it was a very large pill for them or the people to swallow."

Many women—and men—are not ready to have any part of it. Brigham Young is conflicted and desires the grave, feeling to "envy the corpse" and "regret that [he] was not in the coffin." Fellow

Apostle John Taylor feels that "as a married man that this was to me, oustide of this principle, an appalling thing to do. . . . Nothing but a knowledge of God, and the revelations of God, and the truth of them" can get him "to embrace such a principle as this."

Some select men and women called to live this principle under the direction of Joseph Smith initially experience hesitancy and frustration, but they receive individual confirmations. Many record miraculous experiences with angels as well as remarkable visions.

Also confronting Joseph this humid summer is another arrest warrant. Governor Reynolds of Missouri sends the new governor of Illinois, Ford, a letter stating Joseph Smith has now been indicted for treason. A Missouri special agent is sent to apprehend him. Ford gives in to Missouri's request, notwithstanding the habeas corpus trial that freed Joseph in January. Joseph Smith doesn't know of the attempt to apprehend him. He leaves Nauvoo with Emma and their children on June 13 with little stress. They are making their way to Dixon, Illinois, about 210 miles northeast of Nauvoo. They are en route to visit Emma's sister and her family.

Hyrum Smith receives news about the arrest warrant on June 21. Joseph has been gone for eight days. Hyrum sends Stephen Markham and William Clayton quickly to Dixon to interrupt his brother's stay with his in-laws. After sixty-six hours of hard riding and little rest, they find Joseph. He tells his weary friends to "not be alarmed. I have no fear." Instead of making an immediate return to Nauvoo, he feels safer to remain in Dixon. "I shall find friends, and Missourians cannot hurt me, I tell you in the name of Israel's God." Markham and Clayton rest peacefully.

Though at peace, Joseph Smith cancels a large speaking engagement in Dixon. The residents and citizens in surrounding communities are disappointed.

Just outside Dixon, Joseph and Emma quietly find refuge at Emma's sister's farm home. Two days behind Markham and Clayton are Joseph Reynolds, the special agent from Jackson County, and Harmon Wilson, a constable from Carthage, Illinois. The two men are clever in their apprehension of Joseph Smith. Markham and Clayton go into Dixon to get a feel for what is going on and see if anyone has arrived looking to arrest Joseph. They are acting as Mormon missionaries. They dupe Markham and Clayton into obtaining an interview with the Mormon prophet. Caught entirely in a hoax, Markham and Clayton hire a man and his team to take the deceivers to Joseph Smith. This pleases Reynolds and Wilson because they had nearly "run their horses to death."

Reynolds and Wilson arrive at 2 p.m., while Emma and her sister's family are sitting down to dinner. Joseph is crossing the yard to enter the barn when Reynolds steps "to the end of the house" and sees him. He quickly approaches Joseph Smith and immediately collars him. Wilson joins Reynolds. They both cock their pistols and burying them in Joseph Smith's chest, threatening to shoot him if he chooses to "stir."

"What is the meaning of this?" Joseph inquires.

"I'll show you the meaning, by G—; and if you stir one inch, I'll shoot you G—d—you," Reynolds boast. Courageously, Joseph challenges his captors. "I am not afraid of your shooting; I am not afraid to die." He bares his broad chest and tells them to shoot. "I have endured so much oppression, I am weary of life; and kill me, if you please. I am a strong man, however, and with my own natural weapons could soon level both of you; but if you have any legal process to serve, I am at all times subject to law, and shall not offer resistance." Reynolds answers Joseph's boldness with more cursing, stating he would shoot him if he opens his mouth one more time. "Shoot away; I am not afraid of your pistols," Joseph proclaims.

Reynolds doesn't shoot.

They turn their pistols on him and press him to walk. Markham and Clayton return to the farm and feel terrible knowing they were duped. Markham is a strong and bold man, but Joseph calms the situation by saying, "You are not going to resist the officers, are you, Brother Markham?"

"No, not if they are officers: I know the law too well for that."

Without allowing him to say good-bye to his family, Reynolds and Wilson haul Joseph off. They present no writ or warrant from a legal officer. When he asks to obtain a writ of habeas corpus, they curse him and punch him in both sides of his midsection with their pistols. Markham intervenes by delaying the horses. This gives Emma enough time to bring Joseph his hat and coat.

For more than eight miles Joseph has the pistols thrust into his side, bearing the cowardice as a "defenseless prisoner." He is held up for the evening in a tavern. He has still not been allowed legal process in the arrest. "I wish to get counsel."

"G—d—you, you shant' have counsel," Reynolds blurts out. He threatens to shoot him again.

"What is the use of this so often? I have repeatedly told you to shoot," Joseph replies.

A citizen walks by the tavern. Joseph yells out the window that he is being falsely imprisoned. "I want a lawyer," he yells at the citizen. Two lawyers come but have the door to the room holding Joseph Smith slammed in their faces. Reynolds and Wilson threaten to shoot the lawyers. The residents of Dixon are beginning to see the illegal farce taking place in their community. Reynolds and Wilson need to get moving with their prisoner. The owner of the tavern calls out Reynolds's rascality. "If that is [your] mode of doing business in Missouri, they had another way of doing it in Dixon. They were a law-abiding people and Republicans." He demands a fair treatment and trial for Joseph Smith. If Reynolds and Wilson don't comply, the citizens of Dixon will take the matter into their own hands to see justice through.

By evening Markham has obtained a writ by the justice of the peace for the arrest of Reynolds and Wilson, who had threatened his life and the life of his friend Joseph Smith. The attempt to kidnap Joseph is slowly unraveling for Reynolds and Wilson. As the legal squabble continues, a shallow politician who is running for Congress, Cyrus Walker, comes to Joseph but says he can't be his attorney unless Joseph Smith and many Saints commit to vote for him. Since he is known as the "greatest criminal lawyer in that part Illinois," Joseph retains him as counsel. This pleases Walker, who desperately wants a seat in Congress.

Justice is bearing down on Reynolds and Wilson. They are arrested for private damage and false imprisonment of Joseph Smith. They slowly change their attitude. Yet, they obtain a writ of habeas corpus and are freed. When the back and forth legal bickering settles a bit, Joseph is still in custody. Thirty miles from Dixon, they have placed Joseph in another tavern.

Word spreads that Joseph Smith is in town. The next morning, a large gathering takes place in the largest room of the tavern. The citizens request Joseph to speak. Reynolds boastfully informs the people he is in charge, Joseph Smith is his prisoner, and there will be no public meeting. An aged man approaches Reynolds. He strikes his hickory walking stick upon the floor and bluntly rebukes Reynolds. "You damned infernal puke, we'll learn you to come here and interrupt gentlemen. Sit down there, and sit still. Don't open your head till General Smith gets through talking."

Wilson sits down in silence. Joseph Smith speaks for an hour and a half.

By Sunday, June 25, loyal men in Nauvoo have caught wind of Joseph's situation. One hundred and seventy-five men leave on horseback with their horns and flasks filled with rifle powder. In the meantime, Joseph Smith has received a legal venue in Quincy, Illinois, to go before none other than Stephen A. Douglas. Even with the legal venue in Quincy pending, there are Missourians in the area looking to kidnap Joseph and drag him violently to their state.

Joseph Smith's loyal followers know this and that they need to get to him first. And they do. Two Mormon men approach Wilson and Reynolds while they are transporting him. Within a minute, seven more loyal men show up. Joseph Smith smiles at Reynolds and says, "I am not going to Missouri this time. These are my boys."

Joseph mounts his horse Joe Duncan, named after an Illinois politician. Neither Joseph Smith nor any of his men touch or abuse Reynolds or Wilson, but both men are trembling. They fear the retribution owed them. One of the Mormon men asks Wilson, "What is the matter with you? Have you got the ague?"

The route immediately changes to Nauvoo. In doing so, they rendezvous with over sixty more men loyal to Joseph Smith. Two of the men are William and Wilson Law, questionably still loyal. They eagerly dismount their horses and affectionately throw their arms around him, shedding tears of joy. But in coming months, their tender act may be seen as Judas betraying the Savior with a kiss. Their public affection is misrepresenting the private negative feelings they are beginning to have for Joseph Smith.

The Prophet returns to Nauvoo on June 30 to music played by the Nauvoo Brass and Martial Bands. Hundreds of citizens meet them east of the rising temple. Joseph enters Nauvoo in a buggy. Courteously, he allows Reynolds and Wilson to ride with him.

On the outskirts of town, Joseph steps from the buggy and embraces Emma. He then embraces Hyrum, his brother. He climbs upon one of his horses, "Old Charley," and rides next to Emma. The people gather and line the streets for his return. He is "greeted with the cheers of the people and firing of guns and cannon." His emotions can't be held back. At his home on the corner of Main and Water Street, Joseph lights off Old Charley and affectionately greets his mother. His children express their joy. "Little Fred" says, "Pa, the Missourians won't take you away again, will they?"

Some locals from Dixon followed the escort all the way back to Nauvoo and stand in awe at the "enthusiastic attachment of . . . family and the Saints toward" this religious leader they have heard and read so much about. At dinner, Emma and Joseph host a large gathering, with more than fifty people. Sitting at the head of the table are Reynolds and Wilson.

Notwithstanding the Smiths' kindness, Reynolds and Wilson slip out of Nauvoo after dinner while Joseph is speaking to a large congregation. They threaten to go to Carthage and raise a militia to take Joseph Smith from Nauvoo by force. The Nauvoo Charter, which sustains an armed militia and the power of the Nauvoo court to release him on habeas corpus, is keeping his enemies in check.

But Joseph Smith's patience is wearing thin with those who are constantly trying to disrupt his life and discredit his character. A tax collector named Bagby serves a notice on one of Joseph's properties in August. Joseph discusses the notice with some of his clerks near the temple late one afternoon. Bagby, who is nearby, joins the conversation. He denies any knowledge of the notice, but one of Joseph's men, who manages the property, has the notice in hand. "I had always been ready to pay all my taxes when I was called upon," Joseph Smith tells Bagby, "and I don't think it gentlemanly treatment to sell any of my lots for taxes." Bagby calls Joseph a liar and picks up a stone to throw at him. The action enrages Joseph, who follows Bagby for a few steps striking him a few times.

A respectable non-Mormon in Nauvoo, Daniel H. Wells, steps between Joseph and Bagby. Joseph realizes his hasty mistake. He tells Wells, who is a justice of the peace, to assess a fine for the assault. He wants to pay the fine, not considering himself above the law. Wells doesn't consent and drops the matter. The decision doesn't satisfy his conscience. Joseph goes to the home of another officer, Alderman Whitney, a Mormon, and confesses to his physical ill treatment of Bagby. Whitney imposes a fine, and Joseph pays it. Bagby stays a few more hours in Nauvoo "muttering threats against" him.

For the remainder of the summer, Joseph is busy speaking to the people on religious doctrine and political issues. He interviews candidates seeking national office. He also speaks at funerals. He works on his farm and spends leisure time with family and friends, like excursions on the Mississippi River on the boat *Maid of Iowa*, of which he is part owner.

He also spends some private time with Emma. It is at this time the revelation on plural marriage is put to paper. After promptly rejecting the written explanation of plural marriage, Emma leaves for six days to go to St. Louis and conduct some of her husband's personal business matters, because it is not safe for him to attend to them himself.

Reynolds is back in Missouri and has a story to tell that is sure to get enemies of Joseph Smith worked up to greater anger. Missourians who want his blood are regrouping. But there are also men of the same spirit swelling in Illinois. The enemies are getting closer and closer to Nauvoo. Some are even beginning to come from Church membership and camouflage themselves as confidants of Joseph, though bitterly opposing him in secret meetings.

Joseph Smith has less than ten months to live.

Chapter 25

SEPTEMBER 1843

Nauvoo and Carthage, Illinois

IAGONAL FROM THE homestead Joseph and Emma have occupied since coming to Nauvoo, a beautiful two-story Greek revival home is finished. It is built of white pine and is ready for Joseph and Emma to occupy. The immediate traffic of guests and exploding expenses force Emma and Joseph to turn the home into a hotel known as the Mansion House. "In consequence of my house being constantly crowded with strangers and other persons wishing to see me, of who had business in the city, I found myself unable to support as much company free of charge, which I have done from the foundation of the Church," Joseph states. "My house has been a home and resting-place for thousands, and my family many times obliged to do without food, after having fed all they had to visitors; and I could have continued the same liberal course, had it not been for the cruel and untiring persecution of my relentless enemies," he expresses.

Visitors are coming from various parts of the United States to see the Mormon prophet. One ill-mannered visitor insults one of the hired girls working in the Mansion House. When Joseph learns of it, he confronts the stranger. "I understand that you insulted one of the employees of this house last evening." The stranger stammers his words and attempts to justify his position. Joseph in "unmistakable language" tells the man to immediately leave and that he doesn't want any of his "money, or any other men of your stamp." The stranger "cut a lively exit."

As he leaves, more and more converts are arriving. One new arrival at this time is a recent convert to the Church from New Hampshire. Upon meeting Joseph and hearing him speak on several occasions in the autumn of 1843, he concludes that the Mormon prophet "does not pretend to be a man without failings and follies. He is a man that you could not help liking as a man, setting aside the religious prejudice which the world has raised against him. He is one of the warmest patriots and friends to his country and laws that you ever heard speak on the subject."

Contrasting reports on Joseph Smith's character are bouncing all around the papers and in social circles. In early September, outspoken Illinois citizens and professed anti-Mormons from surrounding communities meet in Carthage. They write a preamble and resolutions regarding their expanding neighbors in Nauvoo. "They have obtruded themselves upon us," the preamble states, "calling themselves Mormons, or Latter-day Saints, and under the sacred garb of Christianity, assumed, as we honestly believe, that they may the more easily, under such a cloak, perpetrate the most lawless and diabolical deeds that have ever, in any age of the world, disgraced the human species." As evidence of their charge, they write: "We find them yielding implicit obedience to the ostensible head and founder of this sect, who is a pretended prophet of the Lord, and under this Heaven-daring assumption claiming to set aside, by his vile and blasphemous lies, all those moral and religious institutions which have been established by the Bible."

Joseph Smith teaches repeatedly from the Bible. "I believe in this sacred volume. In it the 'Mormon' faith is to be found. We teach nothing but what the Bible teaches. We believe nothing, but what is to be found in this book." But Joseph Smith also holds that all God wanted His children to know personally or collectively as a Church was not limited to what was in the Bible. "I thank God that I have got this old book; but I thank Him more for the gift of the Holy Ghost. I have got the oldest book in the world; but I have got the oldest book in my heart, even the gift of the Holy Ghost."

The gathering enemies in Carthage pledge their support to help the authorities of the state of Missouri apprehend "the body of Joseph Smith."

One of the ringleaders in this Carthage gathering is Thomas C. Sharp of Warsaw, a community about twenty-two miles south of Nauvoo. Sharp is a young man in his twenties and is initially a "neutral observer" of the Mormons, even being invited to the cornerstone ceremony of their temple in April of 1841. But for various reasons, Sharp uses his persuasion and position as editor of the *Warsaw Signal* to lambaste the Latter-day Saints. Outspoken non-Mormons in Hancock County are increasingly jealous over the rising economical, political, and religious power of the Latter-day Saints.

Sharp is especially critical of the Nauvoo militia. In it he sees the seeds of "militant fanaticism." He is also "alarmed" by the prospects of Mormons filling county offices. William Smith, the Prophet's brother, upset Sharp in an 1842 election for a seat in the House of Representatives. This set off a war of words. William Smith at this time is editor of the *Wasp*, a weekly paper in Nauvoo. In his paper, he takes on Thomas Sharp's anti-Mormon rhetoric. He expressively refers to Sharp in print by his first name—"Thom-ASS." Such a reference draws plenty of laughs but also incites further anger.

By September of 1843, Sharp becomes one of the loudest mouthpieces for those who want Joseph dead or dragged off to Missouri. He will use plenty of ink in the *Warsaw Signal*.

Somehow Joseph Smith gets a complete copy of the preamble and resolutions of the men gathering against him in Carthage. He asks William Phelps to write a reply to Governor Ford, who thinks Joseph and the Mormons are over anxious about the danger before them. In the reply letter, Phelps sends a copy of the conspiring men's resolutions at Carthage, specifically the intention to apprehend the body of Joseph.

Setting all reports and resolutions aside, Joseph is able to preach. He also tolerates and listens to visiting ministers and other political philosophies. A Unitarian minister speaks on persecution. A socialist is allowed to address another gathering of Saints. Joseph listens respectively and then offers his feelings and opinions at the conclusion. Everyone is "freely tolerated."

On the night of September 28, a special counsel of trustworthy brethren meets with Joseph Smith. William Law is one of them, but he is close to turning bitterly against Joseph. He is disgruntled that Joseph promised Cyrus Walker the Latter-day Saints' votes. Hyrum had publicly told the Saints in a large gathering to vote for Joseph P. Hoge, Walker's opponent. Joseph didn't question the suggestion because Hyrum had said he knew so by revelation. Law thinks Joseph is manipulating politicians and using "trickery." Law begins to be more critical of Joseph Smith. It's an immediate strain in their relationship and his position in the Church.

By the end of September, Joseph's two counselors, Sidney Rigdon and William Law, have become distant and aloof from Church decisions and documents. Rigdon goes silent for the most part; Law becomes more belligerent and is more critical to the ecclesiastical control over politics, economy, and social life he perceives Joseph is wielding. He is also critical of Joseph Smith's introduction of the plurality of Gods and the plurality of wives doctrines. Law desires to destroy Joseph's influence in the streets of Nauvoo and in the hearts and minds of the Latter-day Saints. His association and closeness to the Prophet is coming to an abrupt end.

A heavy rain and a strong west wind pound Nauvoo on the last day of September, a blunt sign what Joseph Smith is facing from combining enemies.

MEANWHILE, PORTER ROCKWELL is still enduring confinement in a Missouri jail. A grand jury, for the lack of proof, cannot indict him for attempting to kill former Governor Boggs. But an attempted jail break keeps him confined. "We are glad," a Nauvoo paper editorializes, "for the sake of suffering innocence, that Mr. Rockwell stands clear in the eyes of the law." But why continue to hold him when there is no proof. "They wish to [slaughter] him, and, by offering him as a sacrifice, glut their thirst for innocent blood."

Chapter 26

OCTOBER–NOVEMBER 1843

Nauvoo, Illinois

JUDGE JAMES ADAMS of Springfield has been telling Joseph he has been having impressions that his death was near. He dies of cholera rather quickly, and the Saints hold an honorable funeral for him.

Adams was an immediate friend to Joseph from late 1839, and Joseph allowed Adams to be in many of the most intimate circles as he unfolded the practices (ordinances) relating to the house of the Lord, the temple the Saints are building. His death is a somber time for the Prophet.

A large gathering occurs for Adams's funeral. In a doctrinal tone, Joseph states: "All men know that they must die. And it is important that we should understand the reasons and causes of our exposure to the vicissitudes of life and of death, and the designs and purposes of God in our coming into the world, our sufferings here, and our departure hence. What is the object of our coming into existence, then dying and falling away, to be here no more? It is but reasonable to suppose that God would reveal something in reference to the matter?"

He continues: "If we have any claim on our Heavenly Father for anything, it is for knowledge on this important subject. Could we read and comprehend all that has been written from the days of

Adam, on the relation of man to God and angels in a future state, we should know very little about it. . . . Could you gaze into heaven five minutes, you would know more than you would by reading all that ever was written on the subject."

Joseph then gives his deceased friend a kind benediction. "When men are prepared, they are better off to go hence. Brother Adams has gone to open up a more effectual door of the dead." His teachings allude that the dead are not dead, just in another realm of existence, and that those who die in the gospel of Jesus Christ are needed in the world of spirits to minister to those who died without the gospel.

A few days later, he leaves the topic of death and turns to liberty. Joseph preaches a sermon on the Constitution of the United States. Near the rising temple edifice, he proclaims: "I am the greatest advocate of the Constitution of the United States there is on the earth. In my feelings I am always ready to die for the protection of the weak and oppressed in their just rights." He expresses one fault with the Constitution: "It does not provide the manner by which that freedom can be preserved, nor for the punishment of Government officers who refuse to protect the people in their religious rights, or punish those mobs, states, or communities who interfere with the rights of the people on account of their religion."

Clarifying his position, he remarks, "Its sentiments are good, but it provides no means of enforcing them. It has but this one fault. Under its provision, a man or a people who are able to protect themselves can get along well enough." This could be one reason why Joseph sees the Nauvoo Charter as a means of protecting the Latter-day Saints' rights to worship. "But those who have the misfortune to be weak or unpopular are left to the merciless rage of popular fury," Joseph continues to preach. The fury of Missouri has never been checked in behalf of the Mormons, and he wants the world to know it. He also sees the fury once again at the doors of Illinois.

His religious rights to govern a people who want to be governed in their economic, political, and social behaviors according to acceptable laws of the land are protected under the US Constitution. Joseph Smith isn't known to be an iron fist. "I teach my people correct principles and they govern themselves." This irks many outside the Church and a few inside because the Latter-day Saints readily governed themselves according to Joseph Smith's vision of community and existence.

By early November, leading Mormons, under Joseph's direction, write to five candidates seeking the presidential chair in the 1844 election. They want to know what the national candidates would do "in relation to the cruelty and oppression" the Saints "suffered from the state if Missouri." The letter copied to all five candidates posed this question: "What will be your rule of action relative to us as a people, should fortune favor your ascension to the chief magistracy?"

John C. Calhoun of South Carolina receives a letter. He is a proponent of states' rights and limited government. Lewis Cass of Michigan receives a letter. He is a territorial governor and a general. Richard M. Johnson receives a letter. He is a former vice president of the United States during Van Buren's administration and a current senator from Kentucky. Perhaps Joseph Smith met him when he went to Washington in 1839–40. Henry Clay receives a letter. He is an on-again-off-again senator from Kentucky and has recently founded the Whig Party, which Abraham Lincoln unites with. Martin Van Buren receives a letter even though he had been voted out of office. Van Buren's aspirations are to secure the presidential chair again. In his letter, the Mormon prophet inserted a postscript reminding him of the "coldness, indifference, and neglect, bordering on contempt" he gave Joseph when he visited Washington.

Calhoun, Clay, and Cass respond to the letters. They are noncommittal in tone and depressingly unsatisfactory to Joseph Smith and the Mormon leaders.

On a state political front, a new convert, James Arlington Bennett—baptized by Brigham Young in August of 1843—writes to Joseph Smith in a flattering manner. James Bennett is an established attorney, newspaper publisher, educator, and author, which helps his finances and social standing. His political ambitions are swelling. He expects, he tells Joseph Smith in a letter, "to be yet, through your influence, governor of the State of Illinois."

Joseph likes James Arlington Bennett but has to caution him on soliciting his help in the political realm. "Shall I, who have witnessed the visions of eternity, and beheld the glorious mansions of bliss, and the regions and the misery of the damned,—shall I turn to be a Judas? Shall I, who have heard the voice of God, and communed with angels, and spake as moved by the Holy Ghost for the renewal of the everlasting covenant, and for the gathering of Israel in the last days,—shall I worm myself into a political hypocrite?" And then with a little tongue in cheek he concludes, "Shall I stoop from the sublime authority of Almighty God, to be handled as a monkey's cat-paw, and pettify myself into a clown to act the farce of political demagoguery? No—verily no!"

Joseph will change his political neutrality in the coming months.

Confident in this role as one who communed with God and angels, Joseph Smith tells the leading men of the Church of his intention to write a proclamation to the kings of the earth. A revelation he received three years earlier has directed him to write a proclamation. He also expresses interest in "petitioning Congress for a grant to make a canal . . . or a dam to turn the water [of the Mississippi] to the city, so that we might erect mills and other machinery." He wants to expand the economic power of Nauvoo.

On a clear cold day near the end of November, Joseph visits with Colonel John Frierson, a liaison for an R. B. Rhett, congressmen from South Carolina. Rhett expresses his interest in sharing the Saints' Missouri persecutions in a memorial with Congress. Rhett is a dear friend and interested observer in John C. Calhoun's presidential run. Joseph Smith sends Frierson with a copy of a memorial and asks him to stop in Quincy and get reputable signers to attach their names to the memorial before he shares it with Congress.

To once again draw attention to their sufferings in Missouri, Joseph makes eleven copies of the memorial for circulation. He also writes to the quintessential political group of liberty, the Green Mountain Boys of Vermont. Joseph Smith was born in Vermont and thought to prevail on their senses. "[My] rights and privileges, together with a large amount of property, have been wrested from me, and thousands of my friends, by lawless mobs in Missouri, supported by executive authority; and the crime of plundering our property, and the unconstitutional and barbarous act of our expulsion, and even the inhumanity of murdering men, women, and children, have received the pass-word of 'justifiable' by legislative enactments;

and the horrid deeds, doleful and disgraceful as they are, have been paid for by Government."

Joseph Smith then presents two appeals as he brings his letter to a close. He asks that the Green Mountain Boys rise up in the "majesty of virtuous freemen" and help bring Missouri before the "bar of justice." He also asks they help "frustrate the wicked design of sinful men." He signs off by conveying, "As a friend of equal rights to all men, and a messenger of the everlasting Gospel of Jesus Christ, I have the honor to be, Your devoted servant, Joseph Smith."

Mormon Apostle Parley P. Pratt takes leave of Nauvoo and goes to New York and Vermont with the specific mission of distributing the appeal to the Green Mountain Boys. The appeal is also sent to press.

As Joseph Smith and his friends once again reflect on the injustices they experienced in Missouri, it causes strong emotion. Joseph Smith tells his men, "When mobs come upon you, kill them. I never will restrain you again, but will go and help you." Brigham Young chimed in that he would never hold another brother back again when he or his family were being "abused" by mobs. John Taylor, speaking of what they had to experience in Missouri, says he will "never submit to such treatment again."

The three men voicing their emotions strongest this evening will be in their own time the first three President-prophets of the Church. Though they speak under strong emotion on this occasion, the fact is, they will submit time and time again to their enemies. They will choose peace over conflict and turn the other cheek when smitten. They will "wield a pen" before a sword. In the end, these tough words on a night that brought strong emotions will be subdued by reality and the nature of their characters.

Chapter 27

DECEMBER 1843

ECEMBER BEGINS WITH Joseph Smith administering to the sick and reading reports sent from missionaries laboring in different states. Joseph is also initiating more of the Church's Apostles and faithful members in their temple rites and instructions in the priesthood.

On the night of December 4, a large number of citizens gather in the assembly room on the second floor of Smith's Red Brick Store. Two Missourians squirm their way into the meeting. Either they are vocal about whom they are or it is discerned immediately whom they are; the congregation becomes a bit unsettled. Joseph encourages everyone to "be calm and cool, but let the spirit of '76 burn in [your] bosoms, and when occasion requires, say little, but act; and when the mob comes, mow a hole through them."

The two Missourians know they are surrounded by more than one hundred and twenty loyal followers of the Prophet. They stand quietly by and make note of the rhetoric. They have no qualms about acting part of a mob. The meeting goes for two and half hours, with Joseph Smith recounting the "circumstances" the Latter-day Saints endured in Missouri. The meeting concludes with both the memorial to Congress and his letter to the Green Mountain Boys of Vermont being read to the congregation. No threat on his life or illegal arrest transpires.

Just south of Nauvoo, illegality is taking place. In Warsaw, a Mormon man by the name of Daniel Avery and his young son have been kidnapped by men from Missouri. Avery and his son Philander are accused by Levi Williams of being horse thieves. When he isn't running around with Missourians trying to capture "Joe Smith" and trouble other Mormons, Levi Williams is a Baptist minister. He is a married man with five kids, a farmer, a cooper, and a colonel in the Illinois militia. Williams stays busy, but he finds himself preoccupied with Joseph Smith and the Mormons. He is friends with Thomas C. Sharp, another Warsaw resident. It could be argued by this time that "if Thomas C. Sharp [is] the leading spokesman of the anti-Mormon cause, then Levi Williams [is] probably the leading actor."

Joseph Smith quickly sends an affidavit to Governor Thomas Ford on the events of the kidnapping. Ford responds to Joseph saying he cannot interfere with such crimes against the Latter-day Saints. He counsels him to seek redress through judicial power. Avery will spend most of December in a Missouri prison and will obtain a release by Christmas.

Porter Rockwell is also finding relief in Missouri. His mother visits him. They have to huddle in the corner of his cell and speak in whispers to avoid the guards. She commits each word of her son's conversion to memory. He has a personal message for Joseph. Whatever is told her impels her to leave for Illinois that night. She goes immediately to Joseph when she arrives in Nauvoo.

Wandle Mace, an architect on the Mormon temple, is standing with several men on the temple grounds. "Boys, has Bonaparte any friends in the French Army?" Joseph Smith shouts out from sitting upon his horse. "Of course," Mace and all the others shout back. Joseph then conveys that he has just learned from "the mother of O. P. Rockwell, that for the sum of a hundred dollars she could obtain Porter's release from prison."

Mace sees Joseph Smith pull money out of his pocket, which represents only a portion of the sum needed. He asks for those present to assist him. All present responded heartily. Those who have money with them give it to him, and some go to their homes for the money. While waiting for the men to return, Joseph dismounts from his horse and engages in a friendly wrestle with some of the "boys," as he calls them.

Shortly, Rockwell's mother is sent back to Missouri with more than one hundred dollars.

While his mother is in Illinois, Rockwell could have obtained his freedom by accepting cash and goods. Sheriff Reynolds, who failed at yanking Joseph illegally from Illinois, has returned, and he tells Rockwell of his failed attempt. Reynolds, in some crazed desperation to apprehend Joseph Smith, says to Rockwell, "You deliver Joe Smith into our hands and name your pile." Reynolds fixation to apprehend the Mormon prophet is not entirely understood.

Rockwell doesn't even flinch. He tells Reynolds, "I would see them all damned first and then I won't." His remarkable loyalty to Joseph Smith once again exemplifies a fired stiffness under trying circumstances.

As the release of Rockwell nears, Joseph Smith has to deal with the disloyalty of his two counselors in the First Presidency of the Church, who flank his right and left.

During the fall months and into December, Joseph has made clear in private circles and before the Saints in large gatherings that he is "dissatisfied" with Sidney Rigdon as a counselor. He argues that Rigdon hasn't been helpful and is aloof of his calling as a counselor since their escape from Missouri five years previous. At a large meeting, Joseph Smith lays out Rigdon's questionable activities managing the post office, specifically his "correspondence and connection with John C. Bennett, with Ex-Governor Carlin, and with the Missourians, of a treacherous character." And then to further charge Ridgon of selling out, he presents information and testimony that Rigdon was the one who told Sheriff Reynolds how to find Joseph at Dixon to arrest him.

Rigdon is present at the meeting and allowed to speak. He pleads his case of innocence and addresses his follies. Through his remarks, he wins the affections of the people. Five reputable men in the Mormon community stand in Rigdon's defense. Even Joseph's brother Hyrum stands and "remarks on the attributes of mercy in God . . . and the importance of the Saints exercising the same attribute towards their fellows, and especially towards their aged companion and fellow-servant in the cause of truth and righteousness," Sidney Rigdon.

In what may be one of the few times Joseph loses his case before the Saints, they vote that Sidney Rigdon "retain his station as Counselor in the First Presidency." Joseph Smith, in complete disagreement, arises and boldly asserts before the large gathering of Saints, "I have thrown him off my shoulders, and you have again put him on me. You may carry him, but I will not."

The conference is brought to a close by singing and a prayer. In growing irony, Joseph Smith's other counselor, William Law, is voice for the prayer.

William Law and his wife, Jane, are familiar with the inner circles of Mormonism. They are privy to the ordinances associated with Joseph's introduction of temple rites he calls the endowment. They are also privy to the implementation of plural marriage. By December, Law has a breaking point with Joseph Smith.

The events that transpired between Joseph Smith and William Law and his wife, Jane, are full of "he said, they said." The practice of plural marriage was ultimately rejected by them, but only after Joseph Smith apparently refused to seal them as husband and wife for eternity under the priesthood. Up to this time, William Law and his wife believe Joseph rightfully exercises this divine authority. It is not known for what reasons Joseph Smith denies their eternal marriage covenant. Hyrum Smith at this time places in the records of the Church that William Law had confessed adultery to him. It is possible Joseph eventually married them according to the eternal covenant in December.

SOME EVEN ARGUE that Joseph Smith approached Jane Law, or rather Jane Law approached Joseph as her husband's spiritual decline spiraled, wanting an eternal marriage covenant to take place between them. The details are unknown. William and Jane Law's son Richard spoke of the feelings of both Joseph Smith and his father at this time. At nine years old, Richard said that he was present when his father and Joseph Smith had an interview in 1843. He recounts that his father threw his arms around the Prophet's neck and was "pleading with him to withdraw the doctrine of plural marriage." With tears in his eyes, his father tells Joseph that "Mormonism would, in fifty or one hundred years, dominate the Christian world." According to the son, the Prophet Joseph Smith, also in tears, replies to William Law "that he could not withdraw the doctrine, for God had commanded him to teach it, and condemnation would come upon him if he was not obedient to the commandment."

Law's son Richard has left on record that the interview between the two men was "a most touching one" and that he has no doubt that Joseph believed he had received the doctrine of plural marriage from the Lord. The Prophet's manner is exceedingly earnest, so much so, "that Mr. Law was convinced that the prophet was perfectly sincere in his declaration."

The sincerity in both men can't deflect the tension that is growing between them. Law confides that in December he thought seriously about siding with Joseph and the practice of plural marriage. But by the end of the month to early January, he turns against the practice and more so against Joseph Smith. He claims Joseph is a fallen prophet. From this time, William Law desires to be the head and sit in the prophetic chair for the Latter-day Saints. To obtain the position, Law has to destroy Joseph Smith's influence. He has to begin crying "transgression."

Joseph Smith reminds the Saints of something he taught in the spring of 1839 when his Missouri accusers were crying transgression: those who "cry transgression do it because they are the servants of sin, and are the children of disobedience themselves."

ON CHRISTMAS NIGHT, Porter Rockwell stumbles into Nauvoo. He is a free man but tattered and emaciated. He makes it to the Smith home while Emma and Joseph are entertaining fifty couples. They are enjoying a "cheerful and friendly manner" when a man, seemingly drunk, enters the room. According to fourteen-year-old Charles Stoddard, a hired hand in the house of Joseph Smith, Rockwell is "terribly thin and weakened; his hair was long and matted with filth and his body swarming with lice." Those holding him in jail "left him to stench in his own dirt."

When Joseph sees his childhood confidant, he weeps and hugs him "in spite of his condition."

The Prophet asks Charles and another man to clean Brother Rockwell. They burn his "rags he had one time called clothes." When it comes to his hair, they have a "terrible time . . . it was so snarled and filthy. They had decided the best thing to do was to shave his head but Joseph intervenes and then he promised Brother Rockwell that as long as he did not cut his hair our enemies would have no power over him." Charles's mother, privy to the situation and to the character of Rockwell, says he is "an uncouth man, even vile of tongue but [Joseph] discerns men for what they are inside and though Charles says he reprimands Brother Rockwell at times for his bad language he still loves and respects him and trusts him as much as he does anyone, even the apostles."

Joseph also trusts Charles, his hired hand. He asks Charles to take a position of work at the home of William Law. Charles in no way wants to take the position but does so only at Joseph Smith's urging. He trusts and honors Joseph and his close association. Charles's mother observes, "The prophet is such a kindly man though Charles says he has seen his anger rise. All he has to contend with, is it any wonder? Wrathful outsiders as well as weak and selfish people right among our own ranks. Being a prophet of the Lord, I guess, makes him able to deal with all those whom he comes in contact in a just and noble way. There are many among us who would gladly give our lives that the prophet might be spared the humiliations he has to undergo at the hands of the so-called 'law.' . . . People either love the prophet or hate him."

Charles loves Joseph Smith and is willing to go into the midst of his enemies. The young boy is counseled to keep "his eyes and ears open" as he takes the position at the home of William Law.

Joseph is also soliciting the help of the newly formed Nauvoo police. Forty men are sworn in to uphold the ordinances of the city and the "instructions of mayor"—Joseph Smith— "according to the best of their ability." These men are a large bodyguard for Joseph Smith. They work night and day, holding off the rogues.

One rogue is Joseph Jackson, who stumbled into Nauvoo in May of 1843. At that time, he told Joseph he was "out of employment and destitute of funds." Joseph takes "compassion and employs him as a clerk to sell lands, so as to give him a chance in the world." But Joseph Smith has better discernment after the Bennett ordeal. After three days, he tells William Clayton, "Jackson is rotten hearted." At the end of December, Jackson wants to hear more about Joseph Smith's experiences in receiving revelation from the beginning days of the Church. His interest really isn't religion. The real reason he wants to be in Joseph's presence is to solicit his help on a personal matter involving a young woman he would like to marry, the daughter of Hyrum Smith.

Joseph Jackson doesn't get Hyrum's daughter, and his rotten heartedness begins to be surface.

Porter Rockwell was a childhood friend of Joseph Smith. He had a unique character for religious leanings and affiliation. Along with Joseph Smith, he was wanted for the attempted assassination of ex-Governor Boggs of Missouri. He was accused of pulling the trigger; Joseph Smith was accused of ordering it.

Martin Van Buren was the eighth President of the United States. He entertained an interview with Joseph Smith in November 1839. After Joseph Smith recounts the Saints' sufferings in Missouri, Van Buren says: "What can I do for you? I can do nothing for you, if I do anything, I shall come in contact with the whole State of Missouri."

John Reynolds was a US congressman from Illinois. He was serving in Washington when Joseph Smith arrived in November 1839. He treated Joseph cordially and attended the interview Joseph had with Martin Van Buren. He urged his colleagues in the House of Representatives to "give [Smith] the civilities and attention that was due him."

John C. Bennett was remarkable at hiding his true character. He practiced immoral treachery and was a world-class fake. Witnesses in Ohio said he had a wife and children there. After abusing them, he abandoned them. He seduced Mormon women and preferred to live a life driven by lust rather than responsibility. He was exposed for his double life by both Mormons and non-Mormons.

Brigham Young was an adamant defender of the Mormon prophet. He labored diligently as a missionary and an Apostle. He was severely sick in November of 1842 and never forgot the kindness and awareness Joseph Smith extended to him. Much of the burden of the Church fell on his shoulders after Joseph's death. Some say he slept with one eye open and one leg out of bed during the trek West.

Emma Hale married Joseph Smith in January 1827. She shouldered many afflictions and trials. In 1842, she was appointed the first president of the Relief Society, a women's organization within the Church. She decided not to go West under Brigham Young's leadership and spent the remainder of her life in Nauvoo. She died in 1879. Before taking her last breaths, she rose up in her bed, extended her left hand, and said "Joseph, Joseph, Joseph."

Eliza R. Snow was as a plural wife of Joseph Smith. Like Emma, she was blessed with the gift of expression. She wrote poetry, kept a good personal history, and did not hesitate to address the principles and doctrine in the scriptures. She emphatically declared that she was not manipulated or coerced into her marriage relationship. She had her own witness of plural marriage and, much like her husband, knew she had the Christian world staring her in the face.

Stephen A. Douglas was an aspiring politician when Joseph Smith was gathering thousands of Latter-day Saints in Western Illinois. In one setting, Joseph Smith told him: "Judge, you will aspire to the presidency of the United States; and if you ever turn your hand against me or the Latter-day Saints, you will feel the weight of the hand of the Almighty upon you; and you will live to see and know that I have testified the truth to you; for the conversation of this day will stick to you through life." He publicly ridiculed the Saints, and particularly Brigham Young, in an 1857 political speech. His political career and his life come to an abrupt end four years after he turns his hand against the Saints and nearly eighteen years after Joseph Smith's prophecy. He died of typhoid fever rather quickly.

Mansion House ca. 1840s. Joseph Smith and his family moved into this home at the end of August 1843. They hosted many events and guests in this home. Joseph and Emma tried to be free with their means, but it became a financial burden. They started running the home as a hotel. It was close to a dock

on the Mississippi River. On June 29, 1844, approximately ten thousand people walked through the home and viewed the bodies of Joseph and Hyrum Smith.

Justin Butterfield served as Joseph's legal counsel during the January 1843 habeas corpus hearing in Springfield, Illinois. Justin Butterfield promised Joseph: "I will stand by you, and see you safely delivered from your arrest." Butterfield was sure Joseph Smith would be granted a discharge given the legal rights and procedures of habeas corpus. He told Smith in a letter that his opinion "accords with the opinions of every intelligent man."

$\mathcal{A}$N UNFRIENDLY RAINSTORM accompanies the New Year. This will be Joseph Smith's last New Year celebration. He and his wife Emma host a celebration dinner with food, music, and dancing. The festivities last until morning. However, a melancholy spirit rests upon Joseph as he spends much of the evening and early morning hours in his private room with his family.

He has premonitions of the year ahead, actually the months ahead. There is an urgency to make sure the records of the Church are up to date. He has three clerks working for him around the clock. These men "cheerfully devote" their time but have no means to support their families. "Their hands are palsied and their pens stayed, more or less." Brigham Young, as acting President of the Quorum of the Twelve Apostles, sends a letter to a branch of the Church just outside Nauvoo requesting they supply resources for the Prophet's clerks. Branch members respond and provide the clerks with the necessary comforts and resources to continue their labors.

This relieves Joseph Smith, who is bombarded with correspondences, legal matters, business items, and the proceedings of Church affairs. People are constantly seeking interviews with him. Accounts of these meetings are often recorded by one of his clerks. One correspondence of interest has just arrived in Nauvoo. It is a reply from presidential candidate John C. Calhoun.

His words fall terribly short in Joseph Smith's opinion. "Candor compels me to repeat what I said to you at Washington, that, according to my views, the case does not come within the jurisdiction of the Federal Government," Calhoun expresses.

Joseph uses one of his burdened clerks to pen a lengthy reply to Calhoun. "If the General Government has no power to reinstate expelled citizens to their rights, there is a monstrous hypocrite fed and fostered from the hard earnings of the people. . . . If the Latter-day Saints are not restored to all their rights and paid for all their losses, according to the known rules of justice and judgment, reciprocation and common honesty among men, that God will come out of His hiding place, and vex this nation with a sore vexation."

Joseph Smith takes an even harder swing at Calhoun's political thinking and personal character. "And let me say that all men who say that Congress has no power to restore and defend the rights of her citizens have not the love of the truth abiding in them." If that wasn't enough, he closes his correspondence by saying, "I would admonish you [to read] . . . the 8th section and 1st article of the Constitution of the United States, the first, fourteenth and seventeenth 'specific' and not very 'limited powers' of the Federal Government."

Then turning biblical, Joseph Smith says he hopes that the "God, who cooled the heat of a Nebuchadnezzar's furnace or shut the mouths of lions for the honor of a Daniel, will raise [Calhoun's] mind above the narrow notion that the General Government has no power." Joseph doesn't hesitate to challenge one of the political giants of the day. The next generation of politicians will agree with Joseph Smith's logic and pass the fourteenth amendment. A vexation, in the eyes of Latter-day Saints, will begin to occur seventeen years later at the outbreak of the Civil War, beginning in Calhoun's home state, South Carolina.

ON JANUARY 3, William Law has heard that the Nauvoo police, Joseph's bodyguard, was told to "put [him] out of the way." William

Law is edgy for some reason. He believes Joseph Smith is using his authority to take him out for falling away from the faith. Law hears that the police are talking among themselves expressing that there is a "Judas in General Smith's cabinet,—one who stood next to him; and he must be taken care of, and that he must not be allowed to go into the world, but must be taken care of; and he [is] not only a dough-head and a traitor like Judas, but an assassin like Brutus."

William Law assumes this is a direct reference to him and that it fell from the lips of Joseph Smith.

Police officers are summoned into a city council session and asked if they have ever "received a private oath" from Joseph Smith to dispose of or trouble William Law. In unison the police shout, "No." Joseph calls on William Law to present the individual officer who said such an oath was made. What Law heard was a conversation between two officers. He infers they are talking about him. One of the officers did suppose from the conversation that William Law was the "Judas" and the "dough-head."

The city council investigates the situation nearly one full day. By adjournment all evidence shows nothing more than imagination and surmises of a certain police officer. This calms Law's agitation and uneasiness but not his dissension from Mormon ranks. Under the façade of loyalty, he shakes hands with Joseph Smith and calls on the body of the council and the police to observe his public statement that he would stand by Joseph Smith to the death.

Other Latter-day Saints are becoming dissatisfied with Law because of his questionable behavior and hypocrisy. On the evening of January 7, a close-knit group to Joseph Smith and his temple initiations gather for a meeting. This group is called at times the quorum of the anointed. It includes women. One of the Apostles' wives on this evening notes that a vote is taken on the standing of William Law in the quorum of the anointed and on his position as a counselor in the First Presidency of Church. Law and his wife, Jane, had removed themselves from quorum attendance three weeks prior. Their support of Joseph Smith is quickly waning.

Law is becoming more volatile with every passing day. He says one thing to his former friends in one setting, and quite another to dissidents and non-Mormon company. He is becoming more vocal.

His wife, Jane, advises him to "keep still." Law doesn't follow his wife's counsel. He is taking his angst against Joseph Smith behind closed doors with those who want Joseph dead.

One individual Law is winning over to his company is William Marks, a stake president over several Mormon bishops in Nauvoo. He is also trying to turn Emma Smith against her husband's teachings and practices. Near this time, Joseph has printed, "All the sorrow [I] ever had in [my] family [has] arisen through the influence of Wm. Law." Under great difficulties, Emma sides with her husband.

On January 8, Joseph Smith and William Law meet on one of the streets of Nauvoo. It is not entirely known what is said during this street conversation. But Law is dropped from his position as a counselor to Joseph Smith. The Mormon prophet does not wait for a public Church meeting to transact the business. He acts solely and immediately in his role as President and Prophet of the Mormon Church. This makes Law even more rigid in his behaviors and more irritated with Joseph Smith for going against Church protocol. Having told a public crowd three days earlier that he would stand by Joseph Smith to the death, Law will now turn to the underground and mingle with Joseph Smith's enemies. His brother Wilson will join him.

Francis M. Higbee, in his thirteenth year as a Mormon, has found some solace in William Law's shadow. Higbee sends Joseph a letter on January 10 accusing him of "slandering his character." Something had been printed about his waywardness. In writing, Higbee demands Joseph Smith arrange a "public trial before the Church." His letter doesn't deny any of the charges against him. Higbee doesn't get a public trial before the Church. According to numerous witnesses, he turns to slanderous and abusive language.

Higbee has a day of penitence and confesses his wrongs and false accusations against Joseph Smith and other Saints. Joseph readily accepts it, telling the city council that the "difficulties between me and F. M. Higbee [are] eternally buried." Higbee tells the council of men, "I will be [Smith's] friend forever, and his right-hand man."

Higbee's declaration, like William Law's, is shallow. He and his brother Chauncey join the Law brothers, as they hold secret meetings to plan the destruction of Joseph Smith.

About this time, another set of brothers, Robert and Charles Foster, also join the ranks of those dissatisfied with Joseph Smith. Robert Foster is the physician who accompanied Joseph to Washington in the winter of 1839–40. The Foster brothers, like the other two sets of brothers, consider Joseph Smith a fallen prophet, not a false prophet. His introduction of plural marriage and other doctrines against their religious traditions, along with Joseph's political and economic power he is wielding, are reasons they remove themselves from Latter-day Saint ranks. These six men will form a tight knit group. Joseph Jackson will join them after being shunned by Hyrum when he asks for Lovina's hand (Hyrum's daughter) in marriage. Hyrum finds Jackson to be "a wicked, unprincipled man, whom his daughter should never marry." According to Lucy Mack Smith, the mother of Joseph Smith, Jackson continues from this time forth to seek out and befriend the enemies of the Smith family. He positions himself as a key participant in the conspiracy to kill Joseph Smith.

These seven men seem to be the epitome of Joseph Smith's words during the John C. Bennett scandal a year and a half earlier: "Those who have associated with us and made the greatest professions of friendship, have frequently been our greatest enemies and our most determined foes; if they became unpopular, if their interest or dignity was touched, or if they were detected in their iniquity, they were always the first to raise the hand of persecution, to calumniate [make false charges about] and vilify their brethren, and to seek the downfall and destruction of their friends."

ESIDES WITHERING APOSTATES in the fold, Joseph Smith also has national politics on his mind. A mild January day allows him to take the speaker's stand. Nauvoo has a few places designated for public meetings: a few in groves, one near the temple on the bluff, and one near Joseph Smith's home. He preaches in the open air to a large congregation. He gives a lecture on the Constitution of the United States and the presidential candidates lining up for the 1844 election.

Two days later, Joseph turns back to religious doctrine. He appeals to Biblical teachings as he stands near the rising temple to declare that the Lord promised to send Elijah, the ancient prophet who lived about 900 BC back to the earth before the "dreadful day of the Lord." Joseph Smith declares a fulfillment of the prophecy, quoting the prophecies of Malachi and proclaiming his own experiences on April 3, 1836, in the Kirkland Temple. He declares that Elijah did appear to him and Oliver Cowdery—something Oliver Cowdery never denied, even though he fell away from the Church for ten years.

"Elijah," Joseph Smith announces, "[shall] turn the heart of the fathers to the children, and the heart of the children to their fathers, lest I [the Lord] come and smite the earth with a curse." He teaches that the word *turn* should be translated "bind or sealed." He also teaches that *fathers* refers to those who have lived and are now dead. *Children* are those living in the flesh. The gospel in Joseph Smith's religious teachings must go to all in both realms of existence. The living Saints, according to another Biblical teaching, are to become "saviors on Mount Zion."

"How?" Joseph Smith loudly asks the gathered congregation.

"By building temples," he answers, and by "erecting their baptismal fonts, and going forth and receiving all the ordinances, baptisms, confirmations, washings, anointings, ordinations and sealing powers upon their heads [in temples], in behalf of all their progenitors who are dead, and redeem them that they may come forth in the first resurrection and be exalted to thrones of glory with them; and herein is the chain that binds the hearts of the fathers to the children."

These teachings are foreign to the Christian mainstream and Joseph Smith knows it. But some are heeding the words and the call to gather.

Fervent followers are expanding their proselytizing efforts. The working-class society to the high-class society of England are quickly becoming aware of the Mormon movement. Many favorable English artisans have boarded ships for America and left their mother country to follow an American-born prophet. Thousands of reputable, hard-working Europeans are en route to Nauvoo.

Joseph is regularly welcoming new converts to Nauvoo.

MOB "PARTIES" CONTINUE to gather from "Carthage, Warsaw, and Green Plains," all close in proximity to Nauvoo. These parties continue their "agitation," Joseph Smith records. To counter his enemies' agitation, Joseph sends an Apostle, Orson Hyde, to preach at Carthage. No record is left how it went, only that Hyde does return unharmed.

Joseph Smith's clerks are constantly sending letters to local and state leaders reporting on the mob threats and the violence buildup in certain local communities. Strikes against Mormons living on the prairies away from Nauvoo are becoming more frequent. Many are weary with the threats and the destruction to their property and move to Nauvoo for safety.

On the night of January 29, 1844, Joseph Smith gathers with his brother Hyrum and the Church's Twelve Apostles. They take up discussion on Joseph's pursuit in the coming presidential election. At the time of this meeting, two men had definitely put their names forward for the executive office: Martin Van Buren, again, and Henry Clay. At the meeting, Joseph makes clear, "It is morally impossible for this people, in justice to themselves, to vote for the reelection of President Van Buren—a man who criminally neglected his duties as chief magistrate in the cold and unblushing manner which he did, when appealed to for aid in the Missouri difficulties."

Not going lightly on Van Buren this evening, Joseph Smith tells those gathered with him that Van Buren's "heartless reply burns like a firebrand in the breast of every true friend of liberty—'*Your cause is just, but I can do nothing for you.*'" Joseph feels no connection to Henry Clay either. His response in November was "cool contempt of the people's rights," Joseph reminds the participants. "You had better go to Oregon for redress," Clay told Joseph. The response "would prohibit any true lover of our constitutional privileges from supporting him at the ballot box," Joseph tells the men in the meeting.

The Latter-day Saints love their American heritage but find themselves in a political quagmire.

Willard Richards, one of the Apostles in the meeting, refuses to settle for their political predicament. He puts forth the idea that the Latter-day Saints will have an "independent electoral ticket, and that Joseph Smith be a candidate for the next Presidency; and that we use all honorable means in our power to secure his election."

The vote is unanimous.

Joseph Smith seizes the moment and his thoughts to direct the campaign: "If you attempt to accomplish this, you must send every man in the city who is able to speak in public throughout the land to electioneer and make stump speeches, advocate the 'Mormon' religion, purity of elections, and call upon the people to stand by the law and put down mobocracy." Advocating the Mormon religion is Joseph's central message. He already has missionaries traveling abroad in nearly every state. They just need to get word to expand their duties to include political stump speeches. Joseph wants his run for the White House to bring attention to the ruthless mobocracy he and his people have faced since 1830, which is surfacing again in Western Illinois.

He gives his campaigners some lines to use. "Tell the people we have had Whig and Democratic Presidents long enough: we want a President of the United States. If I ever get into the presidential chair, I will protect the people in their rights and liberties." Joseph Smith feels the network he has put in place for the preaching of the gospel can fulfill a dual role. "There is oratory enough in the Church to carry me into the presidential chair the first slide." He has a prominent collection of citizens from probably every state in the Union who have left their family and friends and gathered with him in Western Illinois. It's time for some of these prominent men to return to their mother state and do some talking.

The meeting ends with all the men optimistic. A non-Mormon visitor from Quincy, Illinois, who is in the meeting will drink a toast, "May Nauvoo become the empire seat of government!"

Joseph Smith's record keepers record no reaction to the toast. But the Mormons have made an indelible impression in Illinois and Iowa territorial politics. What was an uninhabitable swamp land five years earlier is now recognized as a swelling city, with several satellite communities. The flood of converts coming from England and other parts of Europe has the attention of all the leading US newspapers. This encourages Joseph Smith's confidence. However, his statement in late 1843 about not wanting to be "a clown to act the farce of political demagoguery" is swept under the rug.

The meeting amongst his friends puts Joseph in a political sprint. Before dinner he dictates a first draft to one of his scribes on his "Views on the Powers and Policy of the Government of the United States": the foundational document for his presidential platform. The words must have been rolling from his tongue, because the document is sizable.

He doesn't draw attention to the Missouri persecutions; "instead, [he] offers solutions for many of the nation's most pressing problems." Joseph Smith wants to give the president "full power to send an army to suppress mobs . . . [without requiring] the governor of a state to make the demand." He sees the degrading state of those enslaved. All men are created equal, "but at the same time some two or three millions of people are held as slaves for life, because the spirit in them is covered with a darker skin." He has a resourceful way to free them: "Pay every man a reasonable price for his slaves out of the surplus revenue arising from the sale of public lands, and from the deduction of pay from members of Congress. Break off the shackles from the poor black man, and hire him to labor like other human beings." He wants to accomplish this by 1850.

Joseph Smith despises the numerous seats in Congress. He proposes two members of the House of Representatives for every one million citizens and reduce their pay three-quarters. Privy to the inaugural addresses of the "illustrious Washington," the "elder Adams," the "venerable Thomas Jefferson," and "Mr. Madison," the candidate prophet turns to their words to put forth his own feelings on virtue in citizenry, patriotism in leaders, national pride, and "peace and friendly intercourse with all nations."

Other political philosophies set forth in his views on government are "extensive prison reform, forming a national bank, and annexing Oregon and Texas." Like Jefferson and many others, he desires the United States boundary to be "from the east to the west sea." His views are considered "an intelligent, comprehensive, forward-looking statement of policies, worthy of a trained statesman." Many of his ideas will eventually come to fruition.

But his decision to enter the national stage of politics will speed the evil intentions of his enemies. They are far too familiar with his charisma and his powerful network to disseminate a message. In many ways, Joseph is politically attractive to the average American. His enemies don't discredit his chances of winning the highest political seat in the nation.

As January comes to a close, Governor Ford sends a letter to the residents of Hancock County. He is tiring of the threats, the demands, the accusations, and the lies coming to his desk. He conveys in his letter a warning: if a "state of war ensue[s] . . . I will be compelled to interfere with executive power. . . . I wish in a friendly, affectionate, and candid manner, to tell the citizens of Hancock

County, Mormons and all, that my interference will be against those who shall be the first aggressors. I am bound by the laws of the Constitution to regard you all as citizens of the State, possessed of equal rights and privileges, and to cherish the rights of one as dearly as the rights of another."

Statesmanlike words, but Governor Ford will suffer political amnesia a few months later and go contrary to his own declared wisdom.

Chapter 30
FEBRUARY 1–24, 1844
Nauvoo, Illinois

THE POLITICAL MEETING among his friends at the end of January has lifted Joseph Smith's spirit. Not all editors and non-Mormon citizens are against him and his people. One editor publishes a compliment to the Mormon people for their industry and ability to make fine farms on the prairies. "Although much complaint has been made about the Mormons," the editor writes, "we saw on our late trip evidences of improvement on our prairies which we consider highly creditable to the Mormons who made them, without whom we doubt whether they would have been made for many years to come. All those who have traveled over the large prairie between Fort Madison, Warsaw and Carthage, remember how dreary it was a few years since. Now it is studded with houses and good farms."

As cohesive and productive a people, the Mormons are diminishing the economical and political position of Warsaw and Carthage. Nauvoo and the satellite Mormon communities are winning, quite impressively, the development and population battle. The editor concludes, "We think such enterprise is worthy to be mentioned. As long as the Mormons are harmless, and do not interfere with the rights of our people we think they should be treated well." He then adds why they should be treated well, "We shall never convince them that they are a deluded people, as far as their religious notions are concerned, in any other way."

Joseph Smith rests well on the night of February 1. He arises the following morning and relates the following dream he had to three friends.

> I was standing on a peninsula, in the midst of a vast body of water where there appeared to be a large harbor or pier built out for boats to come to. I was surrounded by my friends, and while looking at this harbor I saw a steamboat approaching the harbor. There were bridges on the pier for persons to cross, and there came up a wind and drove the steamboat under one of the bridges and upset it.
>
> I ran up to the boat, expecting the persons would all drown; and wishing to do something to assist them, I put my hand against the side of the boat, and with one surge I shoved it under the bridge and righted it up, and then told them to take care of themselves. But it was not long before I saw them starting out into the channel or main body of the water again.
>
> The storms were raging and the waters rough. I said to my friends that if they did not understand the signs of the times and the spirit of prophecy, they would be apt to be lost. It was but a few moments after when we saw the waves break over the boat, and she soon foundered and went down with all onboard.
>
> The storm and waters were still very rough; yet I told my friends around me that I believed I could stem those waves and that storm, and swim in the waters better than the steamboat did; at any rate I was determined to try it. But my friends laughed at me, and told me I could not stand at all. . . . The waters looked clear and beautiful, though exceedingly rough; and I said I believed I could swim, and I would try it anyhow. They said I would drown. I said I would have a frolic in the water first, if I did; and I drove off in the raging waves. I had swam but a short distance when a towering wave overwhelmed me for a time; but I soon found myself on the top of it, and soon I met the second wave in the same way; and for a while I struggled hard to live in the midst of the storm and waves, and soon found I gained upon every wave, and skimmed the torrent better; and I soon had power to swim with my head out of water: so the waves did not break over me at all, and I found that I had swam a great distance; and in looking about, I saw my brother Samuel by my side.
>
> I asked him how he liked it. He said, "First rate," and I thought so too. I was soon enabled to swim with my head and shoulders out

of water, and I could swim as fast as any steamboat. In a little time it became calm, and I could rush through the water, and only go in to my loins, and soon I only went in to my knees, and finally could tread on the top of the water, and went almost with the speed of an arrow.

I said to Samuel, See how swift I can go! I thought it was great sport and pleasure to travel with such speed, and I awoke.

Coincidentally, Joseph Smith had taught a group of Saints a year earlier that "to dream of swimming in deep water signifies success among many people, and that the word will be accompanied with power." The dream appears to be a conspicuous pattern of his life.

By February 7, Wilson Law has his first publication in the *Warsaw Signal* with aid of the contemptible anti-Mormon Thomas C. Sharp. Sharp is glad to have a new writer and recent defector from Joseph Smith's movement. Wilson Law attempts to camouflage his own immorality, which has been publicly exposed, by writing gibberish about Joseph Smith's "want for more wives." While Sharp pushes a scandalous paper, Governor Reynolds of Missouri continues to send officers into Illinois to "harass" and apprehend the Prophet. "He [is] determined to destroy" Joseph Smith.

Joseph meets with the Twelve Apostles on the night of February 7. They go before God in prayer. Joseph Smith acts as voice. He asks "God to deliver him from the power of that man"—Governor Thomas Reynolds. Joseph declares in his prayer that he is innocent before God "and that his heart [is] heavy under the persecutions he endured."

Two days later, Thomas Reynolds locks himself in the governor's executive office. He pulls the blinds and the trigger. He dies of a self-inflicted gunshot wound. A note lies hauntingly on the desk next to his slumped over body: "I have labored and discharged my duties faithfully to the public, but this has not protected me from the slanders and abuse which has rendered my life a burden to me. . . . I pray to God to forgive them and teach them more charity."

Joseph Smith had prayed for deliverance from Reynolds, not for his death. As Reynolds's sad account reaches Nauvoo and as more enemies combine their vitriol at Joseph Smith, he matter-of-factly teaches, "The Lord once told me that what I asked for I should have. I have been afraid to ask God to kill my enemies, lest some of them should, peradventure, repent."

Slightly relieved of enemy pressure, Joseph spends the rest of February acting as mayor and as prophet. He remits the taxes of widows and the poor who are unable to pay. He discourses on strict obedience to receive salvation and pushes the work on the temple along. He holds more political meetings and instructs on the "interests of the General Government." He also calls the Twelve Apostles and other men together to give instructions "regarding supplies for the Oregon and California exploring expedition" he is planning. He wants an exploration of all the mountain country westward, knowing the Latter-day Saints will be driven once again.

Brigham Young, who sits quietly and cautiously by, takes mental notes. Eight men sign up to be part of the expedition.

A cold wind batters Nauvoo from the north, but the real deadly storm is coming from the south.

Chapter 31

FEBRUARY 25–26, 1844

Nauvoo, Illinois

O N FEBRUARY 25, Joseph Smith is more prophet than presidential candidate. He preaches at the temple block amid a large congregation. Hyrum preaches as well. They share their personal witness of the reality of Jesus Christ. They stand as pillars in the Church, which has now reached nearly 27,000.

After leaving the temple block, Joseph and Hyrum attend a prayer meeting with many faithful Latter-day Saints. They pray that "General Joseph Smith's Views of the Powers and Policy of the United States, might be spread far and wide, and be the means of opening the hearts of the people." Fifteen hundred pamphlets of his views on powers and policy are being printed. The pamphlets will be sent to many leading statesmen and citizens of the states through the missionaries.

Before the gathering adjourns, Joseph Smith utters another prophecy: "Within five years we [shall] be out of the power of our old enemies, whether they were apostates or of the world." It will take great sacrifice, lots of grit, and lots of muscle, but a large body of Latter-day Saints fulfills the prophecy by trekking over the continental divide and into the Great Salt Lake Basin, far from Missouri and the looming Civil War.

The following day, "the first meeting to organize a conspiracy to destroy the Smiths [is] held at William Law's home." Law is quickly demonstrating that there is no neutral ground. As much as he was for Joseph Smith, he is now as much against him. A man once told Joseph that if he ever left the Church, he would leave the Church alone and not fight against it like some apostates. The Prophet warned him: "Before you joined this Church you stood on neutral ground. When the gospel was preached good and evil were set before you. . . . There were two opposite masters inviting you to serve them. When you joined this Church you enlisted to serve God. When you did that you left the neutral ground, and you never can get back on to it. Should you forsake the Master you enlisted to serve it will be by the instigation of the evil one, and you will follow his dictation and be his servant."

William Law and the other core disgruntled men are seeking recruits for their cause. They make private invitations throughout the week to gain an audience for a private meeting on the Sabbath night of February 26. Law and a recently new recruit, Austin A. Cowles, a member of the Mormon Church in name and holding a high position, approach Robert Scott and Dennison Harris, both young men in their late teens. They are invited to the secret meeting and asked to tell no one of the meeting except Emer Harris, Dennison's father. Dennison tells his father. Emer is alarmed at the nature of the request and the older men preying on the innocence of boys. Emer immediately sets off for an interview with Joseph Smith.

Joseph tells Emer to send the boys to him. In the morning, Robert and Dennison visit Joseph Smith. They tell him of the invitation and are instructed by the Prophet to attend the meeting and "pay strict attention and do the best [they can] to learn, and remember all the proceedings."

This is the first of three meetings Robert and Dennison attend as informants for Joseph Smith. At this first meeting, considerable time is given to "working up the system and planning how to get at things the best. . . . They [are] plotting how and what they [can] do against Joseph." Robert and Dennison are invited back for two consecutive secret meetings the following two Sabbaths.

Prior to each meeting, the boys visit Joseph Smith. On the day of the third meeting, Joseph tells them, "This will be your last meeting; this will be the last time they will admit you into their council, and they will come to some determination. But be sure . . . that you make no covenants nor enter into any obligation. . . . Be strictly reserve, and make no promise either to conspire against me or any portion of the community. Be silent and do not take any part in their deliberations. . . . They may shed your blood, but I hardly think they will, as you are so young, but they may. If they do I will be a lion in their path. Don't flinch, if you have to die, die like men. You will be martyrs to the cause, and your crown can be no greater. . . . I hardly think they will shed your blood."

DENNISON'S OWN WORDS portray the scene the two boys had to pass through for this third and final meeting:

> That day we were received and welcomed by William Law and Austin Cowles. We passed up the alley. On each side were men on guard. . . . There was a great deal of counseling going on with each other. And every little while Austin Cowles would come and sit by my side and put his arm around my neck to ascertain how I felt with regard to their proceedings, and at the same time William Law would do the same thing with Robert Scott. They talked about Joseph, denouncing him and accusing him. We told them that we did not know anything against Joseph or about the things they were charging him with, that we were only young men, and therefore had nothing to say. They would then try to convince us by relating things to us against him, but we told them that we knew nothing about them, and did not understand them, that we had been reared in the Church and always esteemed Brother Joseph highly. Robert had been reared by William Law, and I had been a neighbor of Austin Cowles and consequently they esteem us as friends, and we did them. They continued to persuade us, we being the only ones who did not sympathize with their proceedings, but they failed to convert us.
>
> Finally they went on to administer the oath to those present. Each man was required to come to the table and hold up the Bible in his right hand. When Brother Higbee would say, "Are you ready?"

The man being sworn answered, "Yes." He would say, "You solemnly swear before God and all holy angels and these your brethren, by whom you are surrounded, that you will give your life, your liberty, your influence, your all for the destruction of Joseph Smith and his party, so help you God!" Each one was sworn in that way. . . .

After all in the room had taken the oath but Robert and me, we were labored with by those two brethren, William Law and Austin Cowles. They sat together side by side, with Brother Cowles on one side and Brother Law on the other. Their arguments were to try to convince us that Joseph was wrong; that he was in transgression, that he was a fallen prophet, and that the Church would be destroyed except action be taken at once against him—a strong one. . . . We told them that we were young . . . and that we knew nothing at all about their charges. . . . After laboring with us in this way with a view of trying to get us to take the oath, we told them we could not do it.

They then told us that they were combining and entering into a conspiracy for the protection and salvation of the Church, and that if we refused to take the oath they would have to kill us. They could not, they said, let us go out with the information that we had gained, because it would not be safe to do so. And someone spoke up and said, "Dead men tell no tales." They gathered around us and after threatening they perceived that we could not be frightened into it. They again commenced to persuade and advise us in this way: "Boys, do as we have done. You are young, you will not have anything to do in this affair, but we want that you should keep it a secret and act with us."

We then told them that we positively could not. They then said that if we did not yield to their requirement that they would have to shed our blood, and they went so far as to start us down stairs in charge of two men armed with guns [and] with bayonets, and William and Wilson Law, Austin Cowles and one of the Fosters started down [the] stairs into the cellar. There they said they would cut our throats if we refused to take the oath. We told them positively that we would have to die then because we could not receive the oath, but that we desired to be turned loose. They said they could not turn us loose with the information that we had received, because it would not be safe to do it.

They then walked us off with one man on each side of us, armed with sword and bowie knife and two men behind us with loaded guns, cocked, with bayonets on them. We were started to the cellar, but we had not gone more than about fifteen feet when someone cried out, "hold on, let us talk this matter over." We were stopped, when they commenced to counsel among themselves, and I distinctly remember one of them saying that our fathers knew where we were, and that if we never returned it would at once cause suspicion and lead to trouble. They became very uneasy about it, for if they shed our blood it would be dangerous for them, as it was known where we were.

Finally they concluded to let us go if we would keep our mouths shut. We were escorted out. . . . They took us toward the river, and still cautioned us about being silent and keeping secret everything we had heard, for, said they, if we opened our mouths about it, they would kill us anywhere—that they would consider it their duty to kill us whenever or wherever the opportunity afforded, either by night or by day. I told them it would be in our interest and to our peace and safety never to mention it to anybody. They said they were glad we could see that, and after warning us in strong terms, and before the guard left us, I saw Brother Joseph's hand from under the bank of the river.

He was beckoning us to him. They turned back but were yet watching us and listening to us, and one of us said, "Let us go toward the river." The guard made answer and said, "Yes, you better go to the river." With this we started off on the run, and we ran past where Brother Joseph was, and Brother John Scott was with him—he was one of his bodyguard. They slipped around the bank and came down to the same point where we were.

We all walked down the river quite a piece, nearly a quarter [of a mile]. . . . Joseph said, "Let us sit down here." We sat down. Joseph said, "Boys, we saw the danger you were in. We were afraid you would not get out alive, but we are thankful that you got off."

He then asked us to relate the results of the meeting. We told him all that had happened. We also told him the names of those who were there. After Joseph heard us he looked very solemn indeed, and he said, "Oh brethren, you do not know what this will terminate in." He looked very solemn, and not being able to control himself he broke right out. Brother Scott rose, and putting his arm around Brother Joseph's neck, said, "Oh Brother Joseph, Brother Joseph, do you think they are going to kill you?" And they fell on each other's necks and wept bitterly for some time. We all wept.

After Joseph recovered himself, Brother John repeated the same question. Brother Joseph lifted Brother John's arms from off his neck and said, "I fully comprehend it." But he would not say that he was going to be killed. But he said in the conversation, "Brethren, I am going to leave you. I shall not be with you long; it will not be many months until I shall have to go." Brother John said, "Brother Joseph, are you going to be slain?" He never answered, but he felt very sorrowful.

JOSEPH SMITH REGAINS his composure. He arises without fear the next morning. The events unfolding do not paralyze him. How it all will end is clear. Spiritual intuition and scriptural precedence have told him. "For where a testament is, there must also of necessity be the death of the testator," the writer of Hebrews wrote. "For a testament is of force after men are dead; otherwise it is of no strength at all while the testator liveth." So Joseph Smith resolutely moves forward. Church affairs consume his time, and there is plenty to do in the next four months. He will spend considerable time with the Quorum of the Twelve Apostles preparing that body of Church government for his absence.

Chapter 32

MARCH 1–9, 1844

Nauvoo, Illinois

THE ENEMIES OF Joseph Smith and the Church are increasing. Joseph is now aware of the names of men who swore an oath against him. The early part of March gives him a window to instruct the Quorum of the Twelve Apostles and prepare them for their missions throughout the states to preach religion and politics.

He conveys to them that he has "conferred upon them all the ordinances, authority, and keys necessary to do so." Speaking to the quorum assembled, he conveys metaphorically, "I roll the burden and responsibility of leading this church off my shoulders on to yours. Now, round up your shoulders and stand under it like men."

Many disregard his sentiments, knowing he has escaped the hands of his enemies time and time again. For fifteen years he had been hounded, and for fifteen years he has come out of the trouble. There is so much yet to do: Finish the temple and introduce the observances to the body of the Church. Send missionaries to all nations of the earth. Gather Latter-day Saints into a united body and build up Zion, a people of "one heart and one mind." For these things to happen, the Latter-day Saints need Joseph Smith at his best, with the power and authority he has exhibited so many times in his life. But Joseph Smith knows otherwise. He tells the Twelve Apostles in March 1844, "The Lord is going to let me rest awhile."

NOT KNOWING THE exact day and time of his departure, Joseph Smith resolutely pushes ahead. He suggests to other leading men of the Church that James Arlington Bennett of Long Island be a candidate for vice president. This was unbeknownst to James Bennett. James Bennett wants to make a run at the governor's chair of Illinois. Joseph Smith a few months earlier told Bennett that he couldn't get involved in his aspiration and "stoop from the sublime authority of Almighty God, to be handled as a monkey's cat-paw, and pettify myself into a clown to act the farce of political demagoguery."

Joseph's difficult predicament with his enemies and jealous politicians in his own state, along with his disgust for the men putting their names forward for President of the United States, forces an abrupt change of mind. He is ready to be a leader for the mistreated, for justice, and for constitutional principles.

Willard Richards, a member of the Church's Twelve Apostles and ever diligent secretary for Joseph, sends James Bennett, who is in the East, a letter. Richards writes to James Bennett in a persuasively positive tone about the Prophet's political situation. "I have recently mailed to you General Smith's 'Views of the Powers and Policy of the Government of the United States,' which were drawn forth in consequence of his friends selecting him as a candidate for the next Presidency, which he very reluctantly acquiesced in, and it seems would not, only to support a favorite maxim—'The people must govern.'"

Joseph Smith operated upon that maxim. He would also use his own maxim to emphasize self-government and republicanism: "I teach my people correct principles and they govern themselves."

Richards presses Bennett with his political disposition: "If I had not felt disposed to uphold him before the people, I never would have been the first to urge his nomination; and during the short space since his name has been published, his friends have been astonished at the flood of influence that is rolling through the Western States in his favor, and in many instances where we might have least expected it." Richards is behind his candidate 100 percent. "I need not assert what the wisest of the wise admit without argument—that General

Smith is the greatest statesman of the 19th century. Then why should not the nation secure to themselves his superior talents, that they may rise higher and higher in the estimation of the crowned heads of the nations and exalt themselves through his wisdom?"

Richards then draws attention to James Bennett's aspiration to be governor of Illinois. "Your friends here consider your letter about the Governorship of Illinois just like every man in your quarter, mere sport, child's sport; for who would stoop to the play of a single State, when the whole nation was on the board?—a cheaper game!"

Richards persuades the recent convert to the faith quite easily. Bennett joined the Church in August of 1843, being baptized under the hand of Brigham Young. But "his motives were not founded on faith" and reflect more of an opportunist.

However, Richards's efforts to lure Bennett as a running mate will have to be withdrawn. Shortly after the proposal for him to join Joseph Smith on the ticket, there arises a conflict about Bennett being born in Ireland. When the opportunity is lost, Bennett is lost from the faith. He will try for one more opportunity among the Mormons in 1845. But Brigham Young will discern his intentions and will reject his positioning. Bennett later described his baptism into the Mormon Church as a mere "frolic in the clear blue ocean."

Once again Joseph Smith doesn't have very good luck with men named Bennett.

By May, Sidney Rigdon is nominated as candidate for vice president of the United States. Joseph doesn't object to his friend's nomination, even though he wants him dropped from the Church's First Presidency.

The war of words is intensifying, and Joseph Smith is more vocal in public about his enemies. Some of his enemies stand by while he delivers remarks.

On the "splendid day" of March 7, with a warm wind from the south, a vast assembly of people gathers on the bluff at the temple. The purpose of the meeting is to push the work along on the temple and have it closed in with the roof on by December. Hyrum Smith speaks first and stays on topic: "We can do anything we undertake. We have power, and we can do great things. . . . Isaiah said we should perform a marvelous work and a wonder. I don't wonder . . . if he saw this vast multitude; and I think this people is abundantly able to build this temple, and much depends upon it for our endowments and sealing powers; and many blessings depend upon it."

Joseph arrives to the assembly as his loyal brother is finishing his remarks. Abruptly Joseph Smith wants to discuss the city ordinances and the difficulty the officers are having in administering them. "We are republicans, and wish to have the people rule; but they must rule in righteousness. Some would complain with what God Himself would do." Joseph Smith thunders his frustration at the meeting. "Those who complain of our rights and charters are wicked and corrupt, and the devil is in them. The reason I called up this subject is, we have a gang of simple fellows here who do not know where their elbows or heads are. . . . From this time I design to bring such characters who act against the interests of the city before a committee of the whole; and I will have the voice of the people, which is republican, and is likely to be the voice of God; and as long as I have a tongue to speak, I will expose the iniquity of the lawyers and wicked men. I fear not their boiling over nor the boiling over of hell, their thunders nor the lightning of their forked tongues."

He continues his hot sermon. "There is another person I will speak about. He is a Mormon—a certain man who lived here before we came here; the two first letters of his name are Hiram Kimball. When a man is baptized and becomes a member of the Church, I have a right to talk about him, and reprove him in public or private, whenever it is necessary, or he deserves it."

Joseph Smith then turns on the society of lawyers who have infiltrated Nauvoo and are looking to take lawsuits out of Nauvoo to the county seat in Carthage. He and his brother Hyrum have had to answer to illegal lawsuits and false accusations long enough. They speak out. Joseph declares: "When they appeal to Carthage, I will appeal to this people, which is the highest court. I despise the lawyers who haggle on lawsuits, and I would rather die a thousand deaths than appeal to Carthage."

"I want to speak about the lawyers of this city. I have good feelings towards them; nevertheless I will reprove the lawyers and doctors anyhow. Jesus did, and every prophet has; and if I am a prophet, I shall do it: at any rate, I shall do it, for I profess to be a prophet."

This doesn't sit well for those few in the audience who feel he is a fallen prophet, especially Charles Foster, one of the major conspirators to destroy the Smiths.

Joseph takes a short speaking respite, and Hyrum changes his tone and takes off right were his brother left on the harangue of corrupt lawyers. "Polliwogs, wigglers, and toads," he says. "Like tree toads, they change color to suit the object they are upon. They ought to be ferreted out like rats. You could describe them as you would a hedgehog: they are in every hedge, stinking like a skunk."

Conspirator Charles Foster, who had taken the oath to destroy Joseph Smith less than two weeks earlier, is near the speakers stand. He angrily ignores Hyrum to confront Joseph. He blurts out, "Do you mean me, Joseph?"

Joseph says, "I will reply by asking you a question."

"That is no way."

Joseph replies, "Yes, that is the way the Quakers do. But Jesus said, 'Whose image and superscription is this? Why did you apply the remarks to yourself? Why did you ask if we meant you?"

"Then I understand you meant me."

"You said it."

"You shall hear from me."

"As Mayor, I fine you $10 for that threat, and for disturbing the meeting."

An agitated Foster is losing this public fight.

Joseph and Hyrum are ferreting out the rats, at least drawing attention to them so the public can be made aware. The language Charles Foster uses, "you shall hear from me," is another legal challenge coming Joseph's way, and most likely a violent physical threat. Joseph is aware of the oath and Foster's real intentions, and the situation is elevating Joseph's temper.

Charles's brother Robert Foster comes to his defense and asks Joseph Smith to wait a minute. "He has not threatened you," Foster yells before the crowd. "He has," contests Joseph. "No one has heard

him threaten you," Foster shouts back. At this point in the escalating contention, hundreds privy to the whole interchange exclaim
in unison, "I have!" Foster begins to rant against the proceedings;
Joseph calls him to order, saying that if he does not hold his tongue
he would fine him. The crowd, the situation, and the person is too
much for the Foster brothers. They belligerently walk away uttering
their threats.

To fulfill their oath, they will have to get Joseph Smith away
from Nauvoo and his bodyguard, but more important, the twenty
thousand Saints who will sustain and defend him at all costs.

ONE PARTICULAR LAWSUIT taken to Carthage is by Orsimus F. Bostwick. He accuses Hyrum of low moral character acting upon women
in Nauvoo, especially the widows, many of whose husbands died by
the hand of Missouri mobs. Hyrum allows the women to respond
to Bostwick. They arrange and publish a document known as "The
Voice of Innocence from Nauvoo." When it is published, it is given
the shorter title of "Virtue Will Triumph." Written by the leading
minds of the female Relief Society, it speaks of the virtue spring-
ing from Nauvoo as opposed to the nonsense being portrayed by
enemies of Joseph Smith.

Emma Smith calls out Bostwick for his boast that "he could
take a half of bushel of meal, obtain his vile purposes, and get what
accommodation he wanted with almost any woman in the city."
Emma in her own prophetic tone scolds such thinking: "Wo to the
wretch that can thus follow the blood stain mobbers of Missouri in
their hellish career and deal his slander about the streets of Nauvoo."
Bostwick is out of the same mold as John C. Bennett, and Emma
draws the connection. "While we render credence to the doctrine
of Paul that, 'neither the man is without the woman; neither is the
woman without the man in the Lord,' yet we raise our voices and
hands against John C. Bennett's spiritual wife system as a scheme of
profligates to seduce women."

Bostwick is another profligate roaming the streets of Nauvoo
for lustful purposes. The virtuous women of Nauvoo are tiring of

such characters. Emma's frustration is evident as she concludes the publication that was adopted by a large number of the Relief of Society. "While the marriage bed, undefiled is honorable, let polygamy, bigamy, fornication, adultery, and prostitution, be frowned out of the hearts of honest men to drop it."

Emma is in a unique situation. She is married to the man whom over twenty thousand people regard and sustain as a prophet of the living God. She knows this herself, having seen and testified of the power granted him in bringing forth the Book of Mormon and other revelations, subduing enemies, gathering people, building temples, healing individuals, and preaching powerful sermons. Yet, she is married to him, knows of his goodness and tenderness as well as his weaknesses and struggles, and has to share him with others. Emma uniquely and remarkably shoulders the difficult teaching concerning plural marriage. She openly challenges him and yet sustains him at other times, both publicly and privately.

Her words reflect her struggle to accept her husband's teaching on plural marriage and at the same time denounce his enemy's practice of adultery and spiritual wifery. In the eyes of Latter-day Saints, there is a unique distinction between the fidelity, honor, and eternal implications of plural marriage and the lustful and fleeting practice called polygamy. A blurred distinction for many, but not for many of Joseph Smith's followers who believe he is restoring truths with biblical precedence or truths hidden from the world. Joseph introduces the concept of eternal families and posterity.

Chapter 33

MARCH 11, 30–31, 1844

Nauvoo, Illinois

On THE MORNING of March 11, Joseph Smith meets with a handful of leading men of the Church, whom he "organized into a special council." He is contemplating suggestions and ideas to settle in Texas or in the mountains, Sante Fe, California, and the Oregon Territory. To withdraw his followers in a mass exodus from Illinois and settle in a new region in the West will take some order and several months of preparation. By the time the meeting ends, Joseph Smith has organized a "Council of Fifty." The men occupying a position on this council are a "hand-picked body selected by Church leaders [and] operated out of public view."

Joseph Smith and the Quorum of the Twelve Apostles occupy their portion of the fifty seats. There are at least three non-Mormons on the council. The Church is to put forth the spiritual matters while the Council of Fifty will play a civic role including "interactions with states and nations to achieve the Church's political and social objectives." The council is established with a vision set to the time when a "perfect government would exist on the earth, with the Lord reigning as king. In a simple way, the earthly political council symbolizes that future, heaven-directed civil Kingdom of God on earth."

Joseph sees the introduction of this Council of Fifty and the Church he has organized as divine reflection of the idea planted by

183

Isaiah: "Out of Zion shall go forth the law, and the word of the Lord from Jerusalem." Joseph Smith, like most Christians of his day, believes that in the end, God's government will override all earthly governments. So he moves with great confidence that he is playing a significant role in the assimilation of the kingdom of God on earth with the kingdom of heaven about to come.

The council is charged to "follow God's law and seek to know his will." They are to obtain revelation and in all decisions be unanimous. This council was not to challenge the operating government of the United States but more so be a "symbol of the future theocratic kingdom of God." By going west, the Saints would be leaving the boundaries of the United States and would perhaps use the council as a governing body in the wilderness. The council is to "assist with the strategic planning for the Church."

Joseph Smith is thinking ahead as the turmoil continues to swell. His forward thinking and organization helps align Brigham Young for what is about to be placed on his shoulders.

Meeting with the Quorum of the Twelve Apostles and disseminating their ecclesiastical responsibilities and charge, along with meeting with the Council of Fifty, Joseph Smith has a full month of meetings. By the end of March, he is back in political mode and requesting from the US Congress that he have the "privilege of raising 100,000 men to extend protection to persons wishing to settle Oregon and other portions of the territory of the United States, and extend protection for the people of Texas."

Of course some of the persons wishing to go west are the Mormons and the places considered are where General Joseph Smith wants 100,000 men at his command. Some Latter-day Saints sense that their welcome in Western Illinois is about to come to an end. Their leader senses his life is about to come to end. Going west could draw their enemies' attention away from Nauvoo, which will give the Latter-day Saints a chance to finish their temple and outfit European converts. Joseph is willing to blaze some trails west with the help of the Federal Government. He isn't reluctant to send his grandiose request to Congress and to the president of the United States, John Tyler. The request will get people's attention, particularly newspaper editors and willing souls desiring to be part of the 100,000. This is perfect timing for the campaign blitz coming and for securing some votes of male-only elections.

To sustain his religious and political feelings, Joseph Smith defends a black man named Chism accused of robbing a store. Two Missourians whip the man so severely that he is lacerated from his shoulders to his hips. Both men are found guilty; one even admits his guilt. They are fined and held in custody for a short time. Joseph's defense of a black man doesn't sit well with many of his enemies.

Chapter 34

APRIL 4–7, 1844

Nauvoo, Illinois

I N LESS THAN five years, the Latter-day Saints have created a community from a considerable swampland that draws the attention of a variety of people from around the United States and Europe. It is "Joe Smith," "Brother Joseph," the "American Prophet" they want to see with their own eyes. They want to see someone who has developed a persona of being suspect, curious, and revered in name. The Native Americans of various tribes are among these visitors. Joseph Smith's fame as a prophet and seer resonates with them. On April 4, eleven Native Americans visit Joseph. Not much is said of the details of the encounter, but Joseph notes "an impressive interview." Over the years, many Native Americans have found a friend in the American prophet. Hundreds will return a month later.

Joseph Smith has been teaching the Latter-day Saints that "friendship is one of the grand fundamental principles of 'Mormonism;' [it is designed] to revolutionize and civilize the world, and cause wars and contentions to cease and men to become friends and brothers." Joseph is uniquely cordial and personable with all people, with few exceptions. He has several interviews with the poor, the downtrodden, politicians, and sycophants, as well as the refined and the rough. In most cases, all love him and think of him as genuine and likable. Only a handful of his most vehement enemies think otherwise. And many have been eyewitnesses over the years that "even his most bitter enemies were generally overcome if he could once get their ears." Those who turn against him, in almost all cases, never say he is a false prophet but rather a fallen prophet.

Joseph expresses his confidence by stating, "This generation is as corrupt as the generation of Jews that crucified Christ; and if he were here today, and should preach the same doctrine He did then, they would put Him to death." And then his bold confidence rises. "I defy all the world to destroy the work of God; and I prophesy they never will have power to kill me till my work is accomplished, and I am ready die." He sees his work as God's work and knows no man or combined enemy can destroy it.

Friday, April 5, Sidney Rigdon is one of the first speakers at a general conference of the Church. Thousands gather. Thousands more are en route to the conference. Rigdon recounts the birth of the Church in New York fourteen years earlier, when just a few early converts occupied an "old log house 20 feet square." In those days, "we began to talk about the kingdom of God as if we had the world at our command. . . . We looked upon men of the earth as grasshoppers." Rigdon has an aggressive speaking style and can get people emotionally charged. Joseph Smith listens on as Rigdon reminisces. He is still suspicious of his dear friend's motives and loyalty.

On Saturday, April 6, Hyrum Smith is to address the congregation. There are even more gathered than the day previous. Joseph Smith makes some preliminary remarks before his brother speaks, reminding the police who are on the outskirts of the crowd "to keep order. . . . God almighty calls you, and we command you to do it." Some of his enemies are in the congregation.

Hyrum stands to speak. "I cannot make a comparison between the House of God"—the temple rising in their midst—"and anything now in existence. Great things are to grow out of this house. There is a great and mighty power to grow out of it. . . . Knowledge is power. We want knowledge." And no one is to be excluded excepting the hypocrites and the godless. He then announces, "You sisters shall have a seat in that house," a contrary invitation to the women's involvement in such things in their day.

ON THE THIRD day of the conference, April 7, twenty thousand Latter-day Saints have gathered to hear Joseph Smith speak. It is a significant gathering for the outdoor arrangements of the mid-nineteenth century. Four men trained in reporting and note-taking ready their hands. They are positioned comfortably with chairs and a table to do their work. The thirty-eight-year-old prophet stands and begins to speak. He has had no uninterrupted time to prepare lengthy sermons. He speaks impromptu, no notes, no script, nothing memorized.

Joseph Smith by this time is wise enough to know when he is speaking politically and when he is speaking as a professed prophet. "Tis right, politically, for a man who has influence to use it," he told the Saints a year earlier. "In relation to politics, I will speak as a man; but in relation to religion I will speak in authority." In this lengthy sermon, he speaks in relation to religion. The words Joseph Smith conveys makes it clear he doesn't question or doubt his authority or position in God's eyes.

Using the Church conference, Joseph sets up his remarks as the funeral sermon for a dear friend named King Follet, who died in an accident while digging a well. Joseph Smith addresses several subject matters, such as the character of God, God as an exalted man, man's relation to God, and the creation. His teachings on this late afternoon challenge Christian creeds, which he argues are warped in tradition rather than grounded in truth. He begins one of his last major doctrinal discourses, appealing to the hearts and ears of the Saints:

> Beloved Saints: I will call [for] the attention of this congregation while I address you on the subject of the dead. . . . I want your prayers and faith that I may have the instruction of Almighty God and the gift of the Holy Ghost, so that I may set forth things that are true and which can be easily comprehended by you, and that the testimony may carry conviction to your hearts and minds of the

truth of what I shall say. Pray that the Lord may strengthen my lungs [and] stay the winds.

With the absence of wind and the power granted to his lungs, Joseph Smith's voice is able to reach the ears of many: "I do not calculate or intend to please your ears with superfluity of words or oratory, or with much learning; but I calculate [intend] to edify you with the simple truths from heaven."

Brigham Young once said that Joseph Smith had the ability to take "heaven, figuratively speaking, and [bring] it down to earth; and he took the earth, and brought it up, and opened up, in plainness and simplicity, the things of God. . . . He reduced heavenly things to the understanding of the finite. . . . No man was able to teach as he could." Joseph starts the substance of his remarks with the character God:

> It is necessary for us to have an understanding of God himself in the beginning. If we start right, it is easy to go right all the time; but if we start wrong we may go wrong, and it will be a hard matter to get right. . . . If men do not comprehend the character of God, they do not comprehend themselves. . . . I want to ask this congregation, every man, woman and child, to answer the question in their own hearts, what kind of a being God is? Ask yourselves; turn your thoughts into your hearts, and say if any of you have seen, heard, or communed with Him? The scriptures inform us that 'This is life eternal that they might know thee, the only true god, and Jesus Christ whom thou has sent.' . . . For there can be eternal life on no other principle."

Joseph Smith believes that if he can get people to comprehend the true nature of God, they may be able to discern between a false teacher and a prophet and stop the shedding of blood. To that end, he explains:

> God himself was once as we are now, and is an exalted man, and sits enthroned in yonder heavens! That is the great secret. . . . I say, if you were to see him today, you would see him like a man in form— like yourselves in all the person, image, and very form as a man; for Adam was created in the very fashion, image and likeness of God, and received instruction from, and walked, talked and conversed with Him, as one man talks and communes with another. . . .

It is the first principle of the gospel to know for a certainty the character of God, and to know that we may converse with Him as one man converses with another, and that He was once a man like us; yea, that God himself, the Father of us all, dwelt on an earth, the same as Jesus Christ Himself did; and I will show it from the Bible.

The scriptures inform us that Jesus said, as the Father hath power in himself, even so hath the Son power—to do what? Why, what the Father did. The answer is obvious—in a manner to lay down his body and take it up again. Jesus, what are you going to do? To lay down my life as my Father did, and take it up again. Do you believe it? If you do not believe it you do not believe the Bible. The scriptures say it, and I defy all the learning and wisdom and all the combined powers of earth and hell together to refute it.

How consoling to the mourners when they are called to part with a husband, wife, father, mother, child, or dear relative, to know that, although the earthly tabernacle is laid down and dissolved, they shall rise again to dwell in everlasting burnings in immortal glory, not to sorrow, suffer, or die any more, but they shall be heirs of God and joint heirs with Jesus Christ. What is it? To inherit the same power, the same glory and the same exaltation, until you arrive at the station of a god, and ascend the throne of eternal power, the same as those who have gone before.

He goes on to teach that salvation and exaltation must be sought for diligently.

When you climb up a ladder, you must begin at the bottom, and ascend step by step, until you arrive at the top; and so it is with the principles of the gospel—you must begin with the first, and go on until you learn all the principles of exaltation. . . . It is not all to be comprehended in this world; it will be a great work to learn our salvation and exaltation even beyond the grave. . . .

Having a knowledge of God, we begin to know how to approach Him, and how to ask so as to receive an answer. When we understand the character of God, and know how to come to Him, He begins to unfold the heavens to us, and to tell us all about it. When we are ready to come to Him, He is ready to come to us.

Joseph Smith continues to expand the minds of the people by explaining that God could not create something out of nothing.

You ask the learned doctors why they say the world was made out of nothing, and they will answer, "Doesn't the Bible say He created the world?" And they infer, from the word create, that it must have been made out of nothing. Now, the word create came from the word *baurau*, which does not mean to create out of nothing; it means to organize; the same as a man would organize materials and build a ship. Hence we infer that God had materials to organize the world out of chaos—chaotic matter, which is element, and in which dwells all the glory. Element had an existence from the time He had. The pure principles of element are principles which can never be destroyed; they may be organized and re-organized, but not destroyed. They had no beginning and can have no end. . . .

When I talk to these mourners, what have they lost? Their relatives and friends are only separated from their bodies for a short season: their spirits which existed with God have left the tabernacle of clay only for a little moment, as it were; and they now exist in a place where they converse together the same as we do on the earth.

Joseph Smith then explains his understanding of whom God is and what His purposes are.

I might with boldness proclaim from the house-tops that God never had the power to create the spirit of man at all. God Himself could not create Himself. God Himself, finding He was in the midst of spirits and glory, because He was more intelligent, saw proper to institute laws whereby the rest could have a privilege to advance like Himself. The relationship we have with God places us in a situation to advance in knowledge. He has power to institute laws to instruct the weaker intelligences, that they may be exalted with Himself.

This is good doctrine. It tastes good. I can taste the principles of eternal life, and so can you. They are given to me by the revelations of Jesus Christ; and I know that when I tell you these words of eternal life as they are given to me, you taste them, and I know that you believe them. You say honey is sweet, and so do I. I can also taste the spirit of eternal life.

After describing God's purposes in bringing forth His children to the earth, Joseph Smith addresses man's relation to God and our responsibility for ourselves and our dead in knowing and having all the ordinances of the gospel that lead to salvation. He speaks of the unpardonable sin, the forgiveness of sins, and the second death, which is a spiritual death to all the disobedient. He concludes this lengthy sermon by declaring his innocence in a most unique way:

> I have intended my remarks for all, both rich and poor, bond and free, great and small. I have no enmity against any man. I love you all; but I hate some of your deeds. I am your best friend, and if persons miss their mark it is their own fault. If I reprove a man, and he hates me, he is a fool; for I love all men, especially these my brethren and sisters. . . .
>
> You don't know me; you never knew my heart. No man knows my history. I cannot tell it: I shall never undertake it. I don't blame anyone for not believing my history. If I had not experienced what I have, I would not have believed it myself.
>
> I cannot lie down until all my work is finished. I never think any evil, nor do anything to the harm of my fellow-man. When I am called by the trump of the archangel and weighed in the balance, you will all know me then. I add no more. God bless you all. Amen.

Joseph leaves the speaking stand exhausted. He sits down two hours and fifteen minutes after he began.

As he returns home, the imminence of his death looms. On the last day of the conference of the Church, Joseph Smith stands and delivers a few words. The day before wore him out. "It is just as impossible, for me to continue the subject of yesterday as to raise the dead. My lungs are worn out. There is a time to all things, and I must wait. I will give it up."

The Church conference ends on April 9. "The weather has been beautiful . . . and they have been the greatest, best, and most glorious five consecutive days ever enjoyed by this generation," a report says. "Much good was done. Many spectators were present from Quincy, Alton, Warsaw, Fort Madison, and other towns of less notoriety. . . . The good order that was preserved, when we consider the immense numbers that were present, speaks much in favor of the morality of the city."

Joseph Smith strove to deliver a message in hopes of helping people know God's relation to them and their relation to God. As the spring of 1844 opens, Joseph's enemies are getting some people agitated and dissatisfied with conditions in Nauvoo. His enemies are prevailing on some individuals to question his actions, his personality, and his teachings and doctrine.

Chapter 35
APRIL 13–20, 1844
Nauvoo, Illinois

EFORE AND AFTER this five-day conference, Thomas Sharp is printing numerous articles criticizing Joseph Smith and the membership of the Church. Sharp attacks Joseph Smith's "teachings, political views, writings, and actions as mayor, and Church leader." Non-Mormons who were once neutral are starting to witness firsthand the "rapid growth and influence of the Mormons at Nauvoo." The articles rolling off Sharp's press gets more and more non-Mormons believing that Joseph is a "knave, despot, tyrant, false prophet, fraud, and a dangerous and powerful man whose actions should be watched, and closely scrutinized."Sharp's efforts continue to attract the once loyal Mormon brothers of Law, Higbee, and Foster. Sharp welcomes any dissidents with open arms. It is likely that Sharp is aware of the secret oath these men have taken to destroy Joseph Smith.

On April 13, Robert Foster is called before the Nauvoo City Council. He has to account for a charge of lying and "unchristian-like conduct in general." He had been telling people that Joseph Smith was a money grabber and that he, Robert Foster, had to bare all of Smith's expenses when they traveled together to Washington, DC, in the winter of 1839–40.

Before the council Joseph asks Foster, "Did you bear any part of my expenses?"

"I did not," Foster replies.

"Have I ever misused you any way," Joseph asks.

Foster, trying to avoid damaging his own character and making Joseph Smith look acceptable, says, "I do not feel at liberty to answer under the existing circumstances." He is pressed even more by the Prophet to show the council and others in company, the high council of the Church, that Foster has been treated "honorably" by Joseph Smith at all times. Foster continues to squirm in his predicament. "I shall testify no further at present."

Joseph Smith doesn't squirm. He presents charges against Foster to the high council authority of the Church for "abusing my character privily, for throwing out slanderous insinuations against me, for conspiring against my peace and safety, for conspiring against my life, for conspiring against the peace of my family, and for lying."Foster realizes by this time that Joseph Smith knows of the secret meetings a few weeks back. Foster can't hide after this public meeting where the man he wants to destroy brings charges against him publicly. He leaves the proceedings with increased anger. Joseph leaves the meeting and walks a block to the wharf where over two hundred converts from England have just arrived. He greets them and teaches a short sermon. This is the first time the converts from Europe lay eyes on their American prophet. He will teach again the next day on the deck of the steamboat as a heavy rain presses down on Nauvoo.

These new converts bring a healthy social and cultural climate to Nauvoo. Nauvoo at this time has a well-favored number of brass bands, Church choirs, instrumentalists, and vocalists who play at dances and at a variety of other gatherings.

On April 15, the Quorum of the Twelve Apostles, under leadership of Brigham Young, publishes the names of men who accept mission calls to preach and campaign in various states. Twenty-six states and one territory will be entertaining 337 Mormon missionaries. New Jersey initially has two missionaries assigned to labor, while other states like New York and Ohio have more than forty missionaries to canvas the states. Many men are sent through Illinois, Indiana, Tennessee, Virginia, and Pennsylvania.

The Mormon missionary network is favorable to electioneering. Many of these men are returning to their home states, where they lived before their conversion to Mormonism. They are familiar with political workings, have family and friends throughout the communities, and know the towns and cities of importance. "At the height of the endeavor, over six hundred [are] engaged" campaigning for a "prophet-leader of a religion." Joseph Smith is appreciative of the "cadre of supporters canvassing the nation for him." His enemies are not. His closest enemies know his political power is unmatched and his potential election is possible if not stopped.

As the missionaries and campaigners are packing their bags, Joseph Smith is introducing the concept of theodemocracy in a published letter. "I go emphatically, virtuously, and humanely, for a THEODEMOCRACY, where God and the people hold the power to conduct the affairs of men in righteousness. And where liberty, free trade, and sailor's rights, and the protection of life and property shall be maintained inviolate, for the benefit of ALL. To exalt mankind is nobly acting the part of a God; to degrade them, is meanly doing the drudgery of the devil." And then for those who think Joseph Smith is a mere uneducated buffoon, he signs off, *"Unitas, libertas, caritas-esto perpetua!"*—unity, liberty, charity in perpetuity—"With the highest sentiments of regard for all men, I am an advocate of unadulterated freedom."

In short, Joseph Smith wants communities, states, and nations governed by the people according to the revealed will of God. He wants an "aristarchy"–"a body of good men in power, or government by excellent men." Let men understand correct principles and then be anxiously engaged in a good cause, he continually argues. That is unadulterated freedom. But it wasn't in alignment with the Democratic or rising Whig parties' platforms. "While the Whigs [are] most decidedly anti-Mormon, both parties [are] convinced that the political future of Illinois could be read in changing demographics. Mormon immigration to Nauvoo [is] staggering . . . a powerful voting bloc, acting out their unique vision of theodemocracy. Their support [is] fickle and even a liability. They fit neither party's calculus for political success." Joseph Smith knows this and is trying to draw citizens from both parties. If the Mormons are left alone, Illinois politics will develop quite differently, even derailing young political ambitions found in both parties, namely Abraham Lincoln and Stephen Douglas.

WHILE BRIGHAM YOUNG manages the preaching and campaigning, Joseph takes on local Church issues in Nauvoo. He has learned that Robert Foster and the company of men against him have been paying someone's board at the Mansion House, where Joseph and Emma reside. They want to be able to "catch something against [him]; so that, if the report is true, they may have something to carry back," Joseph tells the dinner table guests on the afternoon of April 18. Perhaps Foster's paid employee is at the table.

After months of extending the olive branch to Robert Foster and William Law, Joseph proposes they be excommunicated, cut off from Church membership for "unchristian-like conduct." Thirty-three men unanimously sustain the action. William Law's wife and his brother Wilson are also cut off. Each of their names and the action taken against them are sent for immediate publication in the *Times and Seasons*, a Church periodical.

Of the thirty-three men in council, one is weakening in the faith and in the prophetic mantle of Joseph Smith. William Marks's spiritual temperament is a shadow of Sidney Rigdon's. Like Rigdon, he desires to be a pillar among the Mormon people but is starting to lean in sympathy with those opposed to Joseph Smith. William Marks opposes plural marriage. He is president of the high council in Nauvoo, a position higher than Mormon bishops. In previous days, Marks was dearly loyal to Joseph, even asking him to speak at his son's funeral in 1842. By the spring of 1844, his indifference is beginning to be noted.

William Marks notifies William Law of his excommunication the morning after the decision is made. Whether he is taking that action on his own or directed by Joseph is unknown. But William

Law hardens and becomes more vocal with his dissent and with his desire to save the Church from ruin under Joseph Smith.

William Law has now built up his reasons to speak out and come out violently against Joseph Smith. He opposes "a growing ecclesiastical control over [Smith's] economic, political, and social life" in Nauvoo, blurring a line of Church and state. Law sees Joseph Smith as "totally ungovernable and defiant" to the laws of the land, particularly state laws and not answering for the extradition request from Missouri state officials. Law also sees Joseph's doctrines of "plurality of Gods," which he explained in the King Follet funeral sermon, and the "plurality of wives" as reasons to destroy him.

But the angst that gave William Law fuel for his opposition is how the proceedings of trial for Church membership unfolded. Joseph Smith had dropped him from the First Presidency in January while conversing with him on the street. He is also denied a chance to speak at the recent general conference of the Church. Now he is being cut off entirely without being present to defend himself or his position. "We consider this cutting off as illegal and therefore corrupt," he writes in his journal after hearing of the decision from William Marks.

On April 20, Law approaches Willard Richards, a member of the Church's Quorum of the Twelve Apostles and a clerk of the proceedings that took action against Law. He wants to see the minutes of the meeting. "There was no record," Richards tells him. Chagrined by procedures, Law writes in his diary, "The Church has as a body transgressed the laws of the Church and of God and every principle of justice and are under deep transgression."

Law's disciplinary council did not follow the Church procedure that was established by the revelations Joseph Smith had received and recorded. William Law sees this action as proof that Joseph is operating with too much power and authority in the Church. Though thirty-three men in the Church hierarchy sustained the action to remove him, Law sees it as another example of the misuse of power Joseph Smith is wielding.

Chapter 36

APRIL 28, 1844

Nauvoo, Illinois

PART OF WILLIAM Law's antagonism toward Joseph Smith stems from his envy. Law is a favored man, well spoken, robust, and passionate. His foothold among the Latter-day Saints is slipping, however, and rapidly. The Latter-day Saints in growing number trust the power and charisma resting in the person of Joseph Smith.

To counter Joseph Smith, William's brother Wilson invites disgruntled members to his home. The purpose of the meeting is to organize a reformed church. The purpose of their church is to "destroy the Smiths and take control of Nauvoo." Ignoring biblical principles upon which most churches are built, the men appoint their Church leaders. William Law is the elected president, his brother Wilson a counselor. Robert D. Foster and Francis M. Higbee are appointed as apostles. Charles Ivins, "hotelier" in Keokuk, Iowa, is recognized as the bishop.

They "appoint a committee" to visit homes of known dissidents and even faithful members to plead their cause and inform people of the newly formed church. They expect many to follow. To help get the word out for the newborn church, William Law and his friends order a printing press to promote their church and present Nauvoo with an opposing paper. Their paper will be called the *Nauvoo Expositor*.

The title of their paper is a clever name for what they are setting out to do. William Law readily accepts his role to "expound, explain, and interpret" his trouble with Joseph Smith's doctrines and practices. To position himself as an alternative religious and civic leader in Nauvoo, Law has to continually print and persuade people that Joseph Smith is a fallen prophet. As William's intentions are coming to light, Joseph Smith preaches before a large audience:

> My enemies say that I have been a true prophet. Why, I had rather be a fallen true prophet than a false prophet. When a man goes about prophesying, and commands men to obey his teachings, he must either be a true or false prophet. False prophets always arise to oppose the true prophets and they will prophesy so very near the truth that they will deceive almost the very chosen ones. . . . In relation to the kingdom of God, the devil always sets up his kingdom at the very same time in opposition to God.

William Law and the others know that Joseph Smith's words about false prophets opposing true prophets are intended for them. Joseph makes it even clearer as he continues to proclaim:

> Every man who has a calling to minister to the inhabitants of the world was ordained to that very purpose in the Grand Council of heaven before this world was. I suppose that I was ordained to this very office in that Grand Council. It is the testimony that I want that I am God's servant, and this people His people. The ancient prophets declared that in the last days the God of heaven should set up a kingdom which should never be destroyed, nor left to other people. . . .
>
> He that arms himself with gun, sword, or pistol, except in the defense of truth, will sometime be sorry for it. I never carry any weapon with me bigger than my penknife. When I was dragged before the cannon and muskets in Missouri, I was unarmed. God will always protect me until my mission is fulfilled. I calculate to be one of the instruments of setting up the kingdom of Daniel by the word of the Lord, and I intend to lay a foundation that will revolutionize the whole world. I once offered my life to the Missouri mob as a sacrifice for my people, and here I am.

Joseph Smith is confident in his declaration concerning the extension of his life. However, he had to reconcile that confidence with constant "forebodings of the Spirit that his ministry on earth was nearing its end."

William Law's fellow apostates practice their own interpretation of biblical principles by barraging him with ongoing charges and law suits—smiting him on the right cheek, suing him at the law. Joseph Smith introduced the Church fourteen years earlier by declaring the ministry of angels, the translation of ancient text, priesthood authority to baptize, and the need for modern prophets and current revelation. Law's church originates on an entirely different foundation—to kill Joseph Smith.

The Nauvoo police are quite familiar with the new church in town and keep an attentive watch on them day and night.

Those loyal to Joseph speak out against his enemies. On the Sabbath day, the Laws, Fosters, and Higbees organize their new church, while Brigham Young takes the stand in an open-air meeting. "Dr. Foster is cursed," Young boldly delivers. The people shout "amen." Young continues his sermon by preaching the first principles and ordinances of the gospel: faith, repentance, baptism, and reception of the Holy Ghost. When he finishes, "several people [are] baptized in the river at the foot of Main Street," right near Joseph Smith's home and not too far distant from Wilson Law's home, where the dissidents are trying to get their church started.

Hyrum Smith in full strength and uncompromising defense of his younger brother also delivers at the open-air meeting a bold statement: "There were prophets before, but Joseph has the spirit and power of all the prophets."

Sunday, April 28, proves to be a memorable day in Nauvoo history. Both his devout followers and his most vehement enemies dig in, either in defense of his life or to take his life. At the end of the day, Joseph still holds the edge against his enemies, and he holds it without a public word spoken. He spends the day at home not feeling well.

Chapter 37

APRIL 29—MAY 9, 1844

Nauvoo, Illinois

FOURTEEN-YEAR-OLD CHARLES STODDARD is troubled. He is now in his fourth month of employment at William Law's home. Law's behavior is becoming more and more unrestrained and is making Charles uneasy about the safety of Joseph Smith's life.

Near the end of April or early May, Charles is awakened by William Law before sunrise. Law is drunk and full of foul language. He has been up all night with a few of his "associates" talking and planning revenge on Joseph Smith. He orders Charles to get "out of bed to clean and oil his gun." As Charles arises and is dressing, Law informs him that he is going "to shoot the prophet . . . old Joe Smith." The remark slows Charles in fulfilling his ordered task to clean and oil the gun. He experiences "fright and anxiety." Law "stands over him [and] prod[s] him with his foot." With Law's physical force, Charles reluctantly prepares the gun.

William Law returns a few minutes later and is "satisfied with the way the gun [is] working." He loads the chamber with one bullet, boasting "that he could kill the prophet with one shot." Dawn not yet breaking, Charles is sent to bring the Prophet to William under the lie that William Law has business that needs to be settled upon.

Charles runs as fast as he can to the Prophet's home about two blocks away. He "begs the prophet not to go to Mr. Law's" for he is "drunk." Charles tells Joseph Smith he is "afraid" that Law is prepared to fulfill his oath. Without any immediate concern, Joseph rises from bed and dresses. Dawn is slowly breaking. He walks uniquely calm. Charles is fidgety. As they approach the "Law residence the prophet reassure[s] Charles that no harm would come to him that day."

Charles is further frightened. He can't shake the one thought "racing through his mind. 'I am the one that cleaned the gun that is going to be used to kill the prophet.'" Joseph Smith sensing the boys sickened state makes a "final attempt to calm" him. "Mr. Law may someday kill me, Charles, but it won't be today."

In the stillness of the morning, a boisterous and "staggering" William Law steps out of his house. He boasts of his intention. Joseph Smith's physical demeanor is resolute and his voice composed as Law approaches him. In a "kindly and unafraid" tone, he asks, "You sent for me, Mr. Law?"

Law spouts out a short blustering oath that "he was now going to do Nauvoo, Illinois, and indeed the whole world a great favor by disposing of the prophet with one shot."

Charles shudders, hoping his eyes and ears do not witness the foul deed. To his surprise, Joseph Smith "calmly . . . unbutton[s] his shirt and bare[s] his chest" and says, "I'm ready now, Mr. Law."

At this point Charles nearly faints. His fear "strangle[s] him until he [is] speechless and paralyzed, unable to move a muscle."

William Law paces disturbingly, uttering words under his breath. Suddenly he "turn[s], aim[s], and presse[s] the trigger. There [is] complete silence." The one bullet reserved for the one man doesn't fire. Charles regains his hope and senses. At this point, the "air [rings] with profanity and Mr. Law turn[s] on Charles, accusing him of fixing the gun so it would not go off." Law then spews out a threat to the young boy that he is going to kill him.

Joseph Smith intervenes in the boy's behalf by suggesting that a "can be placed on the fence post for Mr. Law to take a practice shot." Charles immediately discovers a can and lays it on the closest post. Law once again paces. In his drunken state, he takes aim and fires.

"His 'one shot' streak[s] through the exact center of the bottom of that can." His "well-known . . . marksmanship" is proved again, but not on Joseph Smith.

Stunningly quiet, Law looks at the gun in confusion.

Joseph "buttons up his shirt" and gives "Charles a meaningful look" comforting the boy's heart and easing his mind that everything is going to be okay. Turning to Law, who is still in a state of bewilderment, Joseph says, "If you are finished with me now, Mr. Law, I have other things needing to be done. Good morning."

FRANCIS HIGBEE DOESN'T prepare his gun. Instead he prepares and submits at least two lawsuits against Joseph within five days of each other. He accuses him of slandering his name. Higbee says that months earlier Joseph Smith had called him a "thief, fornicator, whoremaster, murderer, adulterer, and perjurer, with a rotten stinking [venereal] disease." He files his suits in Carthage, the county seat. Higbee and others believe that constant lawsuits will derail Joseph Smith and preoccupy him, but they will also get him out of the jurisdiction of Nauvoo. Higbee's lawsuits fail. Once again, Joseph is spared by a habeas corpus and is "answerable before the Nauvoo municipal court."

Notwithstanding the constant effort to deflect annoyances and false accusations, Joseph Smith meets regularly with people "giving advice" to those "calling for counsel." A wealthy convert family from Pennsylvania has recently arrived. They stay in the Mansion House and have a few interchanges with the Prophet. Their twenty-two-year-old daughter Barbara Neff is collecting autographs of well-known Mormons. Joseph Smith writes a rhyming verse before signing his name in her book,

The truth and virtue both are good
When rightly understood
But Charity is better Miss
That takes us home to bliss
and so, forthwith, Remember Joseph Smith.

As the spring sprints for summer, more and more people gather close to Joseph Smith and the protection in Nauvoo. Many are gathering lasting memories of seeing, hearing, and knowing the Prophet personally. They visit, sing, listen to bands, dance, and ready themselves for an impromptu speech from Joseph Smith or other Church leaders. Joseph and Emma's home is on the corner of Main and Water Streets and near the south dock of the peninsula. Their home is perfectly situated for visitors and newcomers arriving in Nauvoo. It is the center of attention, and Emma and Joseph willingly extend hospitality at great costs.

On the late afternoon of May 5, Joseph has a "large company" around and in his home. He takes the opportunity to speak as a politician and addresses the "true policy of this people in [their] intercourse with the national government." The speech prepares the last few missionaries who are now ready to go east for his presidential campaign and for the gospel. Wilford Woodruff and George A. Smith, two prominent members of the Twelve Apostles, leave on May 9. Before leaving, they visit Joseph Smith. He blesses them "in the name of the Lord" and tells them "to go, and they should prosper and always prosper."

This is the last time Wilford Woodruff and George A. Smith will see their friend and prophet alive. He has just over six weeks to live.

Chapter 38

MAY 14–16, 1844

Nauvoo, Illinois

As THE DAYS roll on, more and more steamers are touching into the docks of Nauvoo. They are carrying not only new converts but also national figures who are curious to see the Mormons and catch a glimpse of, or perhaps an interview with, Joseph Smith.

The steamer *Amaranth* is familiar to the banks of Nauvoo. On the night of May 14, the steamer is carrying two conspicuous eastern politicians—Charles Francis Adams and Josiah Quincy Jr. Charles is the grandson of John Adams and the son of John Quincy Adams. Josiah Quincy, future mayor of Boston, persuades Charles to unload their baggage in Nauvoo to "see something of Joe Smith, the prophet." Charles is "passive" on this journey. He does take note of the "discouraging tales of the disposition of these Mormons" spoken of by some of the passengers.

It is after midnight when the steamer approaches the south dock of Nauvoo. A "certain Doctor Goforth, a living skeleton of a man . . . urged our landing." He wants Adams and Quincy to meet the figure gaining national attention. Goforth had "served under General Jackson at the battle of New Orleans" and is going to Nauvoo to promote the election of Henry Clay to the US presidency. John Quincy adds that Goforth, "not being a Mormon himself . . . told us much that was good and interesting about this strange people. He urged us to see for ourselves the result of the singular political system which had been fastened upon Christianity, and to make the acquaintance of his friend, General Smith, the religious and civil autocrat of the community."

Given the hour of arrival, Adams and Quincy find lodgings in an old mill on the bank of the river. "For at so late an hour we determined not to attempt to disturb the great prophet himself, although he was the keeper of the [Nauvoo Mansion]," Adams writes. Displacing a cat and a several cockroaches, they occupy a bed. They sleep a few hours until discomfort and daylight awaken them.

By morning, someone has notified Joseph Smith of the notable guests who had docked a few hours previous. He sends a carriage— "the prophet's own chariot, a comfortable carryall" as Quincy identifies it—down the street to pick up his visitors. It is a walkable distance, but May 15 is a rainy day. Mud is thick and troubling for their short approach to the Mansion House. As the carriage arrives in front of the two-story home of the Prophet, Adams and Quincy see a man standing in the door. Several other men line the path to the door. They are immediately "introduced to the celebrated Joe Smith." Adams describes him as "middle-aged man with a shrewd but rather ordinary expression of countenance, unshaved and in clothes neither very choice nor neat. The whole air of the man was that of frank but not coarse vulgarity."

Quincy later describes Joseph Smith with even greater detail: "Pre-eminent among the stragglers by the door stood a man of commanding appearance, clad in the costume of a journeyman carpenter when about his work. He was a hearty, athletic fellow, with blue eyes standing prominently out upon his light complexion, a long nose, and a retreating forehead. He wore striped pantaloons, a linen jacket, which had not lately seen the washtub, and a beard of some three days' growth. This was the founder of the religion which had been preached in every quarter of the earth." But nonetheless, Quincy gives Joseph the compliment, "A fine-looking man is what the passer-by would instinctively have murmured upon meeting the remarkable individual."

They are received civilly. The home serving as a hotel has many occupants. Joseph Smith tries to find a vacant room. One room is occupied by someone Joseph knows comfortably well; he approaches the sleeping man in a moment of some humor and "abruptly [slaps him] on the shoulder and [is] notified to quit." Adams feels Joseph's levity is strange. "The awkwardness of this scene was relieved by a call to breakfast, which we all obeyed. The table was amply provided as usual in the Western Country, but without order or delicacy."

Breakfast stirs those sleeping and frees some rooms. Joseph Smith is given a moment to change his clothes. He puts on a "broad-cloth suit." Adams and Quincy sit down and hold a long discussion with the Prophet on his doctrines and his projects in the city of Nauvoo and elsewhere. He declares to his eastern visitors, "The curses of my enemies run off from me like water from a duck's back." Joseph is resolute in his position and conduct. "The prophet refers to his miraculous gift of understanding all languages," Quincy relates. "[He] took down a Bible in various tongues, for the purpose of exhibiting his accomplishments in this particular."

After this initial interview, Joseph shows his visitors some Egyptian mummies and a manuscript he has acquired while living in Ohio. The manuscript is the writing of Abraham, they are told. "If anyone denies it, let him prove the contrary," Joseph tells his educated guests. Charles Adams is entertained at the Mormon prophet's approach. "The cool impudence of this imposture amused me very much," he recounts in his diary. As to proving contrary, he adds, "We were too polite to prove the negative, against a man fortified by revelation." Apparently he or Quincy, or both, feel they have some kind of educational training to "prove the contrary." But most of Joseph Smith's translations are "from the Hebrew, which, presumably, his visitors did not understand, rather than from the classical languages, in which they might more easily have caught him tripping."

Lucy Mack Smith, the Prophet's mother, listens and looks on attentively. She even joins in the explanation of the items and how they came to America and were purchased by the Church. She is earning her pay. The Prophet conveys to his visitors that "his mother was in the habit of receiving a quarter of a dollar a piece" for exhibiting the artifacts. The visitors pay her the sum.

After leaving Lucy's room and the artifacts, they engage in another long conversation about the Latter-day Saints sufferings in

Missouri. By this time, Hyrum and other men of the faith have joined the conversation. Charles Adams is taken aback by what he hears firsthand and what he has had heard in some newspaper reports. He leaves on record, "The severe and shocking persecution which they suffered at the time of their cruel expulsion from Missouri four years ago . . . is one of the most disgraceful chapters in the dark history of slavery in the United States, and shows that the spirit of intolerance, religious and political, can find a shelter even in the fairest professions of liberty." Adams knows the Missourians were not justified. He has disdain for the state for being pro-slavery and knows from other reports they are clever in many corruptions.

The long conversation occupies the whole morning. At one o'clock they dine. By this time, Josiah Quincy has personally observed, "The prophet's hold upon you seemed to come from the balance and harmony of temperament which reposes upon a large physical basis. No association with the sacred phrases of scripture could keep the inspirations of this man from getting down upon the hard pan of practical affairs."

Adams and Quincy want to see his practical affairs up close. They request they be taken up to the bluff where they can see the temple being built. Adams captures his thoughts of when the carriage reaches the bluff and the half completed temple is in full sight. "It is a massive edifice on a most commanding site. . . . The architecture is original—and curious. It is built by the contribution of one-tenth of labor and goods. The prophet seems to have drawn his ideas largely from the Jewish system."

Quincy stands on the bluff and takes in the beauty of the Mississippi River, which occupies three sides of the bluff. "The curve in the river enclosed a position lovely enough to furnish a site for the Utopian communities of Plato or Sir Thomas More," Quincy writes. "Here was an orderly city, magnificently laid out, and teeming with activity and enterprise. And all the diligent workers, who had reared these handsome stores and comfortable dwellings, bowed in subjection to the man to whose unexampled absurdities we had listened that morning." Quincy is in awe but not convinced with the man behind it all.

They pass through the active hammers and chisels on the temple construction site. As they return to the Mansion House down on the flats near the river, Adams is drawn away by a gentleman who is employed by the federal government and needs to discuss some business. He is absent awhile and Quincy acknowledges that he misses "one of the most notable exhibitions of the day."

"General Smith," said Dr. Goforth, when we had adjourned to the green in front of the [Nauvoo Mansion], "I think Mr. Quincy would like to hear you preach."

"Then I shall be happy to do so," was the obliging reply; and, mounting the broad step which led from the house, the prophet promptly addressed a sermon to the little group about him. Our numbers were constantly increased from the passers in the street, and a most attentive audience of more than a hundred persons soon hung upon every word of the speaker. The text was Mark 16:15 ["And he said unto them, go ye into all the world, and preach the gospel to every creature"], and the comments, though rambling and disconnected, were delivered with the fluency and fervor of a camp-meeting orator. The discourse was interrupted several times by the Methodist minister [traveling with Adams and Quincy], who thought it incumbent upon him to question the soundness of certain theological positions maintained by the speaker. One specimen of the sparring which ensued I thought worth setting down. The prophet is asserting that baptism for the remission of sins is essential for salvation.

Minister. Stop! What do you say to the case of the penitent thief?

Prophet. What do you mean by that?

Minister. You know our Savior said to the thief, "This day shalt thou be with me in Paradise," which shows he could not have been baptized before his admission.

Prophet. How do you know he wasn't baptized before he became a thief? At this retort the sort of laugh that is provoked by an unexpected hit ran through the audience; but this demonstration of sympathy was rebuked by a severe look from Smith, who went on to say: "But that is not the true answer. In the original Greek, as this gentleman (turning to me) will inform you, the word that has been translated paradise means simply a place of departed spirits. To that place the penitent thief was conveyed, and there, doubtless, he received the baptism necessary for his admission to the heavenly kingdom."

The other objections of his antagonist were parried with a similar adroitness, and in about fifteen minutes the prophet concluded a sermon which it was evident that his disciples had heard with the heartiest satisfaction.

In the afternoon the visitors and the Methodist preacher take another carriage ride with the Prophet, visiting some of the farms on the prairie. In a more private setting, Quincy records another episode between the Methodist minister and Joseph Smith.

"I suppose none but Mormon preachers are allowed in Nauvoo," said the Methodist minister, who had accompanied our expedition. "On the contrary," replied the prophet, "I shall be very happy to have you address my people next Sunday, and I will insure you a most attentive congregation." "What! do you mean that I may say anything I please and that you will make no reply?" "You may certainly say anything you please; but I must reserve the right of adding a word or two, if I judge best. I promise to speak of you in the most respectful manner." As we rode back, there was more dispute between the minister and Smith. "Come," said the latter, suddenly slapping his antagonist on the knee, to emphasize the production of a triumphant text, "if you can't argue better than that, you shall say all you want to say to my people, and I will promise to hold my tongue, for there's not a Mormon among them who would need my assistance to answer you." Some back-thrust was evidently required to pay for this; and the minister, soon after, having occasion to allude to some erroneous doctrine which I forget, suddenly exclaimed, "Why, I told my congregation the other Sunday that they might as well believe Joe Smith as such theology as that." "Did you say Joe Smith in a sermon?" inquired the person to whom the title had been applied. "Of course I did. Why not?" The prophet's reply was given with a quiet superiority that was overwhelming: "Considering only the day and the place, it would have been more respectful to have said Lieutenant-General Joseph Smith." Clearly, the worthy minister was no match for the head of the Mormon Church.

As they ride through the prairies turned into beautiful farms by many Mormons, the guests marvel at the industry that has transpired in so few years. Many of the Mormons are silently going about their business. Their business is not only in temporal matters but in spiritual matters as well. Such matters are aligned and driven entirely around the teachings and visions of Joseph Smith. After dinner Quincy records his own exchange with Smith:

I should not say quite all that struck me about Smith if I did not mention that he seemed to have a keen sense of the humorous aspects of his position. "It seems to me, General," I said, as he was driving us to the river, about sunset, "that you have too much power to be safely trusted to one man."

"In your hands or that of any other person," was the reply, "so much power would, no doubt, be dangerous. I am the only man in the world whom it would be safe to trust with it. Remember, I am a prophet!"

The last five words were spoken in a rich, comical aside, as if in hearty recognition of the ridiculous sound they might have in the ears of a Gentile. I asked him to test his powers by naming the successful candidate in the approaching presidential election. "Well, I will prophesy that John Tyler will not be the next president, for some things are possible and some things are probable; but Tyler's election is neither the one nor the other."

John Tyler will be defeated in the 1844 election, and it won't be by Henry Clay.

Joseph Smith shares his views of government and policy with Adams and Quincy before leaving them at sunset at the loading dock for another steamer. They have spent the whole day with the American prophet. Marveling in some regards, perplexed in others, the two men reflect on their sunrise to sunset experience. Charles Francis Adams writes in his diary:

> There is a mixture of shrewdness and extravagant self-conceit, of knowledge and ignorance, of wisdom and folly in this whole system of this man that I am somewhat at a loss to find definitions for it. Yet it is undoubted that he has gained followers at home and abroad— and boasts of having twenty-five thousand at Nauvoo and two hundred thousand in the Union. This is an extravagant estimate, but the number must be large. His theological system is very nearly Christian Unitarianism—with the addition of the power of baptism by the priests of adults to remit sin, and of the new hierarchy of which Smith is the chief by divine appointment. . . . On the whole I was glad I had been [to see Joseph Smith]. Such a man is a study not for himself, but as serving to show what turns the human mind will sometimes take. And hereafter if I should live, I may compare the results of this delusion with the condition in which I saw it and its mountebank apostle.

John Quincy summarizes his May 15, 1844, experience with Joseph Smith in more prophetic tones.

> It is by no means improbable that some future textbook, for the use of generations yet unborn, will contain a question something like this: What historical American of the nineteenth century has exerted the most powerful influence upon the destinies of his countrymen? And it is by no means impossible that the answer to that interrogatory may be thus written: Joseph Smith, the Mormon prophet. And the reply, absurd as it doubtless seems to most men now living, may be an obvious commonplace to their descendants. History deals in surprises and paradoxes quite as startling as this. . . . I have endeavored to give the details of my visit to the Mormon prophet with absolute accuracy. If the reader does not know just what to make of Joseph Smith, I cannot help him out of the difficulty. I myself stand helpless before the puzzle.

Joseph Smith is so much to so many, yet so little to others. There are many pieces in the puzzle. However, his call for Latter-day Saints to gather in and around Nauvoo is being heeded by thousands. And those coming as converts see it as a call to gather under the banner of the gospel of Jesus Christ, not the banner of Joseph Smith. Modern-day prophets just happen to be one facet of the gospel Joseph Smith and his followers embrace. Something much deeper moves these people. Something much deeper is preparing them for their eventual movement west.

Adams and Quincy are not in Nauvoo long enough to sense the persecution Joseph Smith is currently facing. As soon as they leave, he will be back to answering the lawsuits, affidavits, and threats against him. As Adams and Quincy's steamer leaves Nauvoo at night, another steamer is approaching from St. Louis. As Nauvoo comes into sight, the passengers abroad begin talking presidential politics. Someone suggest a poll be taken.

"General Joseph Smith, 26 gentlemen, 3 ladies."

"Henry Clay, 6 gentlemen, 2 ladies."

"Van Buren, 2 gentlemen, 0 ladies."

The steamer is in Joseph Smith's territory.

HE APOSTLES NOW on their various missions throughout the US are organizing Church conferences and political conventions. In Nauvoo on May 17, the Illinois state convention is in session in the newly completed assembly hall, also known as the cultural (or social) hall. Joseph Smith accepts his nomination for president of the United States, as does Sidney Rigdon for the office of vice president. The delegates for Joseph begin to organize a national convention to be held in Baltimore in two months' time.

After his nomination, he returns home to comfort Emma, who has taken ill. Later in the evening, Joseph hears some raucous in the street near his home. As he looks out the window, he sees a "large assemblage burn[ing] a barrel of tar in the street." He immediately leaves the home to see the reason for the gathering. They are giving toasts, and as soon as they become aware of his presence, they throw him on their shoulders and parade him around the fire twice. After the display, they escort him back to his home by a band of music.

Their enthusiasm and efforts are perfect timing on the political calendar, but not for their friend's life. He'll never take a breath in July.

The following day, Joseph Smith brushes aside the political excitement and returns to Church business. Francis M. Higbee officially joins the Laws and the Fosters; he is excommunicated by a standing high council of the Church. Three other men of their same demeanor are also cut off from Church membership.

On May 19, a heavy rain and the resulting annoying mud keep Joseph Smith's enemies neutralized. This allows him to spend time with Emma, who is still very sick. The Mississippi River is rising about "8 inches per day." The cresting Mississippi doesn't stop the steamers. Over sixty more Latter-day Saints arrive on May 21 "all in good health and spirits." When a break in the weather comes, Joseph Smith can attend to his own domestic matters. He takes the early evening hours on May 21 to "shovel dirt out of ditch," probably caused by the heavy rain. He puts the shovel down in time to go visit a family who has a severely ill child. While he is gone, another visitor comes to his home "having a summons and an attachment to take [him] to Carthage." Joseph is able to elude another officer seeking to arrest him for some trumped up charges.

The following day, more officers from Carthage are hounding him. He quietly sits in his home "watching" and taking from his bodyguard on the perimeter reports and rumors on the officers' movements in the streets of Nauvoo. Midmorning, a large group of Sac and Fox Indians come to the front yard of his home. Prominent is Black Hawk's brother "Kiss-kish-kee." Black Hawk visited Joseph Smith a few years earlier. But given the lawless individuals prowling around, Joseph has his bodyguard kindly turn them away. Someone conveys to the Indians the difficulty the American prophet is in. The Indians stay in Nauvoo the rest of the day and camp overnight.

The next morning, May 23, they call upon the Prophet again. This time they are admitted into the kitchen in the back of the Mansion House. Kiss-kish-kee speaks and lays before the Prophet the cruelty and robbery of lands his people have suffered at the hands of the whites. Joseph doesn't dismiss their mistreatment. They are a driven and persecuted people. However, the Saints in large numbers are kind and giving to the Indians. The day of relief for the Indians and the Mormons is still a long time coming. Joseph Smith changes the "conversation to peace in the land and the Book of Mormon." These two topics are primary points he consistently brings up with the Indians. He urges the Indians to spread the message of the Book of Mormon, urging them to spread its witness of the reality of Jesus Christ and His gospel of peace.

And then, perhaps to set the stage for Brigham Young and the Latter-day Saints trekking across Iowa, he says to the Indian visitors and their leaders, "When any of our people come to see you I want you to treat them as we treat you." After spending some time with Joseph, the Indians leave his home, cross the street, and stop. They perform "a war dance for about two hours." Citizens of Nauvoo enjoy the entertainment and keep the festivities moving by "striking up the Nauvoo band." Late in the afternoon "a cannon is fired" to end the festivities. It also gets the attention of those not gathered. Before the Indians leave, a request is sent out to the people to collect food for them. Many respond and the Indians depart Nauvoo in gratitude.

This is the last known meeting of the Indians and Joseph Smith. With the Indians happily on their way, Joseph records, "Very pleasant day"—a day in which he keeps his distance from officers trying to illegally arrest him and a day when he enjoys the company of his Indian friends. It is also a pleasant day because Emma's health is improving.

Even so, frustration returns the next morning. He is charged with adultery by William Law. Law's spirit is drowning in hypocrisy. He admitted earlier to Hyrum Smith that he himself was an adulterer.

Joseph Smith's public discourses begin to reveal more and more that his tolerance for his enemies is fading. As May 23 comes to a close, Joseph is walking with his clerk, Apostle Willard Richards, after dark for some exercise. Hyrum joins them near his home. Hyrum sees wisdom in giving his brother some counsel. He cautions his brother not to speak so freely about his enemies and to not use language that provokes them to harder words and actions. Joseph looks at Hyrum and bluntly states that "six months would not roll over [your] head before [enemies] would swear twelve palpable lies about [you] as they had about me."

Notwithstanding the tension growing and the frustration in Joseph Smith's tone and response to Hyrum, the brothers stand ever united. Hyrum will go where Joseph goes and is willing to suffer what he suffers. The lies against Hyrum begin to multiply day by day. Within a month he will further understand his brother's predicament. Nonetheless, Joseph acknowledges Hyrum's counsel is founded in wisdom.

Chapter 40
MAY 24–31, 1844
Nauvoo, Illinois, and Carthage, Illinois

WITH MY FAMILY all day," Joseph inserts into his history for May 24. He spends only an hour out of the home counseling with trusted friends. He orders a city council meeting on the morrow. Election matters and missionary updates need to be discussed.

Willard Richards and W. W. Phelps earlier in the day arranged a letter with others to be sent to a Hugh Clark of the central campaign committee in regards to the presidential matters. Using Declaration of Independence language, they convey that Joseph Smith is "a man with whom we are thoroughly acquainted, and have no fear in pledging our lives, our fortunes and our sacred honor, that, if elected, he will give and secure these inestimable blessings to every individual and society of men, no matter what their religious faith."

Letters from the missionaries preaching and campaigning are arriving constantly. Eleven elders report the results of a conference in Chicago at which "a very favorable impression was made upon the minds of the people" concerning Joseph Smith.

But Joseph Smith's enemies have him pinned. He cannot move freely about because of the constant writs of arrest. On May 25, he once again has to hunker down because of expected writs on their way from Carthage. Joseph Jackson, who was denied marriage to Hyrum Smith's daughter, is in Carthage with Robert Foster, charging Joseph Smith "for adultery with Maria Lawrence and other diverse women." The two men submit the charge not for themselves but for William Law, who said that Joseph Smith "had told him so." Joseph Jackson after making his charge returns to Nauvoo. When Joseph hears through his network that Jackson is in town, he sends the police to arrest him. Jackson has for some time been threatening the Prophet's life and the life of his brother Hyrum.

By the afternoon, Joseph is counseling with several other loyal men. They trust in the Nauvoo Charter's power. They decide "not to keep out of the way of the officers any longer." Joseph is also tiring of being homebound to escape the injustice thrust upon him. He and his followers declare in a correspondence, "Truth will prevail."

As Nauvoo police are trying to track down Jackson, Sidney Rigdon officially resigns from the lucrative position of postmaster. He recommends Joseph Smith as his successor. Rigdon isn't running from Mormonism per se, but he does sense the tension and the building mobocracy that is once again threatening Mormon life and property. He is hanging onto Joseph Smith's coat tails, most likely for political reasons. He has exceptional skills in public speaking and the campaign stage before him will satisfy his political and religious ambitions.

Rigdon is preparing his family and his property for a move to Pittsburg, Pennsylvania. There he can "establish Pennsylvania residency to make him eligible for the vice-presidency." But his relocation also removes him from the persecution soon to press down upon Nauvoo. He wants nothing to with this round of persecution and vengeance coming by Joseph's enemies. Five months prior to relocating, Joseph Smith tried to remove Rigdon as his counselor, but the body of the Church wouldn't allow it. Their relationship since has been neutral and cordial. Rigdon defends the Prophet throughout 1844, even though he opposes plural marriage. When Rigdon goes back east, Joseph seems perfectly content and relieved with his friend's decision to leave.

On Sunday May 26, Joseph takes the stand and begins his discourse by reading 2 Corinthians chapter 11, wherein the ancient Apostle Paul glories in his sufferings for Christ. Going against Hyrum's counsel about "speaking so freely," Joseph Smith says, "I should be like a fish out of water, if I were out of persecutions. Perhaps my brethren think it requires all this to keep me humble. The Lord has constituted me so curiously that I glory in persecution. . . . If they want a beardless boy to whip all the world, I will get on the top of a mountain and crow like a rooster; I shall always beat them."

And that was just the beginning of his rhetoric. He follows Paul's direction of "I may boast myself a little":

> In all these affidavits, indictments, it is all of the devil—all corruption. Come on! ye prosecutors! ye false swearers! All hell, boil over! Ye burning mountains, roll down your lava! for I will come out on the top at last. I have more to boast of than ever any man had. I am the only man that has ever been able to keep a whole church together since the days of Adam. A large majority of the whole have stood by me. Neither Paul, John, Peter, nor Jesus ever did it. I boast that no man ever did such a work as I. The followers of Jesus ran away from Him; but the Latter-day Saints never ran away from me yet. You know my daily walk and conversation. I am in the bosom of a virtuous and good people. How I do love to hear the wolves howl! When they can get rid of me, the devil will also go. For the last three years I have a record of all my acts and proceedings, for I have kept several good, faithful, and efficient clerks in constant employ: they have accompanied me everywhere, and carefully kept my history, and they have written down what I have done, where I have been, and what I have said; therefore my enemies cannot charge me with any day, time, or place, but what I have written testimony to prove my actions; and my enemies cannot prove anything against me.

"Nor Jesus" irks some in attendance. Joseph alludes to John 6, when the Savior taught the bread of life sermon and "from that time many of his disciples went back, and walked no more with him." His words, "I boast that no man ever did such a work as I," are reference to mortal man and his role in following the commands of Jesus Christ in establishing the kingdom of God in the last days.

It is this kind of language Hyrum tried to tame a few days earlier. The discourse is given when legal harassments are high (forty to fifty lawsuits at this time is not an exaggeration), as well as several attempted arrests. "This is an ideal forum to send a strong message, even filled with hyperbole, to those who persecuted him."

Though Joseph is accused of putting himself above the Savior, his enemies fail to recall his teachings and his recorded revelations: "Who, among all the Saints in these last days, can consider himself as good as our Lord? Who is as perfect? Who is as pure? Who is as holy as He was? Are they to be found? He never transgressed or broke a commandment or law of heaven—no deceit was in His mouth, neither was guile found in His heart. . . . Where is one like Christ? He cannot be found on earth."

On another occasion he asks, "Where is the man that is free from vanity? None ever were perfect but Jesus; and why was He perfect? Because He was the Son of God, and had the fullness of the Spirit, and greater power than any man. When we reflect upon the holiness and perfections of our great Master, our hearts melt within us for his condescension." Joseph Smith argues that the work he is doing is the work of Jehovah and he has been fulfilling it and keeping people, the Church, together.

The next day, Joseph and several loyal men, at least twenty, go on horseback to Carthage, Illinois. "[I] felt it best to meet my enemies before the Circuit Court, and have the indictments against me investigated," he states. One of the brothers in the ring of the conspiracy finds a soft spot in his heart. Charles Foster meets Joseph and his entourage about three or four miles out of town. Foster is "more mild than previously, and as though he is almost persuaded that he had been influenced to some extent by false reports."

Samuel Smith, a younger brother to Joseph and Hyrum, hears that his brothers have been taken to Carthage by a mob. He raises a group of twenty-five men by midmorning. In good timing, his arrangement arrives about the same time his brothers arrive in Carthage. Well over fifty men are now in tow. A reputable bodyguard.

They arrive at the Hamilton Hotel in Carthage near noon. The Higbee brothers and Joseph Jackson are in the hotel. They have no soft spots in their hearts. They want to kill Joseph before he makes an attempt to return to Nauvoo. Charles Foster tells Joseph in a private conversation after arriving at the hotel that there is mischief going on against his life. While Charles is talking to Joseph Smith one on one, Robert Foster is also experiencing a temporary softening of the heart. He is conversing with the loyal men protecting Joseph.

He knows many if not all of them. He has shared many spiritually refreshing moments with them in days past. He too conveys "with tears in his eyes that there [is] evil determined against" the Prophet "and that there [are] some persons who [are] determined" to kill him in Carthage this day.

Joseph Smith is able to get a short interview with Judge Thomas. His decision to come to Carthage and clear his name of the trumped-up charges is paying off. Thomas treats him with great respect. Joseph notes Thomas's kindness and nobility in the situation. Three attorneys busily try to advance Joseph's trial for perjury and adultery within the hour. But the prosecutors have no evidence and not one material witness, which is troubling to the judge because they had previously stated they had plenty. Whomever they had as witnesses have fled.

Judge Thomas defers the trial. Once again Joseph Smith is granted freedom. The sheriff also extends kindness by saying he will collect bail another time at his convenience. Joseph and his posse immediately call for their horses. Chauncey Higbee tries to lure Joseph Smith into staying so Joseph Jackson can find the moment to pull the trigger. Joseph Smith denies Higbee's request. As they are riding out of Carthage, they pass the courthouse. Jackson and a handful of others spew out insulting language.

Granted another extension on his life, he returns safely to Nauvoo and spends the last few days of May at home with family and friends.

OSEPH SMITH AWAKENS on Saturday, June 1, to the sound of "gentle showers." This is the last month of his mortal life. "By some of [the conspirators] it [is] declared that there should not be one of the Smith family alive in a few weeks." Emma and her children are not deaf to the threats. Neither are Hyrum and his family.

William Law is trying to find any "sisters" of the gospel who will speak ill of the Prophet Joseph Smith's conduct by swearing an affidavit. He needs some smear because he and his followers have their press nearly ready to go. At this time, they are beginning to set the type on their first publication. Joseph Fielding, a member of Joseph Smith's Council of Fifty, writes in his diary that "the subject of the apostasy of William Law and others has caused some little excitement. They lately purchased a press, etc. and printed the first numbers of the *Nauvoo Expositor*." The press is designed to publish all they can find against Joseph and others loyal to him so they might upset the Church and take over leadership.

On June 3, Joseph receives a letter from a man in Burlington, Iowa. He informs the Prophet that "five to six hundred armed men" are preparing to fall upon Nauvoo to liberate a man who is in a Nauvoo jail. The man writing the letter writes under a pen name,

"Horace." He is a "friend to [Smith's] society," he states. He urges the Mormon prophet not to think his correspondence "humbug," but rather to "prepare yourselves for the coming storm."

Joseph Smith doesn't fret over the threat. As if he is entirely free of every worry, he finishes the day reading German with Alexander Neibaur. He has been reading and studying a German Bible for months. "I have an old edition of the New Testament in the Latin, Hebrew, German and Greek languages," he told the congregation at his King Follet discourse. "I have been reading the German, and find it to be the most [nearly] correct translation, and to correspond nearest to the revelations which God has given to me for the last fourteen years."

Still not fretting over "Horace's" letter concerning the large number of men threatening a move on Nauvoo, Joseph arises on June 4 and reaches out to an individual by the name of Mr. Tewksbury. The man lives in Boston, Massachusetts, and has been cut off from the Church. Joseph and Hyrum, for some unknown reason, personally write him a letter encouraging him to rejoin the fold. "We take pleasure in feeling after you; and therefore would, in the sincerity of men of God, advise you to be rebaptized . . . that you may again receive the sweet influences of the Holy Ghost, and enjoy the fellowship of the Saints." They conclude the short letter with straightforwardness. "The law of God requires it, and you cannot be too good. Patience is heavenly, obedience is noble, forgiveness is merciful, and exaltation is godly; and he that holds out faithful to the end shall in no wise lose his reward. A good man will endure all things to honor Christ, and even dispose of the whole world, and all in it, to save his soul."

Lightning storms, thunder, and heavy rain pound Nauvoo on June 5. But there is still no storm of men from Burlington, Iowa, as "Horace" indicated. Joseph doesn't seem the least bit rattled. He moves freely through the streets of Nauvoo and on the open prairies for two days. He even entertains several strangers in the barroom of the Mansion House—a barroom that was temporary since Emma insisted that it be removed. Part of his entertaining on this day includes reading his letter written to Henry Clay to the strangers. One stranger openly sustains Clay for presidency. Joseph challenges him for some time to "show the subject in its true light, and that no man could honestly vote for a man like Clay, who had violated his oath, and not acted on constitutional principles"

The stranger remains the lone supporter of Clay.

The following two days, Joseph Smith loses the battle of words. The first edition of the *Nauvoo Expositor* goes on sale. Robert Foster has carefully considered the words he and his cohorts publish against his former friend and prophet. He once again wobbles in his intentions. On the eve of the Expositor's release to the public, he attempts to visit Joseph Smith. Foster is hoping to return to fellowship. But he has one condition: he wants to be reinstated in his office in the Nauvoo Legion. Dimick Huntington is a trusted man and does not let Foster through the screen of bodyguards. Joseph relates to Huntington "that if Foster would return, withdraw all the suits he had commenced, and do right, he should be restored." Foster tries to play an important card with Joseph on this eve of slander and potent rhetoric. He has conveyed to Joseph that he "had all the affidavits of the anti-Mormons under his control."

Joseph Smith dismisses the claim as a weak boast. Foster has a restless night.

First thing in the morning, he approaches the Mansion House seeking a private interview with Joseph Smith. Initially it is unclear if his motives of reconciliation are genuine or mere façade in order to carry out murderous intentions. Foster's persistence to see Joseph is paying off. In a preliminary interview in the hall of the Mansion House, and with "several gentlemen" in the hall as witnesses, Joseph tells Foster that he would meet with him in the presence of up to four equal friends. Foster leaves dissatisfied and begins telling people of both Mormon and anti-Mormon leanings that Joseph "would receive him back on any terms, and give him a hatful of dollars into the bargain." His rambling nonsense is a common trait of Foster. By evening Foster sends Joseph Smith "an extremely saucy and insulting letter." Whatever Foster's motives are, it is becoming clear to many that he is emotionally and mentally operating under a disturbed spirit. His teeter-tottering reveals his personal conflict for what he had sworn in dark secrecy.

Foster has reached the point of no return. The anti-Joseph Smith deed of the day has already been done, and Foster's name and support are all over it. On June 7, Joseph Smith's most bitter dissenters—William Law, Wilson Law, Charles Ivins, Francis M. Higbee, Chauncey L. Higbee, Robert D, Foster, Charles A. Foster, and Sylvester Emmons as editor—are able to produce an editorial attacking his character.

Peculiarly, however, they begin the editorial sustaining the Latter-day Saint movement established by Joseph Smith.

> We all verily believe, and many of us know of a surety, that the religion of the Latter Day Saints, as originally taught by Joseph Smith, which is contained in the Old and New Testaments, Book of Covenants, and Book of Mormon, is verily true; and that the pure principles set forth in those books, are the immutable and eternal principles of Heaven, and speaks a language which, when spoken in truth and virtue, sinks deep into the heart of every honest man. Its precepts are invigorating, and in every sense of the word, tend to dignify and ennoble man's conceptions of God and His attributes.

But these are the only pleasantries afforded Joseph Smith. The editorial turns on him and argues his fall from prophetic authority. They attack him and his loyal followers for ill treatment of women. They charge him "with bringing innocent females to Nauvoo under the pretext of religion to add to his harem." In a tone that begs for compassion, the dissenters write, "Our hearts have mourned and bled at the wretched and miserable condition of females in [Nauvoo]." Yet, they can only find a handful of women willing to say it is so. So many other women testify to the contrary.

Not only do they attack Joseph Smith on the plurality of wives doctrine, they attack his teachings on the plurality of Gods. They also try to present him as a dictator and tyrant who is wielding too much political and economic power over the people. "Joseph and his accomplices [are] specimens of injustice of the most pernicious and diabolical character that ever stained the pages of the historian," they write.

They add fifteen resolves as they slander him in this editorial. They cross themselves on one of their own resolves. "Resolved 11th, That we consider all secret societies, and combinations under penal oaths and obligations, (professing to be organized for religious purposes) to be anti-Christians, hypocritical and corrupt." Apparently the apostates didn't remember their secret oath-bound meeting to destroy the Smiths in late February and their organizational meeting setting up their reformed church in April for the sole purpose to destroy the Smiths and take over leadership.

Behind the glaring hypocrisy, the men try to come across priestly in the editorial. "We have called upon [Joseph Smith] to repent, and as soon as he shewed fruits meet for repentance, we stood ready to seize him by the hand of fellowship, and throw around him the mantle of protection; for it is the salvation of souls we desire, and not our own aggrandizement." They feel justified in killing Joseph Smith as a favor to God and the whole world.

Joseph can only silently reflect on the Savior's teachings to earlier Apostles who were also on the precipice of being assassinated. "Whosoever killeth you will think that he doeth God a service. And these things will they do unto you, because they have not known the Father, nor me."

On June 8, Joseph and the city council meet for five and half hours in two non-consecutive meetings. They take into consideration the editorial published by the *Nauvoo Expositor*. No unruly action is taken against the Expositor at present. Their deliberations are interrupted by a group arriving from Burlington, Iowa. Joseph Smith graciously meets the passengers at the dock. Aboard is a "pleasant party"—no mob, no angry storm of men.

The next day he greets several other passengers, this time on a ferry arriving from St. Louis. They too are friendly folks and seem cheery and excited to see the Mormon prophet in person. The man they have come to see or put their religious convictions behind helps carry trunks to the Mansion House.

The summer night of June 9 is bearable. A crowd gathers and a large meeting takes place around the Mansion House. Joseph and Hyrum both preach from a stand just across the street to the south. But Joseph is fatigued. He yields the meeting to Hyrum. Hyrum carries the meeting and will help carry his brother the next two and half weeks. Joseph closes the night by having inserted into his history, "My health not very good, in consequence of my lungs being impaired by so much public speaking."

CITY COUNCIL MEETING is called to order first thing in the morning. This will be a long Monday, and by nightfall, Joseph Smith will have given his enemies more fodder for their madness. For seven and half hours the city council and the mayor discuss the "merits of the *Nauvoo Expositor*, and also the conduct of the Laws, Higbees, Fosters, and others, who have formed a conspiracy for the purpose of destroying [Joseph's] life, and scattering the Saints or driving them from the state."

With the deliberations that took place on June 8, the men have sat in council now for thirteen hours. The decision before them is whether or not to allow the slandering press from their enemies to go forward. A city councilor by the name of Warrington is a non-Mormon. He too is disgusted at what the agitators are doing. However, he urges "that rather than destroy the press the city fathers should impose a fine of $3,000 for every libel published." Financially break them.

But this would require collection or payment on their behalf—an unlikely option. Warrington argues that if this doesn't "curb its slanders, then it could be declared a public nuisance." Joseph Smith rejects Warrington's proposal, "saying that Mormons would have to journey to the county seat at Carthage to prosecute these cases and that their lives would be in danger" in doing so.

Joseph wants to stay out of Carthage. He is quite aware that his most bitter enemies are often gathering there in secret meetings and under the pretense of the law to arrest him.

The *Nauvoo Expositor* "stinks in the nose of every honest man," John Taylor, an Apostle and a city councilman, declares. By 6:30 p.m. the city council passes an ordinance concerning libels.

> Whereas the Saints in all ages of the world have suffered persecution and death by wicked and corrupt men under the garb of a mere holy appearance of religion; and whereas the Church of Jesus Christ of Latter day Saints, from the moment that its first truth sprang out of the earth till now, has been persecuted with death, destruction, and extermination; and, whereas men to fulfill the Scriptures that a man's enemies are they of his own household, have turned traitors in the Church, and combined and leagued with the most corrupt scoundrels and villains that disgrace the earth unhung, for the Heaven-daring and damnable purpose of revenge on account of disappointed lust, disappointed projects of speculation, fraud, and unlawful designs to rob and plunder mankind with impunity; and, whereas such wicked and corrupt men have greatly facilitated their unlawful designs, horrid intentions, and murderous plans by polluting, degrading and converting the blessings and utility of the press to the sin-smoking and blood-stained ruin of innocent communities—by publishing lies, false statements, coloring the truth, slandering men, women, children, societies, and countries—by polishing the characters of blacklegs, highwaymen, and murderers as virtuous; and whereas a horrid, bloody, secret plan, upheld, sanctioned and largely patronized by men in Nauvoo and out of it, who boast that all they want for the word go, to exterminate or ruin the Latter day Saints, is for them to do one unlawful act, and the work shall be done, is now fostered, cherished, and maturing in Nauvoo,—by men, too, who helped to obtain the very charter they would break, and some of them drew up and voted for the very ordinances they are striving to use as a scarecrow to frighten the surrounding country in rebellion, mobbing, and war; and whereas, while the blood of our brethren from wells, holes and naked prairies, and the ravishment of female virtue from Missouri, and the smoke from the altars of infamy, prostituted by John C. Bennett, and continued in the full tide of experiment and disgraceful damnation by the very self-called fragments of

a body of degraded men that have got up a press in Nauvoo to destroy the charter of the city—to destroy Mormonism, men, women, and children as Missouri did; by force of arms—by fostering laws that emanate from corruption and betray with a kiss; wherefore to honor the State of Illinois, and those patriots who gave the charter, and for the benefit, convenience, health, and happiness of said city.

Be it ordained by the City Council of Nauvoo that if any person or persons shall write or publish in said city any false statement or libel of any of the citizens, for the purpose of exciting the public mind against the chartered privileges, peace, and good order of said city, or shall slander (according to the definition of slander or libel by Blackstone or Kent, or the act in the statute of Illinois,) any portion of the inhabitants of said city, or bribe any portion of the citizens of said city for malicious purposes, or in any manner or form excite the prejudice of the community against any portion of the citizens of said city, for evil purposes, he, she, or they shall be deemed disturbers of the peace; and, upon conviction before the Mayor or Municipal Court, shall be fined in any sum not exceeding five hundred dollars, or imprisoned six months, or both, at the discretion of said Mayor or court.

The ordinance is now in place for future violations. But the *Nauvoo Expositor* will not get a second chance to redeem itself. The council passes another ordinance declaring the *Nauvoo Expositor* "a nuisance, and also issued an order to [Smith] to abate the said nuisance." Joseph Smith answers the ordinance to stop the slandering press by "immediately order[ing] the Marshal to destroy it without delay."

The marshal and his posse ascend the bluff and pass the rising temple as they make their way to the building where the *Nauvoo Expositor* has set up shop. Chauncey Higbee and Charles Foster are at the premise. "Higbee's blackguard language [is not] answered" by the marshal or his posse. The order from the city council is carried out quickly and with no notable resistance. "G— d— him," Higbee's rant continues, "I will shoot [Joseph Smith] and all that pertains to him; and before ten suns shall go over our heads, the Temple, Nauvoo House and Mansion shall all be destroyed, and it will be the total downfall of this community." Sometime before 8 p.m. and before the summer sunlight has faded, the press, other components, and paper are removed to the street and destroyed.

The marshal returns to the flats near the river and comes before Joseph Smith at the front of the Mansion House. The marshal now has in tow hundreds of citizens. Joseph stands and delivers a short message that they had "done right and that not a hair of their heads should be hurt for it."

He excludes himself from the prophecy.

He also emphatically states that he "would never submit to have another libelous publication established in the city." The speech is well received as the crowd, constantly increasing, gives three hearty cheers.

Not all Mormons are in agreement with the decision to destroy the press. George Laub notes that some of the "brethren" in alignment with Joseph Smith "murmured." This wasn't the action they felt should have been taken. In the open air meeting by his home, Joseph tells those who thought the action was wrong that "God showed him in an open vision in daylight that if he did not destroy that press . . . it would cause the Blood of the Saints to flow in the Streets."

Many of those disturbed by the action go home satisfied—some do not. They know the action is going to bring their enemies' wrath in untold ways.

Francis Higbee and a few other disenchanted followers make some bold threats of their own. Higbee even takes a stab at prophesying by making it known that "there will not be a Mormon left in Nauvoo" within ten days if the press is destroyed. The prophecy falls flat. But he and the others can do nothing at this time, being severely outnumbered by those standing with Joseph Smith. But Joseph knows that the hair on his head can be hurt for the action taken this day. Nonetheless, he and the council feel justified and do not hide the deed in anyway.

THIS IS NOT a singular event in America at the time. Presses have been stopped or destroyed in other communities. The Mormons had one of their printing presses destroyed by a mob in Independence,

Jackson County, in July of 1833. The mob also tarred and feathered two of the Church leaders on the same day, threatening annihilation if the Mormons were not gone from Missouri within a few months.

Another incident where a press was destroyed was down the Mississippi River in Alton, Illinois. A minister and abolitionist by the name of Elijah Lovejoy had four presses destroyed by Missourians and Illinoisans in favor of slavery. In 1837, the fourth time they came for his press, they not only threw the press in the river, but they killed him. No one was ever brought to justice. This occurrence was known to the Latter-day Saints.

In their deliberations of thirteen hours, Joseph hears witness after witness testify of the illegal behaviors of the Laws, Higbees, Fosters, and Joseph Jackson that have gone on without accounting, such as bogus money making and seducing women. In the end of all deliberations, Joseph asks one question concerning the first print and ultimate objective of the Expositor. "Is it not treasonable against all chartered rights and privileges, and against the peace and happiness of the city?"

Robert Foster and William Law return from Carthage later in the evening and find their families in a distraught situation. While destroying the press and the other items, the marshal and his men also destroyed Foster's private papers. When Foster finds out what has been done, he laments, "exclaiming that he is ruined."

The Fosters and the Laws feel some threat against their families and flee Nauvoo within two days. But they are content in knowing they now have Joseph Smith on the ropes with an action that is sure to win some to their side and bring about the Prophet's destruction. Joseph isn't ignorant to what is forthcoming. "[I] would rather die tomorrow and have the [press] smashed, than live and have it go on, for it was exciting the spirit of mobocracy among the people, and bringing death and destruction upon us."

He is willing to die, but it won't be on the morrow. He has seventeen days.

Chapter 43

JUNE 11–15, 1844

Nauvoo, Illinois

OSEPH SMITH BEGINS June 11 in council with several men at his home. By midmorning he issues a proclamation to the citizens of Nauvoo. He calls upon the officers and citizens of the city to "use all honorable and lawful means in their power to assist [him] in maintaining the public peace and common quiet." He warns in the proclamation his enemies' attempts to incite riot and of their rising "suspicion, wrath, and indignation." To counter the mob spirit swelling around them, he counsels the Saints to repel the gathering mobs by "being cool, considerate, virtuous, unoffending, manly, and patriotic, as the true sons of liberty ever have been, and honorably maintain the precious boon our illustrious fathers won."

Before noon Joseph will have to exemplify his own counsel. A captain of one of the steamers that frequents Nauvoo calls upon him. Their conversation is unknown, but Joseph rides with the captain back to his steamer. Passengers of the steamer are readying themselves for departure. When Joseph and the captain arrive at the dock, Charles Foster calls "the passengers to see the meanest man in the world." Joseph Smith holds his tongue. A Mr. Eaton in a cheerful tone defends Joseph by declaring to all present that Foster is the meanest man in the world. One of Foster's cronies pulls a pistol. Mr.

Eaton in some unique, cheerful way calms him down, and the situation dissolves.

By 2 p.m. on June 11, Joseph Smith is speaking before a large congregation. His tone is a bit stronger than the proclamation sent out earlier in the day. He speaks as one tired of being repressed. "I [am] ready to fight, if the mob compel[s] me to, for I [will] not be in bondage." Testing the spirit of the crowd before him, Joseph asks if they would stand by him. Indisputably the crowd affirms his question with a hearty "yes." He goes home comforted and sustained.

His enemies living in Nauvoo feel threatened. They are trying to dispose of their property and hastily gather their belongings. The Expositor's destruction the day before has them on edge, but "runners have gone out in all direction to try to get up a mob." They may be leaving Nauvoo, but they will regroup in Warsaw and Carthage, two places identified for rallying those against the Joseph Smith. Hyrum is arguably wanted by the murderers just as much as Joseph Smith.

David Bettisworth, a Hancock County constable, arrives in Nauvoo on the morning of June 12. He spends the morning trying to find Joseph Smith's whereabouts. Early in the afternoon, he finds him in his private office on the second level of the Red Brick Store. Bettisworth is anxious because he is the first to read the writ of arrest sent out by an Illinois justice of the peace, Thomas Morrison, a day before. The writ begins with, "The People of the State of Illinois to all Constables, Sheriffs and Coroners of the State, Greeting." Bettisworth gloats as he reads the writ. The command is to bring Joseph Smith and the sixteen other men before Morrison "or some other justice of the peace" for destroying the press. Morrison's words are actually pleasing to Joseph. There are plenty of justices of the peace in Nauvoo. The language of the writ, the Nauvoo Charter, and his loyal friends once again favor Joseph Smith obtaining habeas corpus.

Bettisworth is indignant. He rolls into a rant and severe abuse of Joseph because of his legal blockade. In accordance with the writ, Joseph is before a Nauvoo judge before supper. He is "honorably discharged from the accusations and of the writ."

The next day, Joseph Smith makes sure the other sixteen men are "discharged" in the "Nauvoo Expositor matter." The freed men meet in the evening and converse about their current situation, but, more important, they discuss the gospel and the charge to go take it to all the earth. After a Mormon elder preaches a sermon, Joseph stands to make some observations and give some gospel counsel. He also relates a recent dream he had a few mornings back:

> I thought I was riding out in my carriage, and [a heavenly guide] was along with me. We went past the Temple, and had not gone much further before we espied two large snakes so fast locked together that neither of them had any power. I inquired of my guide what I was to understand by that. He answered, "Those snakes represent Dr. Foster and Chauncey L. Higbee. They are your enemies and desire to destroy you; but you see they are so fast locked together that they have no power of themselves to hurt you." I then thought I was riding up Mulholland street, but my guardian angel was not along with me. On arriving at the prairie, I was overtaken and seized by William and Wilson Law and others, saying, "Ah! ah! we have got you at last! We will secure you and put you in a safe place!" and without any ceremony dragged me out of my carriage, tied my hands behind me, and threw me into a deep, dry pit, where I remained in a perfectly helpless condition, and they went away. While struggling to get out, I heard Wilson Law screaming for help hard by. I managed to unloose myself so as to make a spring, when I caught hold of some grass which grew at the edge of the pit.
>
> I looked out of the pit and saw Wilson Law at a little distance attacked by ferocious wild beasts, and heard him cry out, "Oh! Brother Joseph, come and save me!" I replied, "I cannot, for you have put me into this deep pit." On looking out another way, I saw William Law with outstretched tongue, blue in the face, and the green poison forced out of his mouth, caused by the coiling of a large snake around his body. It had also grabbed him by the arm, a little above the elbow, ready to devour him. He cried out in the intensity of his agony, "Oh, Brother Joseph, Brother Joseph, come and save me, or I die!" also replied to him, "I cannot, William; I would willingly, but you have tied me and put me in this pit, and I am powerless to help you or liberate myself." In a short time after my guide came and said aloud, "Joseph, Joseph, what are you doing there?" I replied, "My enemies fell upon me, bound me and threw me in." He then took me by the hand, drew me out of the pit, set me free, and we went away rejoicing.

As the meeting comes to an end, two Mormon men arrive and notify Joseph that three hundred mobbers are assembled at Carthage, "with the avowed intention of coming against Nauvoo." There is also a "mass meeting at Warsaw." Words are flying off a few presses, particularly Thomas Sharp's. He prints shortly after the Expositor's destruction, "War and extermination is inevitable! Citizens ARISE, ONE and ALL!!! -- Can you stand by, and suffer such INFERNAL DEVILS!! to ROB men of their property and RIGHTS, without avenging them. We have no time for comment, every man will make his own. LET IT BE MADE WITH POWDER AND BALL!!!"

This kind of language rejuvenates Joseph Smith's enemies across the river in Missouri. It is not known how large the meeting is, but the word *mass* pushes the momentum. There are Missourians in the "mass."

A murderous spirit is swelling in those ranks.

Joseph somehow obtains a copy of the minutes of the mass meeting. He has one of his clerks insert the minutes into the records of the Church to show "the unparalleled corruption and diabolical falsehood of which the human race has become capable in this generation." Francis Higbee was at the mass meeting in Warsaw and appealed to the moment. He declares that the Mormons had a "hellish career in Missouri and this state—which has been characterized by the darkest and most diabolical deeds which have ever disgraced humanity." The rhetoric is rising. Joseph and now Hyrum Smith are accused of everything possible. Sharp is the "loudest voice of a nationwide anti-Mormon propaganda. . . . The propaganda war [is] waged to secure personal and public opinion, and the weapons [are] words: word-of-mouth [is] the small arms of the battle, and the newspapers [are] the artillery."

On the morning of June 14, Joseph Smith writes a correspondence to Governor Thomas Ford of Illinois. He explains the action he and the city council took in regards to the *Nauvoo Expositor* being a nuisance. He gets right to the point in his letter. "In the investigation it appeared evident to the council that the proprietors were a set of unprincipled, lawless debauchers, counterfeiters, bogus-makers, gamblers, peace-disturbers, and that the grand object of said proprietors was to destroy our constitutional rights and chartered privileges."

He references William Blackstone, a famous and respected English jurist and judge whose words are read by politically astute Americans and most likely read by Governor Ford. Blackstone is considered an authority on speech and press in free nations.

"The City Council," Joseph tells Governor Ford, "decided that it was necessary for the 'peace, benefit, good order and regulations . . . and for the protection of property . . . for the happiness and prosperity of the citizens of Nauvoo' " that the Expositor should be removed.

Other letters of reputation accompany his correspondence to the governor. New converts from the East and non-Mormons write stating their confidence in Joseph Smith as a mayor and religious leader. They also debunk the reports from the likes of Sharp and others. "I think it my duty to state," one accompanying letter reads, "that I have seen nothing in [Smith's] deportment but what is correct in all his domestic relations, being a kind husband and an affectionate father; and all his affairs, both domestic and official, have not only been free from censure, but praiseworthy, and ought to be imitated by everyone desirous of order and peace."

With these letters dispatched to Governor Ford, Joseph Smith spends a relatively quiet day on June 15. He prepares to deliver his last significant religious sermon on the morrow.

Chapter 44

JUNE 16–17, 1844

Nauvoo, Illinois

WHERE WAS THERE ever a son without a father?" Joseph Smith asks a large group of Latter-day Saints gathered in a grove of trees east of the unfinished Nauvoo Temple. This is his second-to-last Sabbath day in the flesh. He preaches a sermon on the plurality of Gods. "Where was there ever a father without first being a son?" Joseph is setting forth simple logic, yet it is often troubling for the finite mind. He purposefully confronts the sectarian notions that have reduced God to a being of three persons. Joseph Smith emphatically declares the doctrine of the Godhead, where the Father, the Son, and the Holy Ghost are three distinct beings, the Holy Ghost a personage of spirit rather than a resurrected being.

Joseph is aware of the "evolutions and iterations of creeds—and others to come over the centuries—[which] declared the Father, Son, and Holy Ghost to be abstract, absolute, transcendent, immanent, consubstantial, coeternal, and unknowable, without body, parts, or passions and dwelling outside space and time. . . . They are three distinct persons, yet not three Gods but one. All three persons are incomprehensible, yet it is one God who is incomprehensible." Joseph Smith boldly declares this to be false. God is to be sought after, understood, and found.

Joseph relies on the teachings in the New Testament to lay his foundation. "If Jesus had a Father, can we not believe that He had a Father also? I despise the idea of being scared to death at such a doctrine, for the Bible is full of it." He specifically quotes Revelations 1:5–6. "Jesus Christ . . . hath made us kings and priests unto God and *his Father*." The Apostle Paul, he argues, proclaimed that "there are Gods many and Lords many." But to help people understand that, he cautions: "I want to set it forth in a plain and simple manner; but to us there is but one God—that is pertaining to us." Jesus taught it; Peter taught it; Paul taught it. He continues, "But if Joseph Smith says there are Gods many and Lords many, they cry, 'Away with him! Crucify him! Crucify Him!'"

The audience, an amalgamation of the faithful and a handful of defectors and bitter enemies, are silent. They are attentive at Joseph's invitation for all to "search the scriptures, for they testify of things these apostates would gravely pronounce blasphemy." A few apostates are near the stand and a few others scattered throughout the audience. He is calling them out in front of several thousand. He is tired of their threats and doesn't fear their proximity.

Many people go home satisfied with the sermon. There is one God pertaining to them. One God they can pray to as a Father, and an experienced one at that. One who knows the vicissitudes of mortal life having experienced what they are currently experiencing. This is a real God to them, not an invented and incomprehensible God.

In the midafternoon, Joseph is approached by Illinois circuit judge Jesse B. Thomas. He is not ignorant to the tension rising between the Latter-day Saints and their neighbors. Thomas advises the Prophet to "go before some justice of the peace of the county, and have an examination of the charges specified in the writ from Justice Morrison of Carthage." Thomas believes this will satisfy the mob. Some rational citizens from Illinois and Iowa, forty in number, arrive shortly after Thomas counsels Joseph. They want to know of and see the difficulties firsthand and make their own judgments rather than naively join the call of anti-Mormons. They get an interview with Joseph Smith. He presents the Mormons' condition and has Willard Richards read the minutes of the council meeting in which the *Nauvoo Expositor* was labeled a public nuisance. "They express themselves satisfied" and return home distancing themselves from rising mob action.

As they go home satisfied, Joseph Smith goes to a stand near the temple where many Mormon men are gathered. They are not satisfied. They see the troubles of Missouri unfolding again before their eyes. They refuse to be driven again. Joseph Smith doesn't deny their willingness to fight and defend their properties. But he does instruct them to "keep their cool, and prepare their arms for the defense of the city, . . . be quiet and make no disturbances." He is hoping that Governor Ford will see the true aggressors even though he is being barraged with countless lies of Mormon atrocities.

Before night intrudes, Joseph has to turn his attention back to the swelling mobs at Carthage and Warsaw. Thomas Sharp is livid. He, in the same vein of mobocracy as former Governor Boggs of Missouri, calls for the extermination of the Latter-day Saints from Illinois. Sharp is successful in rallying and gathering angry men in the towns and countryside surrounding Nauvoo. Mormons in the neighboring communities are increasingly being harassed and having their homes and properties seized and damaged. Many have no other alternative but to abandon their homes and gather in Nauvoo for protection.

Joseph Smith informs Governor Ford by an express rider that there is an "organized effort to exterminate the Saints from Illinois by force of arms." In his correspondence, he asks that prompt action be taken on Ford's part, namely protection by him and the state against the mobs combining against him and his people. "Come down in person with your staff and investigate the whole matter without delay, and cause peace to be restored to the country; and I know not but this will be the only means of stopping an effusion of blood."

Joseph Smith has a few statements prepared to be sent with his letter to the governor. The statements concur that fifteen hundred Missourians are readying to the cross the Mississippi into Warsaw— Thomas Sharp country—with the intention of going on to Carthage. Before retiring for the night, Joseph Smith directs an officer in the

Nauvoo Legion to be ready to act in a "moment's warning." The beginning of the end is before him.

First thing Monday morning, June 17, Hyrum Smith sends a letter to Brigham Young, who is in the Northeast preaching and spreading politics. Hyrum advises him of the situation and the assembling mobs. "The excitement is very great indeed," he conveys. "It is thought best by myself and others for you to return without delay, and the rest of the Twelve." He also asks Brigham Young to call home all of the elders in the field, hundreds of them, with "stillness and calmness." Hyrum, with the memories of Missouri occupying his mind, says to Brigham, "You know we are not frightened, but think it best to be well prepared and be ready for the onset; and if it is extermination, extermination it is."

Joseph Smith writes to one of his uncles, "We feel determined in this place not to be dismayed if hell boils over all at once. We feel to hope for the best, and determined to prepare for the worst."

Hyrum and Joseph finish their letters just in time to be arrested again. They gladly follow the counsel of Jesse B. Thomas the day before and go before a county court—in Nauvoo. It isn't an immediate discharge, but they are discharged after a trial that occupies the morning hours.

Joseph Smith goes from the morning trial and standing as a defendant into the afternoon standing as a lieutenant general of the Nauvoo Legion. He calls out his staff and guard associated with the legion and gives orders for them to sound the call to other members of the legion to be ready to parade the following morning. He stations guards in different parts of the city as rumors and threats roll in. It is believed that William and Wilson Law are going to attempt to burn the *Nauvoo Neighbor* printing office sometime during the night. Joseph is challenging his physicality every minute of every day. He goes to bed at midnight, "ready to retire to rest."

As if nothing is wrong, Joseph tells one of his clerks to insert the final entry for the day—"Pleasant weather."

Chapter 45

JUNE 18, 1844

Nauvoo, Illinois

THE CLIMATE ISN'T so pleasant the next morning. Reports of mobs organizing and attacking are coming from surrounding communities. "By virtue of the authority vested in me as Mayor, and to preserve the city and the lives of the citizens," Joseph Smith proclaims, "I do hereby declare the said city, within the limits of its incorporation, under martial law." This means the city is under the control of military authority. Joseph Smith is lieutenant general of the Nauvoo Legion. He has no confidence in Governor Ford. He discerns that Ford has chosen his side, thus failing as a civilian authority of the state of Illinois.

The lives of twenty thousand people are being threatened, and the governor has casually sought to resolve the situation from Joseph's perspective. Both Ford and Joseph understand the extent of martial law. But only Joseph sees clearly the looming lawlessness on the horizon. He chooses to take the "extreme and rare measure used to control society during war or periods of civil unrest or chaos." He takes responsibility politically since Ford seems confused, ignorant, or self-conscious in his position as a civic officer. Initially, it seems Ford is adamantly neutral, not willing to placate either side. The mob feels to damn the "Governor as being as bad as Joe Smith." Yet the move by Joseph Smith seems to irk Ford and gives him and the mob another action to be brought into question. This "defensive action" leads to the treason charges that will be "levied against [Joseph] at Carthage."

In the afternoon, Joseph addresses the Nauvoo Legion, who has gathered near his home. In full military uniform, he stands on the frame of an unfinished building across the street from his home. Judge Phelps reads to those gathered Thomas Sharp's call to "all the old citizens" of the area to "assist the mob in exterminating the leaders of the Saints and driving away the people." And then, for about an hour and a half, Joseph Smith addresses the legion. Several individuals report on his message.

"The opposition of these men is moved by the spirit of the adversary of all righteousness. It is not only to destroy me, but every man and woman who dares believe the doctrines that God hath inspired me to teach to this generation," he declares, standing a full body length above his listeners. "We have never violated the laws of our country. We have every right to live under their protection, and are entitled to all the privileges guaranteed by our state and national constitutions," he bellows to his audience. "I call God, angels and all men to witness that we are innocent of the charges which are heralded forth through the public prints . . . and while they assemble together in unlawful mobs to take away our rights and destroy our lives, they think to shield themselves under the refuge of lies which they have thus wickedly fabricated."

To clearly state his actions in proclaiming martial law, Joseph Smith argues for the Latter-day Saints. "We are American citizens. We live upon a soil for the liberties of which our fathers periled their lives and spilt their blood upon the battlefield. Those rights so dearly purchased, shall not be disgracefully trodden under foot by lawless marauders without at least a noble effort on our part to sustain our liberties."

Seeking a hearty approval of his audience, he asks, "Will you all stand by me to the death, and sustain at the peril of your lives, the laws of our country, and the liberties and privileges which our fathers have transmitted unto us, sealed with their sacred blood?"

"Aye!" Thousands shout.

"It is well. If you had not done it, I would have gone out there"—
pointing to the West—"and would have raised up a mightier people."
Going west is one option still available to Joseph Smith, and he
thinks about taking it.

But the spirit of the moment seizes his responses. "Drawing his
sword, and presenting it to heaven," he lifts the emotion within himself and with those standing below him. "I call God and angels to
witness that I have unsheathed my sword with a firm and unalterable
determination that this people shall have their legal rights, and be
protected from mob violence, or my blood shall be spilt upon the
ground like water, and my body consigned to the silent tomb." With
a unique melancholy that only he understands, he says, "I would
welcome death rather than submit to this oppression; and it would
be sweet, oh, sweet, to rest in the grave rather than submit to this
oppression, agitation, annoyance, confusion, and alarm upon alarm,
any longer."

Joseph is showing and expressing his exhaustion. For his listeners, it is a rallying speech; for him, it is a good-bye speech. This will
be the last time many of them will hear him speak. "I do not regard
my own life. I am ready to be offered a sacrifice for this people," he
calmly pronounces. He then asks a somber question to a people constantly pressed down by antagonists: "For what can our enemies do?"
Calling upon the words of the Savior, he answers his own question,
"Only kill the body." When that happens, "their power is then at an
end." The Savior encouraged his friends to "fear him which is able to
destroy both soul and body in hell," referring to Satan.

"Stand firm, my friends; never flinch," he urges in a confident
tone. "Do not seek to save your lives, for he that is afraid to die for
the truth, will lose eternal life. Hold out to the end, and we shall
be resurrected and become like Gods, and reign in celestial kingdoms, principalities, and eternal dominions, while this cursed mob
will sink to hell, the portion of all those who shed innocent blood."
These few last words vibrate more in his prophetic voice than a military voice.

"God has tried you. You are a good people; therefore I love you
with all my heart. Greater love hath no man than that he should lay
down his life for his friends. You have stood by me in the hour of

trouble, and I am willing to sacrifice my life for your preservation." In words of benediction, he finishes, "May the Lord God of Israel bless you for ever and ever. I say it in the name of Jesus of Nazareth, and in the authority of the Holy Priesthood, which He hath conferred upon me."

Joseph Smith has a triumphal moment as a patriarch. He ends his speech to the Nauvoo Legion in solemnity.

Hyrum stands with a tinge of fire usually more common in Joseph. He repudiates Thomas Sharp and his rambling lies in print. Sharp accused Hyrum a few days back of threatening to take his life. Hyrum speaks to the assembly of military men and declares that the accusation is "false as hell—there [is not] a syllable of truth in it." Joseph warned Hyrum that the lies and persecution would be heaped upon him as well. Hyrum has a greater sense of what his younger brother is bearing.

The men of the Nauvoo Legion are anxious and readying themselves for the defense of their city, their properties, and their families. They are ready to stand with Joseph to the death.

Chapter 46

JUNE 19–21, 1844

Warsaw and Nauvoo, Illinois

UST AFTER MIDNIGHT on June 19, the mobs turn against Chester Loveland, a non-Mormon near Warsaw. He is married to Fanny Call, a Mormon. He had been told by James Charles, the constable of Hancock County, the previous day to join another company from Hancock County and go to Nauvoo to arrest Joseph Smith and the city council for their destruction of the *Nauvoo Expositor*. Loveland stands his ground and rejects the command. He discerns the murdering spirit in the hearts of his friends and neighbors. They try to trick him into service by presenting a forged order from Governor Ford. He logically thinks the situation through and distinguishes their intentions.

The men of mobocracy come back a third time just after midnight to coerce Loveland. They are carrying hot tar and feathers, with the intention to lynch him if he fails to agree. Loveland was privy to their returning. He locks down his windows, secures the door, and blows out the candles.

Quietly he sits in his home as the mob tries to enter. He hears them arguing. Some want to break down the door, others want to leave. Loveland doesn't move or speak. A leader of the mob threatens him and tells him to leave the region immediately. Loveland remains perfectly still. They leave. He refuses to be part of the inflaming madness. He acts as a true American rather than an oppressor of rights.

The sun rises for both Loveland and Joseph Smith. But Joseph can't merely lock the windows and doors and blow out the candles. He musters the Nauvoo Legion in the afternoon. Standing in front of his home, he gives orders that the legion take position on "all the roads leading out of the city" and that "all the powder and led in the city [be] secured." The Nauvoo flats are between the bluff and the Mississippi River. Joseph's home is located on the south end of the flats near the river. It is beautiful real estate and a choice place to reside, but it is an unfavorable spot to be in with an impending attack from the high ground. Cautiously Joseph Smith also sends patrols to the riverbank and the alleys of the city. Any eye-catching movement that resembles their antagonist is to be dealt with and reported. Possibly twelve thousand Latter-day Saints and several friendly non-Mormons are dwelling on the flats.

Everyone is alert. No attacks occur.

By 9 p.m. Joseph has one of his clerks note that he is at home. He hasn't been able to go too far from home without a large body guard. His enemies want him away from his friends and away from the Nauvoo Charter and his immediate access to habeas corpus. June 19 ends with the entry into Joseph Smith's history reading, "The city is all quiet."

As he enters the last week of his life, it is affidavit after affidavit and correspondence after correspondence. There are at least ten affidavits filed detailing the mob's actions and intentions on this day. He has all of them read in his presence. The alarm is rising. The documents detail the threats of kidnapping, capturing, and killing Joseph Smith. They record the acts of violence the Latter-day Saints are suffering on the farmlands and surrounding communities to the east of Nauvoo. Members of the Church from surrounding communities who are flooding into Nauvoo on June 20 confirm many of the reports.

Joseph Smith compiles many of the affidavits and writes a letter to John Tyler, president of the United States. "I am sorry to say that the State of Missouri, not contented with robbing, driving and murdering many of the Latter-day Saints, are now joining the mob of this state for the purpose of the 'utter extermination' of the Mormons. . . . And now, sir, as President of the United States, will you render that protection which the Constitution guarantees in case of 'insurrection and rebellion,' and save the innocent and oppressed from such horrid persecution?"

He doesn't expect much from President Tyler. A month earlier Joseph had prophesied to Josiah Quincy that Tyler would not be the next president. Giving him the benefit, Joseph Smith wants to see if the most powerful American will do something for an oppressed people. The letter most likely won't even make it to President Tyler before Joseph Smith takes his last breath.

The Mormon prophet also writes to all the missionaries on assignment preaching and politicking to come home, especially the Twelve Apostles. He writes to Mormons throughout Illinois and Iowa to come to Nauvoo and help the legion defend the city. Captain Almon Babbitt of the legion, with a company of men, is in the community of Ramus. He deflects the orders, telling his men, "If any of you go, not one will ever get to Nauvoo alive." There is good reason to believe so: the mob is substantially growing day by day and has patrols between Nauvoo and the Mormon farming communities. In many cases, they have already attacked Mormon homes. But the community of Ramus has several hundred Mormons. The mob has taken a bold defense of the route between the two communities.

Not all think as Captain Babbitt, particularly the uncle of the Mormon prophet, John Smith. He steps forward and declares with remarkable respect for his nephew, "Every man that goes at the call of the Prophet shall go and return safe, and not a hair of his head shall be lost; and I bless you in the name of the Lord." The unique gift of confidence and prophesy is once again evident in the blood of the Smith family. His uncle speaks in a manner and spirit that wins the hearts of the men of Ramus. "The company immediately [throws] the command upon Uriah H. Yager, who accept[s] of it, and start[s] for Nauvoo, although many of them [are] destitute of boots or shoes."

Uncle Smith's prophecy is tested within five miles from Ramus. A mob double their size can be seen approaching, flying two red flags. The mob takes position in a wooded area adjacent to the road the

Mormons are traveling down. On command, the Mormons spread themselves ten feet apart. As they pass the wooded position, the mob opens fire. With "balls whizzing past their heads," the Mormon men keep their spacing and make it through the hot gauntlet without a hair of their heads being harmed.

They arrive in Nauvoo all accounted for.

The men who arrive didn't fire a shot. Joseph Smith tells them and many others in confidence that "there would not be a gun fired on our part during the fuss." Even so, Joseph can't just sit still. If he and Hyrum are out of the way and removed from Nauvoo, the mob would spare the residents. Joseph Smith knows they want his blood and that if he is either dead or fleeing in the wilderness to the West, it will buy his people time. Late on the evening of June 20, Joseph approaches his brother Hyrum and advises him to take his family "on the next steamboat and go to Cincinnati."

"Joseph, I can't leave you."

In a dismal tone, Joseph turns to those in his presence and says, "I wish I could get Hyrum out of the way, so that he may live to avenge my blood, and I will stay with you and see it out." Both Hyrum and Joseph spend the night under the watchful care of a loyal bodyguard.

By 10 a.m. the next morning, Friday, June 21, Joseph Smith is with his guard on Main Street. He is riding north reviewing portions of the legion. He is in the shadows of the Nauvoo Temple now boasting solid exterior walls. The mob excitement has slowed the construction on the temple. The men have put down the trowels and put their fingers near triggers, even though, according to Joseph Smith, they wouldn't be pulling them.

By midafternoon the Prophet receives a letter from Governor Ford. Instead of going to Nauvoo personally, Ford goes to Carthage (having stopped by Warsaw on his way). This is a fatal blow to Joseph Smith and the Mormons. Ford passes through two of the most anti-Joseph communities. "I arrived at this place (Warsaw) this morning" Ford records. "Both before and since my arrival, complaints of a grave character have been made to me of certain proceedings of your honorable body." Although, he tries to convey a neutral and objective tone, "As chief magistrate, it is my duty to see that impartial justice shall be done, uninfluenced either by the excitement here or in your city. I think before any decisive measure shall be adopted, that I ought to hear the allegations and defenses of all parties."

Ford doesn't want the conflict to escalate, but he doesn't want the Mormon influence to go unmatched and their success to go unchecked. He believes "that if Joseph [is] removed from the scene, the Mormons would scatter and there would be no need to drive them out or exterminate them." With civil authority, Ford tells Joseph Smith that he will "shape [his] course with reference to law and justice." Ford asks Joseph Smith to send responsible individuals to him to tell him their side of the story. For some reason, he isn't willing to go to Nauvoo to see Joseph personally.

Joseph Smith delays his response to Ford. He calls for the city council to convene at 4 p.m. As they meet, more affidavits are read. The scene on the prairies to their east resembles a horrible dark storm on the horizon. John Taylor and John Bernhisel agree to take the Mormons' situation to Governor Ford. Taylor is one of the Twelve Apostles and is a man in whom liberty flows in great measure.

While Taylor and Bernhisel are in Carthage, Joseph Smith pours over other affidavits. Enemy Joseph Jackson tells John P. Greene, a faithful Mormon, that "Joseph Smith [is] the damnedest rascal in the world, and he would be damned if he did not take vengeance on him, if he had to follow him to the Rocky Mountains." Notwithstanding the increasing threats, Joseph Smith entertains an officer in the United States Army. He stays in the Mansion House and receives the hospitality of the Smith family. Joseph also happily receives his attorney from Burlington, Iowa, James W. Woods. Woods is also a recipient of the Smiths' hospitality.

Chapter 47
SATURDAY, JUNE 22, 1884
Carthage and Nauvoo, Illinois, and
Waters of the Mississippi River

OHN TAYLOR AND Bernhisel arrive in Carthage shortly after Ford does. They enter Carthage with every ounce of courage. Up to thirteen hundred men are gathered and another five hundred are gathered at Warsaw. The scene for John Taylor confirms all the reports. Ford boasts that "one of [my] most singular achievements [is] keeping the lid on this trigger-happy lot."

Taylor and Bernhisel wait for an audience with Ford. When he finally comes into their presence, they are "surrounded by some of the vilest and most unprincipled men in creation." Taylor begins to read to Ford the compilation of affidavits and presents to him the Mormon position. As Taylor reads, he is constantly interrupted by the unprincipled men at Ford's side. "That's a lie! That's a G—d–d lie! That's an infernal falsehood! That's a blasted lie! they bellow."

Ford asks Taylor to inform Joseph Smith to come to Carthage immediately to appease the people and answer the original charges of "riot" regarding the *Nauvoo Expositor* destruction. Taylor argues with Governor Ford that Joseph Smith coming to Carthage would be extremely unsafe. At this point, the governor tells Taylor to bring him and to do so without bringing any arms. Ford then "pledge[s] his faith as Governor, and the faith of the state, that [Smith and his followers] should be protected, and that he would guarantee [their] perfect safety."

With these words, Ford defames his own character.

Taylor and Bernhisel leave Carthage at about 5 p.m.

Earlier that day in Nauvoo, Joseph Smith writes another letter to Governor Ford, asking him to personally come to Nauvoo and investigate the situation himself. Messengers Lucien Woodworth and Joseph Smith's attorney set off for Carthage to deliver the correspondence. They will be witnesses to Taylor's words and the scene in Carthage.

As Joseph Smith's messengers are defending him in Carthage, the Nauvoo Legion is receiving instructions. Joseph orders entrenching tools be found and that men take three to four hour work shifts preparing places of defense. But he also gives orders to let people freely pass in and out of the city.

Joseph anxiously spends the afternoon and early evening combing over several more affidavits from Mormons who have been abused in the surrounding country by the gathering mob. He utters a prophecy that "in the sickly seasons sickness would enter into the houses of the mob and vex them until they would fain repent in dust and ashes. They will be smitten with the scab."

By 10 p.m. on June 22, Joseph Smith hears the reports of Taylor and Bernhisel's interview with Ford. Ford sent a letter to Joseph, which beat Taylor and Bernhisel to Nauvoo. "I now express to you my opinion that your conduct in the destruction of the press was a very gross outrage upon the laws and the liberties of the people. It may have been full of libels, but this did not authorize you to destroy it." And then in an attempt to personalize his rebuke, he unwisely tries to make a parallel. "There have been many newspapers in this state which have been wrongfully abusing me for more than a year, and yet such is my regard for the liberty of the press . . . I would shed the last drop of my blood to protect those presses from any illegal violence."

Again, Ford blemishes his character. His own cowardly nature surfaces hour by hour. At this point, Joseph Smith recognizes Ford's shallowness. Joseph has been slandered for over twenty years in the press and in public. He has been tarred and feathered, chased, and physically abused, not to mention illegally imprisoned for six months. He has been driven from several homes and three states in fourteen years by his enemies who spread false reports and thirst for his blood. Ford's political opponents attacking him in the press isn't even a lick of dust compared to what Joseph Smith has endured. Ford gives Joseph Smith one ultimatum: "I can call out no portion of the militia for your defense until you submit to the law." Logic would seem to have the civic authority dispersing the mob and then having the law take its course, but this is not Ford's logic.

Joseph Smith makes two decisions after reading Governor Ford's letter. He revokes martial law and writes a response informing Ford of his gross error in thinking that presses haven't been destroyed in the United States. He cites examples of how presses have been destroyed in Ohio, New York, and Boston for "scurrilous prints." Joseph Smith lets the high-minded governor know that he and the city council thought "the loss of character by libel and the loss of life by mobocratic prints to be a greater loss than a little property, all of which, life alone excepted, we have sustained, brought upon us by the most unprincipled outlaws, gamblers, counterfeiters, and such characters as have been standing by me, and probably are now standing around your Excellency—namely, those men who have brought these evils upon us."

Joseph makes it clear to the governor why he is resisting answering to charges in Carthage. "We dare not come. Writs, we are assured, are issued against us in various parts of the country. For what? To drag us from place to place, from court to court, across creeks and prairies, till some bloodthirsty villain [can] find his opportunity to shoot us."

Joseph Smith is done appealing to Ford. Visitors from the East have arrived in Nauvoo earlier in the day. Joseph's visit to Washington, DC, early in 1840 is paying off in some regards. People of high status come or send messengers to him, especially in the last several months. On this day, two of John C. Calhoun's sons, John C. Calhoun Jr. and Patrick, arrive and are "anxious to see the Prophet." They get an interview with him. As they approach the Mansion House, they are unaware that he is in an upper room with close friends, deliberating what he should do regarding Ford's request to come to Carthage. The two brothers are screened by three men and then "walk past three hundred armed guards" as they are allowed enter the home. They are in his presence long enough to hear of the pressing troubles and hear some aspects of the faith. They also hear him refer to himself as a prophet. Joseph Smith excuses the sons of his political opponent. This isn't a political time for him. The two sons of Calhoun can do nothing for him, only urge him to appeal to the Federal Government. But this has not helped in times past and will not accomplish anything now.

After the men are excused, Joseph Smith returns to Ford's letter, telling his close friends who are in counsel, "There is no mercy—no mercy here."

Hyrum, now seeing where Ford's request has led, answers his brother's stress. "No; just as sure as we fall into their hands we are dead men."

"Joseph replies, 'Yes; what shall we do, Brother Hyrum?'"

Hyrum has no answer, only a sober reply, "I don't know."

Joseph Smith's optimism surfaces, as does his prophetic countenance, which his brother Hyrum and so many others are familiar with. "The way is open," he says. "It is clear to my mind what to do. All they want is Hyrum and myself; then tell everybody to go about their business, and not to collect in groups, but to scatter about. There is no doubt they will come here and search for us. Let them search; they will not harm you in person or property, and not even a hair of your head. We will cross the river tonight, and go away to the West."

Joseph goes outside amongst his guards to make arrangements for his and Hyrum's families to be taken as soon as possible from Nauvoo. He also makes arrangements to cross the Mississippi River with Hyrum within an hour. He turns to one of the guards, takes him by the hand, and expresses faith by declaring, "Now, Brother Hodge, let what will come, don't deny the faith, and all will be well." He makes a move to return inside his home. As he does, he tells Stephen Markham directly to his face, "If I and Hyrum [are] ever taken again we [will] be massacred, or I [am] not a prophet of God."

Though intending to distance himself from his enemies, Joseph knows his blood is about to be spilled. "I want Hyrum to live to avenge my blood," he tells Markham, "but he is determined not to leave me."

Joseph Smith spends a few moments with his wife and children. He tells Emma that he is going west and that preparations are in motion to secure her and the children's safety out of Nauvoo. Hyrum Smith leads the way out of the Mansion House. He extends his hand to Reynolds Cahoon. "A company of men are seeking to kill my brother Joseph, and the Lord has warned him to flee to the Rocky Mountains to save his life. Good-bye, Brother Cahoon, we shall see you again."

Hyrum removes to his home to say good-bye to his family. Shortly afterward, Joseph comes out of his home, leaving the affection and security that only a family can give. "His tears [are] flowing fast." He is holding a "handkerchief to his face" and follows the footsteps of his "Brother Hyrum without uttering a word." The men protecting the Prophet watch somberly as their friend passes through their midst.

Now entirely in the dark, with no clerks except Willard Richards, and no three hundred armed bodyguards except a dear friend, Porter Rockwell, Joseph and Hyrum wait calmly on the banks of the Mississippi River for a skiff to take them across to the Iowa side. The West is before them, and the unfinished temple to their backs. William Phelps, once in the ranks of the apostates but now a dear friend, is told to take the families of Joseph and Hyrum to Cincinnati. He is also told to petition the United States and Congress for a redress of grievances.

Chapter 48

SUNDAY, JUNE 23, 1844

Nauvoo, Illinois, and the Iowa Side of the Mississippi River

Y 2 A.M. a skiff has been brought to Joseph Smith and his company for their passage across the Mississippi River. Rockwell rows the skiff, which is in a terrible condition. It is full of leaks and begins to sink. Rockwell keeps rowing while the three others use their boots to bail out water during the crossing. By the time they reach the Iowa side, their energy is spent. They arrive around daybreak.

It is good timing. A constable and his posse arrive in Nauvoo about the same time to arrest Joseph. Failing to find him and Hyrum, they return to Carthage. One man from the posse stays behind and conveys Governor Ford's views. "If Joseph and Hyrum [are] not given up, he [will] send his troops and guard the city until they [are] found." His predecessor, Governor Carlin, failed to apprehend Joseph Smith after having tried for about a year. And it is well known that Joseph has plenty of decoys to elude his enemies.

Porter Rockwell, thoughtful as ever, agrees to return to Nauvoo immediately to obtain horses and get them across "secretly" that night so the two brothers can keep moving west. Their intentions are to "start for the Great Basin in the Rocky Mountains" as soon as possible.

Friends from the Iowa side give Joseph, Hyrum, and Willard Richards provisions to go west. Porter Rockwell, moving with God's grace, makes it back to Iowa at 1 p.m. Three Mormon men are with Rockwell. While in Nauvoo, Emma asks Rockwell to persuade her husband to come back. One of the Mormon men with Rockwell is Reynolds Cahoon. He is carrying a letter from Emma conveying her request that Joseph come back and go before the law.

Anxiety surfaces in many.

Additional reports are coming in about the swelling numbers of the mob. In the last few days, some Nauvoo merchants and other residents have closed up their shops and homes and left like cowards. People haven't accepted Joseph's promise that they would be safe and that the combining mob wanted his and Hyrum's blood and that was all—that would satisfy their hellish actions. But some do not believe it and have left Nauvoo.

Reynolds Cahoon and two other Mormon men, Lorenzo Wasson and Hiram Kimball, accuse Smith of "cowardice." In Joseph's speech to the legion a few days prior, he wanted to defend the people's rights and throw down mobocracy. His last-minute attempt to flee west is seen by a few as cowardice, a character trait not compatible to his tested life. Cahoon tells Joseph a fable. "When the wolves came the shepherd ran from the flock, and left the sheep to be devoured." His comment stings the Prophet.

Looking in the faces of those loyal to him, Joseph Smith replies, "If my life is of no value to my friends it is of none to myself." Joseph Smith had told the Saints nine months earlier that his enemies couldn't kill him until his work is accomplished and he is ready to die. All the indications suggest his work is near accomplished. He is ready to die.

Singling out his undaunting boyhood friend, Joseph turns to Porter Rockwell. "What shall I do?" The rather coarse Rockwell defers to his dear friend's seniority. "You are the oldest and ought to know best; and as you make your bed, I will lie with you."

Cahoon has engaged Hyrum to try to convince Joseph to return and give himself up. Joseph interrupts Cahoon and says, "Brother Hyrum, you are the oldest, what shall we do?" "Let us go back and give ourselves up, and see the thing out," Hyrum tells his younger brother.

Joseph is solemn in thought. After a few moments of complete silence, Joseph looks expressively at Hyrum. "If you go back I will go with you, but we shall be butchered." Hyrum's optimism tries to lift his brother's spirits. "No, no; let us go back and put our trust in God, and we shall not be harmed. The Lord is in it. If we live or have to die, we will be reconciled to our fate." Hyrum is hoping for deliverance but offering to die. "Reconciled to God's will, and with a perspective of eternal life, Hyrum [can] walk coolly into the face of death, knowing that the next life [is] as real as the mortal one."

Another moment of silence is broken by Joseph Smith. He puts down the letter from his wife. "We had better go back, and if we die, we'll die like men." Joseph tells Cahoon to ready a boat to take them back across the river to Nauvoo.

At 2 p.m. while still on the Iowa side of the Mississippi River, Joseph and Hyrum pen a letter to Governor Ford. They tell him that they feel he is good on his word to protect them as they answer to the law. "[We] now offer to come to you at Carthage on the morrow, as early as shall be convenient for your posse to escort us into headquarters, provided we can have a fair trial, not be abused nor have my witnesses abused, and have all things done in due form of law, without partiality, and you may depend on my honor without the show of a great armed force to produce excitement in the minds of the timid."

Joseph agrees to meet a detachment of the governor's troop at the "big mound," a fifty-foot hill on the side of the road five miles east of Nauvoo. He and Hyrum arrange to be there at 10 a.m. the following morning.

After the letter is written to Ford, the men say good-bye to friends and fellow Latter-day Saints in Iowa. They begin walking to the Mississippi River, a river they will cross one last time. Joseph Smith and Porter Rockwell fall behind the group with a pace of melancholy. The others shout back, urging them to pick up their pace. In a tender moment privy only to Rockwell and Willard Richards, Joseph Smith says, "It is of no use to hurry, for we are going back to be slaughtered." He then tells Rockwell of one more wish. "I wish [I could] . . . get the people once more together, and talk to them tonight." Rockwell tells the Prophet he would have a grand gathering in a few hours and that he then could speak to the Saints one last time by "starlight."

John Murdock, a faithful Mormon from the first days of the Church, watches the men row back across the river. He feels "something in the air; that there was something threatening about [the] situation." This scene is also indelibly planted in the heart and mind of Hyrum's five-year-old boy, who will not be able to "speak of it for the rest of his life without weeping." The boy's aunt watching their return feels "sorrowful forebodings." There is an unnerving feeling starting to rest upon many. They had seen their prophet in dire situations before. When Joseph and Hyrum come ashore on the Illinois side of the river, they go directly to their homes. Both are surrounded by family. Being with family deflects a portion of their anxiety. This last moment of solitude with his family overrides Joseph Smith's desire to preach to the people one last time. He chooses to spend the hours with his family in private. So does Hyrum. Their wives try to comfort them and sustain them. The two women are hoping it all ends like times before, with their husbands being vindicated before the law and free from the entanglements of their enemies.

Amidst the gloominess, Hyrum learns that his oldest daughter, Lovina, has just been married to Lorin Walker, a man a faith—a contrast to the nature of anti-Mormon Joseph Jackson, who sought Lovina's hand a year earlier. Lovina and Lorin spend their first night together knowing her father's life is on the line.

Sadly, two Mormon messengers, Jedidiah M. Grant and Theodore Turley, are told by Governor Ford on this night that there will be no posse or escort to help Joseph arrive in Carthage unmolested. Ford sends the messengers, stressing that Joseph better be in Carthage by 10 a.m. the following morning. Ford, now talking and operating more like a modern-day Pilate, tells the Mormon messengers that if Joseph doesn't turn himself in, "Nauvoo [will] be destroyed and all the men, women, and children that were in it."

With wearied horses, Grant and Turley don't arrive back in Nauvoo until 4 a.m. on June 24. Joseph Smith pushes aside all warnings and pleas from his faithful friends not to go to Carthage. "He [is] determined to go to Carthage and give himself up to the Governor."

Thomas Reynolds was governor of Missouri from 1840–1844. In July of 1842, Reynolds issued a demand to Illinois Governor Carlin for the extradition of Joseph Smith and Orrin Porter Rockwell. Governor Reynolds committed suicide at the governor's office late into his term.

A drawing of Thomas Sharp later in life. He used his position with the Warsaw Signal to express his hatred for Joseph Smith and excite like-minded individuals to come to the cause of mobocracy. "War and extermination is inevitable! Citizens ARISE, ONE and ALL!!!—Can you stand by, and suffer such INFERNAL DEVILS!! . . . We have no time for comment, every man will make his own. LET IT BE MADE WITH POWDER AND BALL!!!"

Governor Thomas Ford turned justice aside as the events unfolded with the illegal arrest and murder of Joseph Smith. His history reveals his conflict in the aftermath: "Carthage Jail, may become holy and venerable names, places of classic interest, in another age; like Jerusalem, the Garden of Gethsemane, the Mount of Olives, and Mount Calvary to the Christian, and Mecca and Medina to the Turk. And in that event, the author (Ford) feels degraded by the reflection, that the humble governor of an obscure state, who would otherwise be forgotten in a few years, stands a fair chance, like Pilate and Herod, by their official connection with the true religion, of being dragged down to posterity with an immortal name, hitched on to the memory of a miserable impostor."

William Law falls out of Mormon ranks by January 1844. He turns bitterly against Joseph Smith and organizes a church with the sole purpose to destroy him. His diary said that he left Carthage on the morning of the assassination (so did Governor Ford, Joseph Smith's attorneys, and many others.) William dies in Wisconsin nearly fifty years after the assassinations.

Willard Richards remarkably did not receive any bullet wounds during the firestorm at Carthage. Richards (Taylor) wrote about the experience and left on record the injustice shown Joseph and Hyrum Smith by Governor Thomas Ford. Richards died in 1854 while serving as a counselor to Brigham Young.

John Taylor received at least four bullet wounds that gloomy day in Carthage. He will live over forty years after the incident. Taylor became the third President of the Church after the death of Brigham Young.

Dan Jones boldly defended Joseph Smith in Carthage. The last midnight before his death, Joseph Smith says to Dan Jones, "Are you afraid to die?" Jones answers back, "Has that time come, think you? Engaged in such a cause I do not think that death would have many terrors." Joseph Smith's prophetic gift surfaces at the dismal moment. "You will yet see Wales," Brother Jones, "and fulfill the mission appointed you before you die."

Hyrum Smith was almost six years older than Joseph. He believed his brother's prophetic call. He said of his brother: "There were prophets before, but Joseph has the spirit and power of all the prophets." Hyrum was the first one killed at Carthage Jail.

A depiction of the last public address of Lieutenant General Joseph Smith. "I call God and angels to witness that I have unsheathed my sword with a firm and unalterable determination that this people shall have their legal rights, and be protected from mob violence, or my blood shall be spilt upon the ground like water, and my body consigned to the silent tomb."

Statue in Nauvoo across the street from the Nauvoo Temple depicting Joseph and Hyrum leaving the city one last time as they make their trek to Carthage. In this vicinity, Joseph is reported to have glanced back at the city between him and the Mississippi River and say: "This is the loveliest place and the best  people under the heavens; little do they know the trials that await them."

Death Masks of Joseph and Hyrum Smith. The death masks were prepared by George Cannon, a convert from England who had recently arrived in Nauvoo. These two remarkable pieces of history are in possession of the historical and museum departments of The Church of Jesus Christ of Latter-day Saints.

The temple was officially dedicated April 30, 1846, nearly two years after Joseph Smith's death. Brigham Young left to go west before it was officially dedicated but initiated temple rites before leaving. In October 1848, the temple was set on fire by an arsonist. Four exterior walls remained standing until May 27, 1850, when Nauvoo was struck by a major tornado that toppled some of the

walls. In 1999, Church President Gordon B. Hinckley announced the rebuilding of the temple on its original site. After two years of construction, the Church dedicated the temple on June 27, 2002, the day Joseph and Hyrum were killed 158 years earlier.

Carthage Jail 1866–67, over twenty years after the assassination.

Carthage Jail today, south wall with front door and windows to the upstairs bedroom. The well is off the east wall. Joseph fell from the second story window when he was murdered The oldest standing structure in Carthage, Illinois. Owned by The Church of Jesus Christ of Latter-day Saints, and tours are available year round.

Door to the room Joseph, Hyrum, John, and Willard tried to physically keep shut as the mob pressed upon them. The hole through the middle panel was made by the gunshot that hit Hyrum in the face.

Interior of the room the prisoners occupied when the mob attacked.

Chapter 49
MONDAY, JUNE 24, 1844
Nauvoo, Illinois, and the Road to Carthage

JOSEPH AND HYRUM have now had two restless nights with little sleep. With less than four full days to live, their stamina is resilient. Emma feels the worst she ever has in her life. She too expects murder, which causes her to acknowledge that her husband's release from his tormentors is near its end.

As the sunrise appears, Joseph and Emma have a tearful good-bye. Hyrum and his family arrive at his brother's home, and he expresses his feelings by reading a selection from the Book of Mormon.

> And it came to pass that I prayed unto the Lord that he would give unto the Gentiles grace, that they might have charity. And it came to pass that the Lord said unto me: If they have not charity it mattereth not unto thee, thou hast been faithful; wherefore thy garments shall be made clean. And because thou hast seen thy weakness, thou shalt be made strong, even unto the sitting down in the place which I have prepared in the mansions of my Father. And now I . . . bid farewell unto the Gentiles; yea, and also unto my brethren whom I love, until we shall meet before the judgment-seat of Christ, where all men shall know that my garments are not spotted with your blood.

Hyrum takes the page he reads from in the Book of Mormon and turns the "leaf upon it." He hands the book to a family member and then bids his family farewell. As Joseph, Hyrum, and those accompanying them mount their horses, a Mormon fellow approaches and says, "If you go there they will kill you."

"I know it," Joseph utters, "but I am going. I am going to give myself for the people, to save them."

The procession to death begins.

They stop by the home of a man named Rosecrantz. Perhaps to solicit his help and companionship for the fiery furnace they are about to enter. Rosecrantz is "acquainted with the governor." A young woman, Mary Rich, hears the conversation unfold between Joseph Smith and Rosecrantz at the gate of the home. She is at the home taking care of Rosecrantz's sick wife. Joseph Smith asks Mary if she is able to bring them a drink of water. Mary returns with water. He acknowledges her kind deed. "Lord bless you," Mary, "you shall have a disciple's reward." Another woman named Mary witnesses the occasion and hears the words fall from Joseph's lips. "Brother Rosecrantz, if I never see you again, or if I never come back, remember that I love you." Though not spoken to her, the words topple her emotions. She removes herself to her sleeping quarters as tears abruptly flow.

Benjamin Ashby, a young boy, is working in his father's garden as Joseph and the others accompanying him pass by at a painstakingly slow pace. In a childlike discernment, he sees the "deep sorrow that cover[s]" Joseph's "noble countenance."

Slowly the men continue the climb to the bluff. The rising temple is in full sight. The man who inspired its construction knows the significance of the edifice and has established the order of the ordinances and covenants to be administered once it is complete. Joseph Smith sets forth that The Church of Jesus Christ of Latter-day Saints is the possessor of the holy priesthood held anciently by patriarchs, prophets, and apostles. And the holy priesthood invests in the Church the "divine commission to erect and maintain temples dedicated to the name and service of the true and living God, and to administer within those sacred structures the ordinances of the Priesthood, the effect of which shall be binding both on earth and beyond the grave"—ordinances and covenants like baptism and marriage.

Anson Call is sitting alone on the west side of the temple as Joseph and the men following him ascend the bluff. As they approach, Anson "discover[s] an unusual melancholy appearance upon [Joseph Smith's] countenance." Anson observes him closely. He knows this type of countenance is foreign to Joseph Smith. Notwithstanding the persecution throughout his life, Joseph has always been given to a "cheery temperament."

At this scene, Joseph surveys the temple and then turns to look down on the Mississippi River. Between him and the river dwell thousands and thousands of Latter-day Saints. After a silent glance and after careful thought, he says to those around him, "This is the loveliest place and the best people under the heavens; little do they know the trials that await them." The gift of prophecy rests upon him even in his gloominess and coming fate. His insights, foresight, and prophecies have resonated with so many. He will take these unique gifts to his grave.

Joseph makes a pass around the temple, "viewing it with very few remarks to any of the workmen." Anson remains on the west side of the temple, waiting for him to reappear around the northwest corner. Next to Anson is a man named Alpheus Cutler. Joseph comes around the temple and picks Cutler out of the men. "Go with me," he tells Cutler. They ride a few hundred feet south of the temple to a tomb that is being prepared for Joseph Smith's father, who had died a few years earlier. It is to be a family tomb. "I want this tomb prepared and I want my body to lay in it with my father if they [the mobbers] do not get it."

His enemies had threatened in print that their intention was to "make catfish meat of him." Not only did they intend to kill him, but they desired to cut up his body and throw it into the Mississippi River, where there were plenty of catfish. Joseph Smith is also aware that Missourians have placed a thousand dollars on his head, "as with John the Baptist, on a platter."

Safely surrounded by loyal men, Joseph begins the foreboding ride to Carthage. They pass several more homes and farms. Some people they acknowledge; others they pass with a gloomy silence. They call upon Daniel H. Wells, a non-Mormon at the time and a Nauvoo city official. He is ill, but Joseph Smith wants to say good-bye to him. "Wells, I wish you to cherish my memory, and not think me the worst man in the world either." Wells will hold Joseph Smith in high regard the rest of his life. He joins the Mormon Church two years later and eventually becomes an Apostle and counselor to Brigham Young.

At least twenty men are still accompanying Joseph. John Butler is one of the guards. He and the others are "all willing to live or die with them." As they push farther away from Nauvoo's city limits, Joseph pleads with Hyrum to take the bodyguard contingent and return to Nauvoo to enjoy the safety of the city and the company of their families. He argues that once he is dead there may be respite for the Saints. Hyrum refuses to leave his brother's side. "Joseph," he responds, "in the name of Israel's God I swear where you go, I will go and where you die, I will die." Joseph Smith takes a solitary glance to the ground. After pondering for a moment, he looks up and says to Hyrum, "Amen." They continue on.

By 10 a.m. they have arrived at Albert G. Fellow's farm four miles west of Carthage. As they come onto the farm, they see a militia approaching under the direction of Captain Dunn, who is sent by Governor Ford with some orders. Outnumbered, the Mormon men hear a tone of confidence from Joseph Smith. "Don't be alarmed, brethren, for they cannot do more to you than the enemies of truth did to the ancient Saints." And then in strange confidence, Joseph Smith says, "They can only kill the body." He could have finished the Savior's words for the brethren, "After that [they] have no more that they can do."

Joseph enters the home of the farm. Captain Dunn presents the orders from Governor Ford that the "state arms in possession of the Nauvoo Legion" be returned. Joseph Smith immediately counter-signs the orders. An appointed guard in the Nauvoo Legion, Henry G. Sherwood, volunteers to go back to Nauvoo ahead of the group and start collecting the arms. Joseph tells him to "do as well as he could in all things." He is submitting to all requests coming from Carthage. Before Sherwood leaves, Joseph Smiths arises and tells all in his hearing, "I am going like a lamb to the slaughter, but I am calm as a summer's morning. I have a conscience void of offense toward God and toward all men. If they take my life I shall die an innocent man, and my blood shall cry from the ground for vengeance, and it shall be said of me 'He was murdered in cold blood!'"

No one utters a word. Joseph then says to Sherwood, "Go, and God bless you." Sherwood rides as "swiftly" as he can to Nauvoo to begin the process of gathering all the state arms.

Dunn requests that Joseph and his bodyguard return to help see the orders through. Joseph, in company with Captain Dunn, backtracks to Nauvoo at a comfortable pace. As they make their way back, Dunn pledges his honor "as a military man" that all will be protected, "even if it were at the expense of his own life." His men give three cheers in agreement with their captain. The spirit of the Mormon men stays the same. They know few can be trusted.

While Joseph Smith returns to Nauvoo with Dunn, he sends a letter to Carthage. He lets Governor Ford know he is going back to Nauvoo to make sure his friends comply. He conveys in the letter that after the arms are secured in Dunn's charge, he will "cheerfully submit to any requisition." Hyrum sends a man by the name of Abram Hodge to Carthage with the letter. When he arrives, two neutral men give him warning. Pointing to the Carthage Greys, the town militia, the two men confirm, "There are the boys that will settle you Mormons." The two men represent the mood of the citizens. No one necessarily wants to see bloodshed, but neither do they want to see the rise and progress of Joseph Smith's movement.

Back in Nauvoo, the social hall is the appointed place to bring the state arms. When Joseph Smith and Dunn arrive back in Nauvoo, it is half past 2 p.m. For three and a half hours the call is made to relinquish state arms. Many reluctantly do so, observing and feeling another "Missouri massacre." With Joseph Smith's assurance, they comply. Governor Ford gives no orders that the militias in other cities give up their state arms. Many of the mobs can keep their arms. This is an alarming injustice and a strike against Ford's pretended impartiality. The Nauvoo Legion has only protected Nauvoo, while the mobs were combining and harassing the Saints in all the surrounding communities far outside their jurisdictions as county militias.

During the collection of the arms, Joseph returns twice to his family to say good-bye. Leonora Taylor, wife of Apostle John Taylor, is in the home when Joseph Smith returns. She witnesses Joseph urging "Emma to go to Carthage with him." Perhaps her presence may stay the violence. But being ill with chills and fever, Emma declines, putting her trust in the God who has delivered her husband countless times. With flowing tears and great anxiety, Joseph and Emma embrace for the last time. She is five months pregnant, perhaps another reason to stay behind.

Joseph's mother, Lucy, in anguish of the departure, says, "My Son, my Son, can you leave me without promising to return? Some forty times before have I have seen you from me dragged, but never before without saying you would return; What say you now my Son?" Joseph gives his mother and all those in the backdrop a different promise this time. "My friends . . . I love you, I love the City of Nauvoo too well to save my life at your expense,—If I go not to them they will come and act out the horrid Missouri scenes in Nauvoo;—I may prevent it, I fear not death, my work is well nigh done, keep the faith and I will die for Nauvoo."

He makes his way back to the social hall before departing for Carthage. In a private conversation with Joseph Noble and Hyrum, he expresses his swelling feelings. He asks Hyrum "what the spirit indicated to him." Hyrum admits that he can "get no satisfactory answer." Joseph fills Hyrum's void, "Well, if they kill me, I shall die innocent and my blood will be required of this nation, this day"

All three men proceed on their horses in muted contemplation.

When they arrive back at the social hall at 6 p.m., Captain Dunn gives a short speech and thanks the "peaceable citizens of Nauvoo." Again he promises to protect them and their leaders as they answer to the law in Carthage. As they prepare to ride away, Joseph Smith sits heartrendingly in the saddle and tells those gathered in a raised voice, "Boys, if I don't come back, take care of yourselves . . . keep the commandments of the Lord; I am going like a lamb to the slaughter." He turns and leaves the flats of Nauvoo for the last time. He emotionally climbs the bluff and passes the unfinished temple once again. He retraces the path to assassination for the second time in a day.

As he passes his farm, Joseph Smith looks back several times. The men traveling with him notice his glances backward. They inquire into his uneasiness. "If some of you had got such a farm and knew you would not see it anymore," he utters "you would want to take a good look at it for the last time." As they near the edge of the woods just outside Nauvoo, Hodge, who had been sent to Carthage by Hyrum, meets them. He has made his flight from Carthage speedily. "Brother Hyrum, you are now clear," Hodge immediately tells him, "and if it was my duty to counsel you, I would say, do not go another foot, for they say they will kill you." Others begin to gather around Hodge and Hyrum. Hodge holds his tongue and backs away as his eyes and shoulders turn down.

A letter from Carthage from Joseph Smith's legal counsel is delivered to him about the time of Hodge's rendezvous. His legal counsel encourages him to have ready all the documents and witnesses to show that the destruction of the *Nauvoo Expositor* wasn't carried out in a "riotous or tumultuous manner." Joseph's legal counsel feels Governor Ford is good on his word in protecting him from the mobs.

John Butler, who faithfully endured the Missouri troubles, is riding near the Prophet. Joseph Smith keeps telling those following him to return to Nauvoo. Butler and the others beg him to not request their return. They are willing to "stay with him and die with him, if necessary." To this Joseph emphatically says "no." They are to return home. Hyrum won't leave, and Joseph has given up on trying to persuade him. Butler witnesses the dear affection between the two brothers. As he and several others prepare to part ways with the two brothers, he feels that "something great [is] going to transpire." Joseph Smith turns to the men, blesses them, and then sends them off. Reluctantly the men bid him farewell.

The men turn their horses and ride nearly twenty miles back to Nauvoo; they go the "whole distance without uttering one word." All are still; even the horses seem subdued. No one can express his feelings. As Butler rides back, his mind and heart are being prepared that "the prophets of the Lord [are] about to be taken from us and that they [are] going to await their doom, the same as the Lord did when he was here upon the earth."

At 9 p.m. Joseph and Hyrum and a few others arrive back at Albert Fellows's farm, a friendly spot before the unfriendly greeting a few miles down the road in Carthage. They are able to rest their horses and themselves for a half hour. They take some refreshments and provisions that have been given to them in Nauvoo. Captain Dunn prepares to escort Joseph and Hyrum the last four miles.

They arrive in Carthage a few minutes before midnight.

Dunn takes them directly to Hamilton's Hotel, where Governor Ford is staying. The owner, Artois Hamilton, is aware of the threats and the intentions of those who have been gathered in and around his establishment for several days. When Joseph and Hyrum arrive, Ford is watching from a second floor window. The public square is full of madmen camouflaged in militias. Ford can hear and see as the Smith brothers precede through the thicket of murderous men. In the dark and a somewhat chaotic scene, someone shouts, "Where is the Damned prophet? . . . Stand away . . . let us shoot the damned Mormons. . . . G—d— you, old Joe, we've got you now. . . . Clear the way and let us have a view of Joseph Smith, the prophet of God. . . . He has seen the last of Nauvoo. . . . We'll use him up now, and kill all the damned Mormons."

Like a "pack of savages," the Carthage Greys are throwing their guns into the ground bayonet first. As they do so, they are "whooping, yelling, hooting and cursing."

Governor Ford turns the spotlight on himself by inserting his position and power as head of state. He speaks up from the window position. "I know your great anxiety to see Mr. Smith, which is natural enough, but it is quite too late tonight for you to have the opportunity; but I assure you, gentlemen, you shall have that privilege tomorrow morning, as I will cause him to pass before the troops upon the square, and I now wish you, with this assurance, quietly and peaceably to return to your quarters."

The bloodthirsty men, seen as "gentlemen" in Ford's eyes, give a feeble, "Hurrah for Tom Ford." They don't care for him but know he is shallow enough to wink at their treachery. They return to their quarters.

Joseph and Hyrum enter the Hamilton Hotel and find that the Law, Higbee, and Foster brothers are also checked into the hotel. Instead of the governor going to Nauvoo, he chooses to walk "arm in arm with Law and Foster" in Carthage. The Mormons "have reason to fear [Governor Ford] has caught their spirit."

The trigger happy Joseph Jackson is also present. But Joseph and Hyrum also have a few friends in the hotel. John A. Hicks, another apostate of the faith from Nauvoo, brags to Cyrus Wheelock, a confidant of Joseph and Hyrum, that he intends to shed the blood of Joseph Smith even if the law clears him. Wheelock tells Ford what Hicks boasted of. Ford looks at Wheelock with "perfect indifference" and does nothing.

Governor Ford defers the Smith brothers' arrest until the morning. With their "foes without" the hotel and "traitors within," Joseph and Hyrum close their eyes for some rest. They are fatigued by the emotional day of saying good-bye to their families, their city, and the people they love.

Chapter 50

MORNING HOURS UNTIL 4 P.M., TUESDAY, JUNE 25, 1844

Carthage, Illinois

AMILTON'S HOTEL IS a block east of the courthouse and public square. The gathering militias and mob can be heard. Many have gathered to get a glimpse of the Prophet. Others have gathered to end Joseph Smith's life. They are anxious to see their prize. Once again, Governor Ford pledges his protection. He tells the two brothers they "should have a fair and impartial trial."

After their breakfast, Joseph and Hyrum "voluntarily submit themselves" to Sheriff Bettisworth, "an overbearing, insolent officer." He holds a writ against them. By 8 a.m. Joseph and Hyrum are arrested for treason against the US government and the state of Illinois. The treason charge is because Joseph activated the Nauvoo Legion and declared marshal law in the city to protect themselves from the growing threats. Their enemies know the law can't get them, nor hold them, for riot in destroying the *Nauvoo Expositor* press. Those who want Joseph Smith dead anticipate "his release on riot." The "plotters" brag all morning that "if the treason charges [don't] succeed, they had eighteen others ready." The charges are lined up to keep Joseph Smith in Carthage. If they can keep him there long enough, eventually the murderers will find a moment to carry out their intentions.

The Hamilton Hotel with its distinguished guests isn't the place.

At 8:30 a.m. Governor Ford orders the troops lingering in and around the hotel to form a "hollow square on the public ground near the courthouse." He leaves Joseph and Hyrum in the hotel. Once the troops resemble some order, formed in a hollow square, Governor Ford stands on a table and addresses the men for over twenty minutes. He speaks flattery and pumps up his own image. His words "excite the feelings of indignation against Generals Joseph and Hyrum Smith." Ford gives his "assent and sanction to the rumors" of Joseph's and Hyrum's dangerous disposition and tyrannical behavior. Ford's "falsehoods and misrepresentations" in his speech incites the blood of Joseph Smith's enemies. Nonetheless, Ford reminds them they are "in the hands of the law, which must have its course."

Ford either ignores the fact or entirely misses it, but Mormons do hear his words to the mob. Joseph gets a report at the Hamilton Hotel before Ford returns at 9:15 a.m.

Governor Ford is ready to start the parade of Joseph and Hyrum Smith. He asks Joseph if he "will walk with him through the troops." Not declining the invitation, Joseph Smith first requests a private conversation with the governor. Ford looks down at his shoes and refuses. His tone and demeanor flip-flop within minutes. Bold and moving in public before hundreds of non-Mormons a few minutes before, he now can't even look Joseph Smith in the eyes in private. Notwithstanding, Joseph and Hyrum prepare to be paraded through the mob who has gathered as if preparing for major military action rather than a court proceeding.

Anxious onlookers also try to position themselves near the public square to get a look at a rising popular figure in America.

Joseph and Hyrum leave the hotel with Governor Ford and Miner Deming, the brigadier general of the Hancock County militia units. The people and troops they first pass on the way to the public square are quiet. The militia groups from McDonough County, east of Hancock County, have the privilege of being first to get a "clear view." Before proceeding to the hollow square, Joseph gets a ten-minute conversation with Ford. Again Ford pledges the "faith of the state" and that Joseph and "his friends will be protected from violence."

With another assurance from the head of the state, Joseph and Hyrum began their walk before the troops, seven minutes before 10 a.m. General Deming is in the middle, Joseph Smith is on his right, and Hyrum Smith is on his left. Three faithful Mormons—Willard Richards, John Taylor, and W. W. Phelps—are right behind them. Some of Deming's men are close behind, some even mingling in the crowd, ready to put down any disturbance. Governor Ford puts himself in the front of the parade. He introduces his guests over twenty times down the line as "General Joseph Smith and General Hyrum Smith."

There is no disorderly conduct, no disrespect to this point.

The demeanor of the parade changes when they approach the Carthage Greys. Threats and hisses roll forth. The Greys reject Ford introducing them as generals. We will "introduce [ourselves] to the damned Mormons in a different style." As their agitation increases, they throw "their hats" and draw their "swords." Ford "mildly" asks them not to "act so rudely." His mild manner only increases the intensity of their words, for they fear no substantial recourse. Ford once again pacifies the Carthage Greys with a matter-of-fact statement that you will have "full satisfaction." Spoken as if Ford knows how it will all end.

Ford, not wanting to break his pledge to the Smiths in public, rushes them back to the Hamilton Hotel. The governor's parade lasts about seven minutes. Joseph and Hyrum—and more friends who have recently arrived—are in two rooms. The Mormon men anxiously wait out the morning hours.

Back at the public square, the Carthage Greys are refusing to following orders. General Deming puts them under guard. By 11 a.m. he has them quieted. One thing has come out of the morning parade—the Carthage Greys are more mob than militia. They have no interest in law and order. By 11:15 a.m. Joseph learns that Warsaw troops are nearing Carthage. Thomas Sharp had published days before "summonses calling the entire militia to gather at Carthage or Warsaw to mobilize against Joe Smith." A few days later, Sharp boasts that his call to action against Joseph and Nauvoo has garnered "7000 armed men ready for the attack." Though Sharp's numbers are exaggerated, the call to mobilize men willing to dispose of Joseph Smith and break down the Mormon stronghold of Nauvoo is working.

A mixture of Warsaw troops and the agitated Carthage Greys only tightens Joseph's predicament. Several leading men in these two groups, along with wandering renegades from Missouri, have been plotting for months to rid the earth of Joseph Smith, and they would be glad to take out Hyrum Smith too. The two brothers are now confined with a few of their friends in two hotel rooms. The bloodthirsty mobs from these militia units have him right where they want him—almost. Joseph is still in Governor Ford's immediate proximity.

After his midday meal, people desire to have an interview with Joseph Smith. One of the men is from Warsaw—Mark Aldrich, a man serving as the US marshal for Illinois. "Several of the officers of the troops . . . and other gentlemen" come to Joseph's room. He cordially meets with them. A group is gathered, pressing to be in his presence. Joseph asks their honest opinion, "[Is] there anything in [my] appearance [that indicates I am] the desperate character [my] enemies represent [me] to be?"

"No sir," they reply. "Your appearance . . . indicates the very contrary . . . but we cannot see what is in your heart, neither can we tell what are your intentions." Joseph replies, "Very true, gentlemen, you cannot see what is in my heart, and you are therefore unable to judge me or my intentions." Not shying away from his prophetic role, he then tells them:

> But I can see what is in your hearts, and will tell you what I see. I can see that you thirst for blood, and nothing but my blood will satisfy you. . . . And inasmuch as you and the people thirst for blood, I prophesy, in the name of the Lord, that you shall witness scenes of blood and sorrow to your entire satisfaction. Your souls shall be perfectly satiated with blood, and many of you who are now present shall have an opportunity to face the cannon's mouth from sources you think not of; and those people that desire this great evil upon me and my brethren, shall be filled with regret and sorrow because of the scenes of desolation and distress that await them. They shall seek for peace, and shall not be able to find it. Gentlemen, you will find what I have told you to be true.

Again Joseph Smith wins the conversation. His listeners have little to say. The Civil War is seventeen years away. Most of the men chasing and hounding Joseph Smith will be at that time in their forties and will experience the atrocities of that war and see firsthand the cannon's mouth.

Ford reappears and tells Joseph Smith that he sent a contingent of men to Nauvoo to co-operate with the Nauvoo police in keeping the peace. Reports of plunder are increasing, and the Mormon men in Carthage request a guard on behalf of their people.

Joseph Smith is able to pen a quick note to his wife midafternoon. He conveys to her that the "Governor has just agreed to march his army to Nauvoo, and I shall come along with him." This promise gladdens his heart, and he hopes it will gladden Emma's. But Ford will not keep his promise.

Joseph Smith also sends word to Porter Rockwell, telling him not to come to Carthage and to stay in Nauvoo. Rockwell obeys his dear friend's request.

Chapter 51

TUESDAY EVENING, JUNE 25, 1844

Carthage, Illinois

*S*TILL SAFELY SEPARATED from the mobs in the Hamilton Hotel, Joseph Smith receives several reports. One report is the firestorm coming from the mouth of the Law, Higbee, and Foster brothers. Knowing that the honest rule of law would in the end vindicate Joseph and Hyrum, the trio of brothers incites the boiling emotions among the Carthage Greys and the Warsaw mob. "There [is] nothing against [the Smiths]; the law [can] not reach them but powder and ball [will] and they [will] not go out of Carthage alive." Such language ties them to the Warsaw mob. Editor of the *Warsaw Signal*, Thomas Sharp, used similar words a few weeks earlier.

They have to keep Joseph Smith in Carthage. To make sure this happens, Joseph and Hyrum are taken to Robert Smith (no relation), the justice of the peace, to answer the charges of riot in destroying the press. Robert Smith happens to be captain in the Carthage Greys. He himself has recently been arrested for mutiny but somehow now is worthy to sit as a justice of the peace. Justice Thomas Morrison of Carthage issued the writ against Joseph, Hyrum, and the others for riot, so legally they were to stand before Morrison. Even Governor Ford concurs. But nothing is done about it. They stand before Robert Smith, a "greater enemy of the defendants."

Joseph's attorneys acknowledge that there is "sufficient cause" to send the trial to the circuit court in session in a few months. However, the enemies know that gives Joseph too much time to flee. Justice of peace Robert Smith wants to be sure Joseph will be in court when the next term of the circuit court is in session. To do so, he makes an attempt to "overreach the wealth of the defendants and their friends." Fifteen Mormons are to give five hundred dollars each to assure their presence at the circuit court. This is a lot of money. In this attempt, Robert Smith is confident he can imprison them for not having bail.

To Robert Smith's surprise, the Mormon men meet the "strength to cover the demand." Many of them have to give the security to "the full extent of their property" to post the bail. But they do so without flinching. Though not behind bars, Joseph is still confined to the hotel, at least for the next three hours. During this time, Joseph Jackson is still spouting off. Pointing to his pistols, Jackson declares, "The balls are in there that will decide this case." One man goes upstairs to the Prophet's room and tells him what Jackson said. It is an unsettling three hours. The hotel is bustling with foot noise, all heading to and from Joseph Smith's room.

By 7:30 p.m. several of the Mormon men who posted bail for the charge of riot leave for Nauvoo. Though posting bail for the charge of riot, the charge of treason keeps Joseph and Hyrum in Carthage under hotel arrest. The Smith brothers are still not entirely alone. Other Mormon men are with them. Joseph and the others seek another interview with Ford to gain passes from the guards for their friends to come and go. Governor Ford approves their request. After their short interview with Ford, Joseph and Hyrum take their supper.

At 8 p.m. the overbearing and insolent Constable Bettisworth reappears, this time with a *mittimus*—"a warrant of commitment to jail or prison." He insists Joseph and Hyrum go to jail. Bettisworth can't produce a copy of the warrant when it is requested, but he again insists they go to jail. Joseph's attorneys step in and remind Bettisworth that any prisoner is "entitled to be brought before a justice of the peace . . . before they [can] be sent to jail." Suddenly, Bettisworth pulls out a *mittimus* from Robert Smith, a member of the Carthage

Greys. It is so blatantly false and illegal he was apparently hesitant to use it. He was hoping they would go to jail voluntarily. Joseph immediately protests against "such bare-faced, illegal, and tyrannical proceedings." The lawyers slow the illegal tyranny down by appealing to Governor Ford.

Governor Ford has lost interest in protecting the Smith brothers. Ford now winks when the Carthage Greys want to place them in jail illegally. Ford says the "executive power could only be called in to assist, and not dictate or control the action" of the local civil authorities. Ford also winks to the fact that Joseph Smith is being forced to answer before his known enemies rather than a partial judge and jury. Fairness and justice before the law are being blatantly abused, and Ford sanctions it.

It is at this time Ford begins to break all of his promises to Joseph and the Mormon people.

The Apostle John Taylor immediately pushes himself into the presence of Ford and calls him out. Taylor is maddened by the ridiculous indifference of Ford, especially when Ford knows the whole schism by the enemies of Joseph Smith is "vexatious prosecution." Ford tells Taylor that he is "very sorry" and that it is an "unpleasant affair, but it [is] a matter over which [I have] no control." Taylor reminds him of his promises regarding the Smiths' safety. Ford responds that if needed he would detail a guard to protect them.

At this, Taylor recognizes the shallowness of the governor. Taylor expresses his disgust in the proceedings to the governor: "If we are subject to mob rule, and to be dragged contrary to law into prison, at the instance of every infernal scoundrel whose oath could be bought for a dram of whiskey, [your] protection avail[s] very little, and we [have] miscalculated [your] promises." John Taylor leaves the wishy-washy governor and returns to Joseph Smith's room. Bettisworth's illegal warrant holds. He anxiously waits to escort Joseph and Hyrum to jail.

After posting excessive bail and without a hearing for the charges of treason, Joseph and Hyrum are led to jail. John Taylor, Willard Richards, Stephen Markham, Dan Jones, and four other men "join the procession." Markham is carrying a large hickory cane he has "nicknamed the rascal beater." Dan Jones "has his own smaller black hickory club." Though no match for the guns and fixed bayonets of the Carthage Greys, the clubs do come in handy to deflect the drunks who break ranks and come at the prisoners with bayonets down. Markham and Jones courageously deflect the blades. It is a dangerous walk; "a great rabble is gathered in the streets." Taylor is convinced the plan is to murder Joseph and Hyrum on the way to the jail. Carthage Jail is three blocks west and two blocks north of the Hamilton House. The distance gives plenty of time and provides plenty of positions for assassins to strike. The daylight is about gone. Darkness is settling in.

Captain Dunn, who had escorted Joseph Smith out of Nauvoo, now escorts him to the jail. Dunn to this point is keeping his word to protect Joseph Smith, "even if it [is] at the expense of his own life." The five-block march feels like five miles. Dunn and his men, along with the eight Mormon men still in close proximity to Joseph and Hyrum Smith, are able to convey them to the jail without serious incident. Because of the tension and behavior of the intensifying mob, the jailer, George Stigall, puts the Mormon men into the criminal cell located on the second story. The cell is dark, dingy, and not a comfortable place for summer visitors. It is a in every sense a "foul-smelling" dungeon. The cell room has one heavily barred window facing west and two ventilating slits in the brick for air and minimal view on the north.

Once the troops and questionable rascals outside the jail disperse for the night, Stigall moves the Mormon men back down to the first floor to occupy the more comfortable debtor's "apartment," which is furnished with a bench, some blankets, and a night bucket.

Here Joseph Smith, with his brother and friends, enjoys "amusing conversation on various interesting topics" dealing with the "secrets of godliness." A sacred feeling rests upon them. At 11:30 p.m. the men kneel for prayer. After the prayer, the men feel the prison has become "the gate of heaven." The sacred evening hours in conversation subdue all their fears. The men find a comfortable position on the floor. Ten bodies fill the floor of the room. The last words of the day are spoken by Joseph Smith. As he closes his eyes, he says, "For the most intelligent dream tonight brethren," expressing his confidence that God would speak to them in their sleep.

Chapter 52

WEDNESDAY MORNING, JUNE 26, 1844

Carthage Jail

JOSEPH SMITH BREAKS the silence of the morning around 6:30 a.m. by hearkening back to his last words the night before. He inquires among the ten men about any intelligent dreams.

Dan Jones responds.

During the night, Jones had a dream portraying Governor Ford and his troops marching across the prairie to Nauvoo without Joseph and Hyrum Smith. They had pled in vain to go, but he brushed them off and purposefully didn't take them. Jones also saw himself in the dream being driven from Carthage, "galloping through the masses," which he describes as a "medley of soldiers, half Indians, and semi barbarians." Jones saw his deliverance from the rowdy masses and his safe arrival in Nauvoo, where he boarded his boat and made way to Quincy, Illinois, fifty miles south of Nauvoo. However, in his dream his boat stopped for a time at Warsaw en route to Quincy. At this point in his dream, he saw the "midst of powder, smoke, death, and carnage" coming from Warsaw.

All the other prisoners acknowledge the dream is from God. Joseph Smith had earlier taught: "We believe that we have a right to revelations, visions, and dreams from God, our Heavenly Father; and light and intelligence, through the gift of the Holy Ghost . . . on all subjects pertaining to our spiritual welfare; if it so be that we keep His commandments, so as to render ourselves worthy in his sight." Jones has proven worthy. A native of Wales and a member of the Mormon Church for just over a year, he has shown his willingness to sacrifice and defend Joseph Smith at all cost. The dream gives Joseph some insight on his temporal welfare. And it is gloomy. He is about to be left in the hands of his enemies as the highest ranking civic officer in the state of Illinois turns his back.

The nine men are captivated by Jones's dream. They sit still and ask no further questions as to the imagery or its meaning. Joseph Smith breaks the silence by commenting that the dream was of God and showed the threatening events before him and his friends. The dream will be fulfilled in a few days. He expresses to Dan Jones and the others that he never believed "the governor would ever take him to Nauvoo alive."

They eat breakfast at 7 a.m. with the jailer, George Stigall, and his family—his wife, his sixteen-year-old son, Henry, and at least two daughters. Stigall sees the rubbish gathering outside and feels Joseph Smith and his company will be safer in an upstairs bedroom with a bed, additional mattresses, and some chairs. Though it is the most comfortable room Stigall can offer, its detriment is three large windows, two on the south side and one on east side. The door to the room is "pine . . . without bolts, lock, or even a latch that [will] shut" properly. The door is warped. Dan Jones spends time hewing the warped door with his penknife to get it to close with the latch. This he does knowing a "night attack" is possible. Jones doesn't like the visibility from the windows. It provides the assassins easy shots into nearly every corner of the room.

Stephen Markham silently observes their predicament. A few days earlier, Joseph Smith told him "that if I and Hyrum were ever taken again we should be massacred, or I was not a prophet of God." The situation and the prophecy bear down upon his spirit. Markham, however, responds to Joseph Smith's request at 7:30 a.m. to take a message to Governor Ford. Dan Jones and a man named Lorenzo Wasson accompany him.

While Joseph awaits their return, he and Hyrum converse with the jailer. Stigall conveys to them that a week ago a mob had made every attempt to attack Nauvoo. After sending "runners to Missouri and all around the counties of Illinois," they could only gather two hundred people. They were hoping for nine hundred, Stigall reports. Their actual numbers depressed their attempt to attack.

Joseph is growing impatient. He asks Stigall if he will take a message to the governor. Stigall agrees. It is a short message. Joseph expresses his disappointment at Ford's rejection the night before and hopes Ford will not deny him an interview this morning. He reminds the governor, "We have been committed under a false mittimus, and consequently the proceedings are illegal." He then expresses, "We desire the time may be hastened when all things shall be made right, and be relieved from this imprisonment."

While Stigall is delivering Joseph's correspondence, Markham and Jones return. The governor made them believe he was surprised at the events of the evening prior "and was sorry." They also report that the governor feels he is doing all in his power and the "wrath of the people [is] about to turn on the head of [Joseph] Jackson, the mob, &c." Twelve minutes before 9 a.m., Stigall returns with a one-line reply from the governor: "The interview will take place at my earliest leisure to-day."

The governor doesn't delay. He arrives at Carthage Jail a few minutes before 9:30 a.m. Joseph Smith is able to present in greater detail the facts "relating to the Expositor press" and the "course pursued by the City Council." He also explains why he called out the Nauvoo Legion and declared marshal law, to protect the city and not present a threat to the state. He then asks why Ford called the "military array" gathered in Carthage. The governor denies he called out the military (mob) array in Carthage and tells Joseph that they assembled "without his orders."

Again Ford pledges that they should be protected and the laws rightfully enforced. He also tells them again he is going to march to Nauvoo and bring them along. Ford acknowledges to Joseph Smith that he and his friends have not been given sufficient time to prepare themselves as defendants. He also admits that Joseph Smith's account of the situation is true. He even tells Joseph that "the people of Nauvoo had acted according to the best of their judgment." Joseph Smith offers to pay for the loss of the Expositor press, but he also expresses he will not allow a libelous paper to be published in Nauvoo.

The interview ends with Joseph stating, "Governor Ford, I ask nothing but what is legal, I have a right to expect protection at least from you; for, independent of law, you have pledged your faith, and that of the State, for my protection, and I wish to go to Nauvoo."

"And you shall have protection," Ford tells him. "I do not know that I shall go tomorrow to Nauvoo, but if I do, I will take you along." Ford abruptly leaves by 10:15. The forty-five-minute interview only sinks Ford deeper and deeper into the river of lies.

He changes his tune and demeanor outside the jail. Thomas Gregg is with the governor and had heard the whole interview with the Mormon prophet. As they are leaving the jail, Ford says aloud in Gregg's hearing, "It is all nonsense; you will have to drive these Mormons out yet!" Gregg fills out the governor's feelings. "If we undertake that, governor, when the proper time comes, will you interfere?" To this Ford replies, "No, I will not." With a sigh and a pause, he adds, "Until you are through." Another officer tells Ford, "The soldiers are determined to see Joe Smith dead before they leave here." Ford quiets the officer, "If you know of any such thing keep it to yourself."

Ford wants Illinois to be rid of the Mormons, but he wants "it done in such a way that he could not personally be tied to the bloodshed."

Joseph Smith, discerning the shallowness of Ford, immediately sits down at the jailor's desk and writes a letter to Judge Jesse B. Thomas, associate justice of the Illinois Supreme Court. He presents his predicament of being in prison on a false mittimus, without having gone before a magistrate. He asks Judge Thomas to go to Nauvoo, at his expense, and make himself comfortable at his home until papers and witnesses can be presented to him. In turn, he also asks Judge Thomas to bring him, Joseph Smith, to Nauvoo on habeas corpus. "Our witnesses are all at Nauvoo," he writes. "The excitement and prejudice is such in this place, testimony is of little avail."

Judge Thomas declines to put forth his legal authority, citing lack of jurisdiction in the treason charge. Joseph, trying to expand his chances of getting out of Carthage for a fair trial, also asks that his attorneys, Reid and Woods, seek a change of legal proceedings to Quincy. Joseph hasn't forgotten the kindness many of the residents of Quincy showed the Saints when they were being driven from Missouri in the winter of 1838–39. Though some have turned against the Saints, Quincy does not have the anti-Mormon spirit so prevalent in Warsaw and Carthage.

Carthage is a death trap, and he knows he has little time before the trap releases on him. He has to get out. Samuel Williams, who has command of the Carthage Greys, admits that many in his company are growing more and more unruly. They are "full of all kinds of hissing, groaning . . . and discordant sounds." Williams is trying to "preserve silence" but has "no more command over them."

Any known Mormons lingering in Carthage are being "harassed" out of town at this time.

Chapter 53

WEDNESDAY AFTERNOON, JUNE 26, 1844

Carthage Jail and the Courthouse

THE THREE WINDOWS in the room where Joseph Smith and his friends are confined are open for ventilation. They can hear much of their enemies' excitement near the jail. They can hear the interchanges between the mob and the six to eight men left to guard the jail. The guards are men from the Carthage Greys. The situation sets up a dangerous afternoon. The prisoners have intermittent moments of calm but with "belying tension."

Willard Richards, the Prophet's scribe and one of the Apostles, is again straining his muscles in his writing hand. Correspondences are being sent in every direction. John Taylor, another Apostle present, is singing. Dan Jones and Stephen Markham are giving their undivided attention to the warped door. They get the door and the latch to finally cooperate. Joseph and Hyrum are preaching to the guards with success. Several of the guards are relieved during their shift because they grow soft and agreeable to the prisoners' position. Many of the men admit they are being "imposed upon" to accept the order to guard the Smiths. Several times Joseph and Hyrum hear the guards who voluntarily walk away say, "Let us go home boys, for I will not fight any longer against these men."

Hyrum Smith is cheered by their ability to win some of the hearts of the Carthage Greys. Perhaps the Lord, "for his Church's sake," will provide a way for his brother to get out of prison unharmed. Joseph's spirit isn't cheered as much as Hyrum's. "Could my brother Hyrum but be liberated, it would not matter so much to me." Joseph desires Hyrum to live and help the Church on its destiny. And then Joseph reflects on Sidney Rigdon, who had been faithfully by his side for nearly ten of the fourteen years of the Church's existence. Rigdon, who in Joseph's eyes has lost his spiritual rigor and common sense, is nowhere close to Carthage. And Joseph is content with that. "Poor Rigdon, I am glad he is gone to Pittsburg out of the way; were he to preside he would lead the Church to destruction in less than five years."

But the destiny of the Church and its next leaders is suspended as the events at Carthage unfold.

The jailer, Stigall, is being kind to the prisoners and not buying the illegality of the mob's requests. Someone from the prosecution wants the prisoners to be examined. Stigall, along with Joseph's attorneys, say the prisoners have already been committed and cannot be removed without due course of the law. Justice Robert Smith and the constable no longer have "control over the prisoners." This doesn't settle well with them, and their anger is heightened.

They keep up their demands. Stigall says he won't let the prisoners out of his jail unless "one or two leaders of the mob" can be "obtained to walk arm in arm with the prisoners" to the courthouse. Joseph receives a letter from General Deming stating that the governor has ordered him to protect Joseph Smith under all circumstances. But Ford is clearly passive on the earnestness of the situation, and arguably so are those following the order.

Nonetheless by 4 p.m., Joseph and Hyrum are forced from prison. They pass Robert Foster, who has recently admitted that Joseph has "done nothing against the law." This is strange irony because Foster had a financial interest in the *Nauvoo Expositor*. Frank Worrell is also present when Joseph and Hyrum are forced from the jail to immediately be taken to the courthouse. Worrell intimidates and threatens Stigall.

Stigall loses the fight to keep them at the jail. He knows Joseph and Hyrum are innocent men.

Joseph, seeing the lot he has been dealt, grabs his hat and walks boldly out of the jail into the "midst of the hollow" formation of the "Carthage Greys."

He expects to be massacred in the streets before arriving at the courthouse. Hyrum is within arms length of his younger brother. Joseph "politely locks arms with the worst mobocrats he [can] see." Hyrum locks onto Joseph's arm. Willard Richards, Taylor, Jones, Markham, and John Fullmer are in tow. The mobocrats have their rifles pointed at them. Once again, Jones and Markham courageously smack back the barrels and bayonets with their clubs. The drunkenness is apparent, and the threats are spewing from the mob. "Now, old Joe, if you are a prophet, how did you come to jail like this?" some shout in his face. Another haunting voice is heard, "If Joe were a prophet, he would soon call for a legion of angels, and we would all be killed, and he would escape."

Joseph Smith's attorneys are bewildered amidst the illegal nonsense. However, a postponement until the next day is granted. Witnesses will be subpoenaed. Justice Robert Smith again orders them back to the jail on the basis of another mittimus.

Passing through the drunken rabble once again, Joseph and his loyal friends hear the screeching. There is plenty of "whooping, hallooing and denunciations." Joseph says nothing as "some tauntingly upbraid him for not calling a legion of angels to release him." Others wonder aloud why he can't deliver himself and "destroy his enemies, inasmuch as he pretends to have a miraculous power." Yet others are squawking for him to "prophesy when and what manner of death awaits" him. The same spirits that mocked Jesus Christ are present. Joseph and Hyrum walk back to the jail unharmed and enter their final evening in confinement, their final evening in mortality.

Chapter 54

WEDNESDAY EVENING TO MIDNIGHT, JUNE 26, 1844

Carthage Jail

OSEPH, HYRUM, AND their friends arrive back at Carthage Jail about 5:30 p.m. It is early summer, which means there is plenty of daylight. The day is proving to be oppressive and long. The heat and humidity compound their discomfort. The windows in the upper room of the jail remain open. Shortly after their return, Joseph and Hyrum hear a familiar voice below trying to get into the jail. It is their uncle John Smith. He miraculously makes it safely to the jail. En route he dodged numerous mobbers along the road. Three times guns shot at him and several others threatened him when they realized who he is.

He abruptly dismounts his horse and makes a bold attempt to go right into the jail.

The guards at the jail reject him. Words are exchanged. Looking down from one of the south facing windows, Joseph can see his uncle's interchange with the guards at the door. "Let the old gentleman come in, he is my uncle." One of the guards looks up at Joseph, "[We] do not care who the hell he was uncle to, he should not go in." The Prophet-prisoner doesn't cower back into the room. "You will not hinder so old and infirm a man as he is from coming in," he yells down at the abusive guards. Then, speaking as if he is the mayor of Carthage or at least the jailor, Joseph Smith says, "Come in uncle."

The guards don't answer in return. "Searching him closely," the guards let Uncle Smith enter.

He stays an hour. Uncle Smith asks about Joseph's sentiments. "Will [you] again get out of the hands of [your] enemies?"

"Hyrum thinks I shall," Joseph replies.

After they visit, Joseph requests that he track down a man in the neighboring town of Macedonia. He would like his help as an attorney for the expected trial the next day.

Uncle Smith leaves his nephews and rides to Macedonia.

About this time the jailor, Stigall, gets a unique request from the governor via a short correspondence. It is growing evident that Governor Ford is tipping his hat to the mob. "I would advise the jailor to keep the Messrs. Smith," he writes, "in the same room in which I found them this morning, unless a closer confinement should be clearly necessary to prevent an escape." He signs it "Governor and Commander in-chief." Ford is helping the mob with this request. The room they are in is arguably the best situation for the growing trigger-driven mob. They can shoot from the landing at the top of the stairs and from outside into the windows of the room.

A letter from William Clayton, one of Joseph's secretaries in Nauvoo, arrives. Joseph is comforted with the kindness of his friends in and around Nauvoo. Clayton conveys that Latter-day Saints are willing and ready to post any amount of bail. "All is peace in Nauvoo," he writes. "Many threats keep coming that the mob are determined to attack the city in your absence, but we have no fears." The correspondence cheers Joseph Smith. He tells the messenger who brought the letter to return to Nauvoo immediately and obtain certain documents for the next day's trial.

Joseph and those with him eat supper at 8 p.m.

As they finish their meal, Joseph's attorneys visit him. They have just learned that Governor Ford held a council with all his military officers in Carthage. The attorneys, Wood and Reid, tell Joseph that the decision by the council is to march to Nauvoo tomorrow morning at 8 a.m., without Joseph and Hyrum. A guard of fifty men (the Carthage Greys under Robert Smith's command) is to be left in Carthage to protect them. Ford also asks that the trial be moved to Saturday, June 29. His contingency will return from Nauvoo on the evening of June 28. Every hour reveals whom Governor Ford is trying to pacify. Though he will try in coming days to distance himself from the events at Carthage, Ford is easily wrapped up in the plot. He isn't ignorant of his position and his role. Before dying, he expresses his fears in writing that he will be immortalized as a Pilot or a Herod.

The attorneys' news isn't very comforting. They stay for nearly forty-five minutes, discussing Joseph's options. His attorneys return to the Hamilton Hotel, not knowing the course they should pursue. Those interested in Joseph Smith's well-being at Carthage are dwindling.

Five men are still with Joseph and Hyrum—John Taylor, Willard Richards, John Fullmer, Stephen Markham, and Dan Jones. At 9:15 p.m., Taylor offers a prayer. After the devotion, Hyrum reads and comments on extracts from the Book of Mormon that describe servants of God in past generations who suffered imprisonments and deliverance for the gospel's sake. Hyrum extends his hope and his confidence while their personal safety is becoming dreadfully dire.

The guards, standing and sitting on the landing at the top of the stairs, listen with interest to Hyrum's words and testimony. When he finishes, Joseph turns his preaching directly to the guards. Dan Jones marvels at his composure and spiritual power as Joseph explains the "divine authenticity of the Book of Mormon—the restoration of the Gospel [of Jesus Christ], the administration of angels, and that the Kingdom of God is again upon the earth."

The guards listen intently, their crudeness and angst against the man is subdued. It is well known that Joseph Smith usually won out if he could get peoples' ears in a fair environment. This is one reason the guards were changed out every few hours. He tells the guards on duty he has violated no law of God or of man. They don't deny it. They leave the prisoners alone in their room. The sun has now fallen behind the west horizon. Joseph and Hyrum lie on the bed. The other men occupy the mattress on the floor next to the bed while Willard Richards records the dealings of the day and responds to correspondences. He has little candle light remaining.

The men are mentally exhausted.

Sometime around 11 p.m., a gunshot is heard near the jail. Joseph, a little anxious about his security, arises from the bed and finds a comfortable position near the men occupying the mattress on the floor.

The candle burns out. Willard Richards takes Joseph's place on the bed next to Hyrum. Dan Jones is lying to Joseph's left, and John S. Fullmer on his right. Joseph extends his right arm to John Fullmer and says, "Lay your head on my arm for a pillow Brother John."

It is late. Some of the men quickly fall asleep.

Joseph, Dan Jones, and John Fullmer converse in soft tones "about the prospects of their deliverance." At this quiet moment, Joseph tells them "several presentiments." He opens up and tells the men he has to die.

THE WORDS OF the writer of Hebrews convey Joseph's forebodings: "For where a testament is, there must also of necessity be the death of the testator. For a testament is of force after men are dead; otherwise it is of no strength at all while the testator liveth." Joseph Smith taught a reality of the Godhead that contradicted Christianity's tenets on who God was and is. He declared that he was a prophet, an instrument that helped establish under divine mandate the Church of Jesus Christ. He introduced temple worship much like Moses did to the children of Israel and the prophets in Solomon's day.

FOR JOSEPH SMITH, this testament will require his blood. He knows he will be brutally killed. He just doesn't know how. The anxiety is building, yet he stays calm and in control. He tells Fullmer and Jones, "I would like to see my family again," and also, "I would to God that I could preach to the Saints in Nauvoo once more." The "once more" expresses his feeling that time is running out. Fullmer tries to "rally" his friend's spirit, suggesting his confidence that he "would often have that privilege." Joseph thanks Fullmer for the hope and "good feelings expressed to him."

Fullmer falls asleep.

After a few minutes of silence, Joseph discerns that he and Dan Jones are the only ones still awake. In a soft whisper, Joseph says to Jones, "Are you afraid to die?"

Jones answers back, "Has that time come, think you? Engaged in such a cause I do not think that death would have many terrors." Joseph Smith's prophetic gift surfaces at the dismal moment, and he says to Jones, "You will yet see Wales, and fulfill the mission appointed you before you die." Jones doesn't entirely understand that mission, but he will step foot in Wales in 1845 and stay for four years. When he arrives, there will be two hundred and fifty Mormons in the country. When he returns home in 1849, there will be "nearly four thousand Welshmen who call themselves Mormons." Dan Jones relies upon this sacred moment lying on the floor of Carthage Jail for the rest of his life. The prophecy will be tested severely for the next sixteen hours.

Both men go silent and fall asleep.

At midnight, Jones is disturbed in his sleep. He arises and goes to the window overlooking the doorway of the jail. He sees a large gathering of men. Jones can hear the men below discussing "who, and how many shall go in." His rustling in the dark room stirs the others, but not until he gave an alarm did they all arise to their feet. Suddenly, the mad dash of men climbing the stairs moves all the prisoners in harmony near the door. They had placed a chair against the door earlier in the evening as "precaution to fortify" themselves. In their urgency to defend themselves, one of the men in the room takes the chair and prepares to use it as a weapon.

They stand by the door awaiting the mob's entrance. The prisoners' quick response and heavy breathing at the door draws out the cowardice in those who storm the jail. They hesitate, and confidence gives way to cowardice. Joseph Smith senses their paralyzing stance. He calls out to them from behind the door. "Come on ye assassins we are ready for you, and would as willingly die now as at daylight." At these words, the mob returns downstairs and consults. They advance and retreat alternately throughout the night, evidently failing to agree, "until the assassin's terror—the morning light" chases the murderers away.

Notwithstanding the mobs nighttime harassment in front of the jail, Joseph is able to obtain some sleep.

Chapter 55

THURSDAY EARLY MORNING HOURS, JUNE 27, 1844

Carthage Jail, Illinois

OSEPH RISES FROM bed at 5:30 a.m. The sole window in the east wall allows him to view his last sunrise. Before sunset, the window will become a passage to another realm of existence.

As soon as all of the men stir, Joseph Smith tells Dan Jones to go downstairs and ask the guards the "cause of the disturbance in the night." A bitter man, an officer of the guard, and a member of the Carthage Greys, Frank Worrell tells Dan Jones abruptly, "We have had too much trouble to bring Old Joe here to let him ever escape alive, and unless you want to die with him you had better leave before sundown; and you are not a damned bit better than him for taking his part." And then in a more threating and mocking tone, Worrell declares, "You'll see that I can prophesy better than Old Joe, for neither he nor his brother, nor anyone who will remain with them will see the sun set today."

Worrell knows his murderous friends are gathering in Warsaw just to the west of Carthage. The plan has been laid, and Worrell is confident the hour of killing Joseph is nigh.

Dan Jones doesn't question Worrell's intentions. He immediately goes to Governor Ford at the Hamilton House. While en route, he hears a man standing before an assemblage giving a speech. "Our troops will be discharged this morning in obedience to orders, and for a sham we will leave the town; but when the Governor and the McDonough troops have left for Nauvoo this afternoon, we will return and kill those men, if we have to tear the jail down." The man's speech gets "three cheers from the crowd." In some regards, the boastful declaration is only partly true. Carthage Jail is a unique structure built from native red limestone and is only five years old. The man giving the fiery speech is flexing more of his tongue than his muscles. The jail will stand through the coming onslaught of assassins.

Jones immediately conveys to Governor Ford all that he has heard from Worrell and the man giving the speech. Without much emotion, Ford blows Jones off. "You are unnecessarily alarmed for the safety of your friends, sir, the people are not that cruel."

Dan Jones is beside himself. He boldly confronts the governor. "The Messrs. Smith are American citizens, and have surrendered themselves to your Excellency upon your pledging your honor for their safety; they are also Master Masons, and as such I demand of you protection of their lives." Jones emphasizes that better men be granted to guard his friends and not "professed assassins."

Jones's words leave Ford pale in the face and nearly speechless. Jones continues his demand and warning to the executive of the state. "If you do not do this, I have but one more desire, and that is if you leave their lives in the hands of those men to be sacrificed"—a quailing Ford musters in a hurried tone, "What is [your desire], sir?"

"It is . . . that the Almighty will preserve my life to a proper time and place, that I may testify that you have been timely warned of their danger." Dan Jones has Ford pinned. He rushes back to the jail, clearly understanding Ford's position and plans. The guards refuse him entrance. Seeking a pass to reenter the jail, he returns to the Hamilton House. But Governor Ford is done with Dan Jones. The man is showing a remarkable stand in behalf of Joseph and Hyrum Smith. Ford needs to rid himself of the man. He rejects Jones's request.

Dan Jones then witnesses another scene of injustice all in the hearing and in the sight of the governor. While Ford is "standing in front of the McDonough troops, who [are] in line ready to escort him to Nauvoo," those acting more mob than militia pretend they are disbanding. They are at the rear of the McDonough troops and can be heard by all "that they were only going a short distance out of town, when they would return and kill old Joe and Hyrum as soon as the Governor was far enough out of town."

It is impossible to not have heard the words of the murders. Jones looks at the governor for a response. Ford says and does nothing.

Mormon apostate Chauncey L. Higbee confronts Jones, "We are determined to kill Joe and Hyrum, and you had better go away to save yourself." Jones stands in awe at the events unfolding. He puts forth his influence and bravery to stop the madness. His life is not in danger. He is granted the desire of his heart to live and testify of the injustice he is witnessing.

It is now 7 a.m. Joseph, Hyrum, and the remaining few have breakfast. A Mr. Crane eats with them and wants to know if the reports he heard about Joseph Smith fainting three times before the troops on Tuesday is true. "He is told it is a false report."

Cyrus Wheelock, another unwavering Mormon, approaches Governor Ford by 8 a.m. Ford has softened a bit, with the fiery Jones not in his presence. He grants Wheelock a pass to see his friends in jail.

Joseph Smith is anxious to get a letter off to his wife. With the help of Willard Richards, he conveys some final sentiments.

> Dear Emma.—The Governor continues his courtesies, and permits us to see our friends. We hear this morning that the Governor will not go down with his troops today to Nauvoo, as we anticipated last evening; but if he does come down with his troops you will be protected; and I want you to tell Brother Dunham to instruct the people to stay at home and attend to their own business, and let there be no groups or gathering together, unless by permission of the Governor, they are called together to receive communications from the Governor, which would please our people, but let the Governor direct.
>
> Brother Dunham of course will obey the orders of the government officers, and render them the assistance they require. There is no danger of any extermination order. Should there be a mutiny among the troops (which we do not anticipate, excitement is abating) a part will remain loyal and stand for the defense of the state and our rights. There is one principle which is eternal; it is the duty of all men to protect their lives and the lives of the household, whenever

necessity requires, and no power has a right to forbid it, should the last extreme arrive, but I anticipate no such extreme, but caution is the parent of safety.

Joseph Smith.

And then in a melancholy postscript he writes:

P. S.—Dear Emma, I am very much resigned to my lot, knowing I am justified, and have done the best that could be done. Give my love to the children and all my friends, Mr. Brewer, and all who inquire after me; and as for treason, I know that I have not committed any, and they cannot prove anything of the kind, so you need not have any fears that anything can happen to us on that account. May God bless you all. Amen.

Joseph Smith's attorneys arrive midmorning. They tell him that the governor is not taking the whole army to Nauvoo, only a portion. Sometime before they arrive, a meeting has taken place with Ford, his officers, and several other men. A friend of the Mormons—Dr. Southwick, who has recently arrived from Louisiana—was in the meeting to learn of the subject matter. He tells Stephen Markham, who is still close to the Prophet in jail, that the "purport of the meeting was to take into consideration the best way to stop Joseph Smith's career, as his views on government were widely circulated and [were taking] like wildfire." Southwick heard them argue that "if he, [Joseph Smith], did not get into the Presidential chair this election, he would be sure to the next time; and if Illinois and Missouri would join together and kill him, they would not be brought to justice for it." Dr. Southwick assures Stephen Markham that Governor Ford and Robert Smith were in the meeting.

Joseph and Hyrum are about to be left solely in the hands of the Carthage Greys. Many of them were under arrest two days earlier for "insulting the commanding general, and whose conduct had been more hostile to the prisoners than that of any other company." Now they are left unfettered to carry out their evil deed. To protect the road coming into Nauvoo, Governor Ford assigns two hundred men eight miles out of town on the Warsaw Road "under the control of Levi William, a notoriously sworn enemy to Joseph." On this road later in the day, drunken men seeking to kill Joseph Smith will make their way to Carthage. Levi Williams will not stop them but will join them.

Ford is aware of the looming actions. So is Cyrus Wheelock. He is about to use his pass to visit his friends and then return to Nauvoo just ahead of Ford and the troops. To Ford, Wheelock expresses, "Sir . . . you have heard sufficient to justify you in the belief that their enemies would destroy them if they had them in their power; and now, sir, I am about to leave for Nauvoo, and I fear for those men; they are safe as regards to the law, but they are not safe from the hands of traitors, and midnight assassins who thirst for their blood and have determined to spill it."

Then with strong emotion, Wheelock says in an earnest voice, "Under these circumstances I leave with a heavy heart."

Ford then admits to Wheelock that the pressure he is getting from Joseph's enemies is conflicting him. "I was never in such a dilemma in my life." Ford is siding with the wrong side of justice and decency. The political pressure, the praise and threats to his person, and the secret meetings to stop Joseph Smith's religious and political career are mounting on his mental faculties. Ford tries to assure Wheelock, "Your friends shall be protected, and have a fair trial by the law; in this pledge I am not alone; I have obtained the pledge of the whole of the army to sustain me." But Ford knows that army is about to set off to Nauvoo and leave Joseph hauntingly alone in Carthage Jail in the shadows of the Carthage Greys.

Having spoken his mind, Cyrus Wheelock somberly makes his way to the jail to see his friends for the last time. He has Ford's pass and easily gets entrance. Because of the wet weather of the morning, Wheelock is wearing an overcoat. Inside the coat he has slipped "an Ethan Allen dragoon-style pepperbox pistol into his pocket," apparently belonging to John Taylor, who still sits in jail with the Smith brothers. It is a "six-shooter." Wheelock places the gun into Joseph's pocket. "Should you not retain it for your own protection?" Joseph asks Wheelock. He declines and considers the situation providential. "Most other persons had been very rigidly searched" the past two days when they made visits.

Joseph then turns to Hyrum and hands him a single barrel pistol he had been given by John S. Fullmer. "You may have use for this," he tells Hyrum. To which Hyrum honestly responds, "I hate to use such things or to see them used."

"So do I," says Joseph, "but we may have to, to defend ourselves."

Hyrum—without protest—takes the pistol.

Joseph stresses to Wheelock that upon his return to Nauvoo he is to urge all commanders of the Nauvoo Legion to not instigate any military action. He is also charged by his prophet-friend to tell all the Saints to "remain perfectly calm and quiet" as the events unfold. And then what might be considered Joseph's last sermon, and before a small audience, he teaches:

> Our lives have already become jeopardized by revealing the wicked and bloodthirsty purposes of our enemies; and for the future we must cease to do so. All we have said about them is truth, but it is not always wise to relate all the truth. Even Jesus, the Son of God had to refrain from doing so, and had to restrain His feelings many times for the safety of Himself and His followers, and had to conceal the righteous purposes of His heart in relation to many things pertaining to His Father's kingdom. When still a boy He had all the intelligence necessary to enable Him to rule and govern the kingdom of the Jews, and could reason with the wisest and most profound doctors of law and divinity, and make their theories and practice to appear like folly compared with the wisdom He possessed; but He was a boy only, and lacked physical strength even to defend His own person, and was subject to cold, to hunger and to death. So it is with the Church of Jesus Christ of Latter-day Saints; we have the revelation of Jesus, and the knowledge within us is sufficient to organize a righteous government upon the earth, and to give universal peace to all mankind, if they would receive it, but we lack the physical strength, as did our Savior when a child, to defend our principles, and we have of necessity to be afflicted, persecuted and smitten, and to bear it patiently until Jacob is of age, then he will take care of himself.

In silence, the small audience contemplates the message.

So much goes unsaid. Wheelock is then given a list of names of men who should come to Carthage by Saturday to be witnesses in the trial. The prisoners give verbal messages to Wheelock to take back to their families in Nauvoo. Willard Richards, the Prophet's secretary, purposes they be written down, fearing they may be forgotten. Hyrum Smith places his hands on Wheelock's shoulders and fastens his eyes upon him. "With a look of penetration" he says aloud for all in the room to hear, "Brother Wheelock will remember all that we tell him, and he will never forget the occurrences of this day."

As Cyrus Wheelock's interview with Joseph ends, Governor Ford lines up his men to March to Nauvoo.

Chapter 56
THURSDAY, 9:30 A.M., JUNE 27, 1844
Carthage Jail, Illinois

IN HIS LAST slumber in mortality, Joseph Smith captures a dream. The morning is hectic, and he is unable to express it. By 10 a.m. he has a moment to outline what rested on his mind a few hours earlier.

"I was back in Kirtland, Ohio," he tells those in his hearing. Kirtland was the headquarters for The Church of Jesus Christ of Latter-day Saints from the winter of 1831 to the winter of 1838. Joseph Smith had to leave in the middle of winter, at night, to escape those who were seeking to kill him at that time. In his dream, he was walking by himself and desired to visit his old farm. When his farm, which he hadn't seen for over seven and half years, appeared in his dream, he found it was "grown up with weeds and brambles, and altogether bearing evidence of neglect and want of culture."

He desired to examine the structures of the farm.

His dream next took him inside his barn. As he went into the barn, he found that the floor had been removed by vandals and thieves. It was also without doors. The weatherboarding was off, and the whole structure was in need of someone to take of it. The condition of the farm and the barn saddened him.

"While I viewed the desolation around me," he tells his friends "[I] was contemplating how it might be recovered from the curse upon it." As he stood in contemplation, "there came rushing into the barn a company of furious men, who commenced to pick a quarrel with me." The dream was vivid and descriptive of the quarrel with men he has had his entire life.

"The leader" of the furious men ordered him to "leave the barn and farm, stating it was none of [his], and that [he] must give up all hope of ever possessing it." In his dream, Joseph responded to the leader of the mob, "I told him the farm was given me by the Church, and although I had not had any use of it for some time back, still I had not sold it, and according to righteous principles it belonged to me or the Church." At this, the agitator turned even more madly on Joseph "and began to rail upon [him] and threaten [him], and said it never did belong to [him] nor to the Church."

As if the dream was really playing out in the flesh, Joseph Smith told the man, "I did not think it worth contending about, that I had no desire to live upon it in its present state, and if he thought he had a better right I would not quarrel with him about it but leave." Joseph's attempt at being a peacemaker fell short. This "did not seem to satisfy him, as he seemed determined to quarrel with me, and threatened me with the destruction of my body."

Suddenly Joseph was spared the man's vengeance of tongue and physical abuse. As "he was thus engaged, pouring out his bitter words upon me, a rabble rushed in and nearly filled the barn, drew out their knives, and began to quarrel among themselves for the premises." At this point in his dream, the mad men forgot about him. At which time, he says he "took the opportunity to walk out of the barn about up to [his] ankles in mud." Though with great difficulty, Joseph Smith was able to distance himself from his enemies. The dream ended with him hearing from a short distance the commotion and fighting in the barn amongst his enemies. He heard them "screeching and screaming in a very distressed manner, as it appeared they had engaged in a general fight with their knives." They began killing each other as he moved farther and farther away.

The scenario affirms a verse from the Book of Mormon, which Joseph Smith testified he translated by the power of God: "But, behold, the judgments of God will overtake the wicked; and it is by the wicked that the wicked are punished; for it is the wicked that stir up the hearts of the children of men unto bloodshed." In his last night of sleep, Joseph has been given a dream indicating his deliverance from his enemies and how in the end they will turn on each other.

By the time he shares it with those present, he is almost seven hours away from being freed from the bitterness, the threats, and the violence of his enemies. The dream designates that he will have to pass through ankle-deep mud in order to separate himself from the mob—this is modest imagery for a man who is about to start walking out of the barn. He is about to be free from all enemy troubles.

"Envy and wrath of man have been my common lot all the days of my life," he wrote a few years before Carthage Jail. "For what cause it seems mysterious, unless I was ordained from before the foundation of the world for some good end, or bad, as you may choose to call it. Judge ye for yourselves. God knoweth all these things, whether it be good or bad." Of the mountainous persecution he has been facing and climbing over, around, and through, Joseph Smith leaves on record, "It has become a second nature to me; and I feel, like Paul, to glory in tribulation; for to this day has the God of my fathers delivered me out of them all, and will deliver me from henceforth; for behold, and lo, I shall triumph over all my enemies, for the Lord God hath spoken it."

This is his confidence and divine assurance. He holds it close to his heart as he nears death. Having declared his last sermon and now conveying his last dream, Joseph gives his last testimony. "Both Joseph and Hyrum give a testimony to the Latter-day work, and the coming forth of the Book of Mormon, and [prophesy] of the triumph of the Gospel over all the earth, exhorting the brethren present to faithfulness and persevering diligence in proclaiming the Gospel, building up the Temple, and performing all the duties connected with our holy religion."

The few Mormon men still in their presence sense the impending fate.

Chapter 57

THURSDAY LATE MORNING TO EARLY AFTERNOON, JUNE 27, 1844

Carthage Jail, Illinois

OVERNOR FORD IS just about to leave Carthage for Nauvoo. He takes with him the guards who are "most friendly to the prisoners." In glaring hypocrisy, Ford not only breaks his word to take Joseph to Nauvoo, he also sets as guards of the jail those who are "known enemies of the Prophet." Privy to the plan, William and Wilson Law, along with Robert Foster, leave Carthage as well. Like Ford, they need to distance themselves from the coming bloodshed. The sham includes protecting key politicians and dissidents of the Mormon faith. The work of death will be carried out by others.

Dan Jones lingers as the events unfold. He is no longer allowed in the jail, so perhaps he is receiving his instructions from Joseph Smith through the upstairs window. Jones does secure a pass for Dr. Willard Richards, Joseph's secretary.

The number of Mormon men in Joseph and Hyrum's immediate presence is dwindling. Men are being sent with messages and on errands. One of Joseph's attorneys, Joseph W. Woods, leaves Carthage about this time to go to Nauvoo with Governor Ford. Woods knows that half of the Carthage Greys assigned to guard the jail are "in conspiracy to murder Joseph Smith." The "Greys," as he calls them, are camped four hundred yards from the jail at the courthouse. Woods also knows that eight men are "detailed" to guard the jail and every few hours are then relieved by eight others. All those appointed for duty are known to breathe out threatenings against Joseph. If they soften in their contempt during duty, they are immediately replaced by someone full of hatred.

Before leaving Carthage, Woods has his last interview with his client. Joseph Smith says to Woods, "[I shall] not live to see another day." Woods discerns the accuracy of the statement and is "fully . . . impressed with the belief that [Joseph will] be murdered." In this interview, Joseph Smith once again "prove[s] himself a prophet."

When Woods leaves the upper room of the jail, only John Taylor and Willard Richards are with Joseph and Hyrum. Though they are in good company, a poignant stillness and loneliness settles upon each of them. Joseph and Hyrum try diligently to get Dan Jones past the guards of the jail. They refuse to admit him.

Jones may be one of two Mormon men still in Carthage outside the jail. The booing and threats of the Carthage Greys and other members of the murderous crowd pound his ears. He courageously refuses to withdraw from the proximity of the jail. He "dares to defend the prisoners and dares them to allow [Joseph and Hyrum] to have a trial next day by the law of their country according to the right of every man." The mob yells and threatens more. Jones extends a promise to his fomenting foes that if the law can "prove them guilty I [will] agree with their verdicts with all my heart." The mob responds to his defense by throwing rocks at him. Joseph can only watch and listen from the windows. A "chief leader" of the mob admits to Jones that "they [cannot] be proven guilty and the law of the land [cannot] not reach them, but powder and ball will." Once again, the language of Thomas Sharp's editorial surfaces; it is the rallying line for the mob. With a secure pass, Willard Richards descends the stairs of the jail and delivers a message to Jones. Jones tells Richards that the mob's intention is to "kill them before nightfall." Richards sees that Jones is in more danger outside the jail. He presses a letter into Jones's hand and conveys the request of Joseph Smith. Jones is to take the letter to Quincy, Illinois.

The "news of the letter goes throughout the mob like the wings of the breeze." Many in the mob believe it is a request for the Nauvoo Legion to come to Carthage and free their friends. Their judgment of what the letter says is another way to manipulate the emotions of all involved. Their assumption of the content of the letter terribly misses the mark. The letter is addressed to Mr. Browning of Quincy, requesting legal services. Dan Jones doesn't get out of town by a casual trot. He calls for his horse amidst growing threats and curses that he will never leave alive if he doesn't turn over the letter.

Jones is "determined to die rather than release it from his hand." He is chased out of town. He is compelled to pass on the road near a set of woods where members of the mob have retreated to take discreet shots at him. Though his chances to get to Nauvoo are slim, Jones "doubt[s] not a bit." The prophecy from Joseph Smith the night before about going to Wales to serve a mission for the Church miraculously impels his flight. He moves with confidence and an unseen protection. As the mob quarrel among themselves, Jones rides hard out of town, "bullets whistling through the air everywhere except where they were aiming," he states. Jones takes the Warsaw road out of Carthage. Recognizing his mistake, he crosses a prairie to the Nauvoo road that puts him in front of Governor's Fords entourage heading to Nauvoo.

Ironically, those coming to kill Joseph Smith are on the Warsaw road coming to Carthage. Jones would have run directly into them within a half mile if he failed to realize his mistake. He makes it to Nauvoo, takes a ferry to Quincy, and delivers the letter as instructed.

Shortly after Jones makes his escape from Carthage, Stephen Markham makes his. He is captured when he is out on an errand to obtain some tobacco for Willard Richards, who has an upset stomach. Markham had minutes earlier been sitting on the bed by Joseph Smith discussing the situation. "I wish you would tell me how this fuss is going to come out, as you have at other times," Markham says to his friend. "Bro. Markham," the Prophet affectionately answers, "the Lord placed me to govern His kingdom on the earth, but the people have so taken away from me the reigns." Joseph is alluding to a few days prior when Mormon men came across the Mississippi River while he and Hyrum were in Iowa preparing to depart for the Rocky Mountains. It was at this point some called him a coward for leaving the Latter-day Saints in Nauvoo.

"The whisperings of the Spirit left me," he tells Markham, "and I am now no more than a common man. I can do nothing for myself except they place me back to my former position. If they don't do it, I am gone."

The words rest heavily on his mind as he goes to the store for the tobacco. An "old man" calls to Markham, "You have got to leave the town in five minutes." Markham replies, "I shall not do it. Neither can you drive me. You can kill me, but you cannot drive me." As courageous as his heart is, the mobs' hearts are brutally cold. The old man turns and charges "upon [him] with his bayonet." Markham knocks him down with his club. This brings the rally of the Carthage Greys. The inn keeper, Hamilton, comes out and addresses Markham: "[You] had better go home as [you will] only get killed if [you] remain. You can do the prisoners no good and I will bring you your horse." Markham is unmoved at Hamilton's bogus mercy. "I was not going home," he tells him. Hamilton shows exasperating emotion and brings his horse anyway. Markham is forced onto his horse by bayonet. He is stabbed in his legs many times. As he rides from the jail, he can feel the blood run down his legs and fill his boots.

Markham is troubled that he can't explain to his friends why he didn't return. But in all likelihood, Joseph Smith is an eyewitness to much of the commotion. From his second-story imprisonment with three large windows, Joseph quietly bids farewell to a dear friend.

The four prisoners' conversations are subdued. Their spirits are "extremely dull and depressed." Though ill with an uneasy stomach, Willard Richards turns to his friend and honorably declares, "Brother Joseph, if it is necessary that you die in this matter, and if they will take me in your stead, I will suffer for you." Richards' words reflect the commitment and love of thousands and thousands of Latter-day Saints.

Chapter 58

THURSDAY 3–6 P.M., JUNE 27, 1844

Nauvoo, Illinois

O̶N THE OUTSKIRTS of Nauvoo, a host of citizens watch as Governor Ford makes his appearance on the plateau. His entourage heads west down Mulholland Street. When they reach the temple on the edge of the bluff, they dismount and desire to tour the rising edifice. William Sterrett, a workman, is assigned to follow them while they tour the temple. Governor Ford and his followers pause at the baptismal font resting on the back of twelve sculptured oxen. They make light of it and then break off some of the horns for souvenirs.

After their light-minded stop at the temple, Ford and his people go straight to the Mansion House. Emma Smith greets the governor and his followers with hospitality. Hearing of his desire to address the people, at least one thousand—perhaps up to five thousand—people gather around the stand where Joseph days earlier had delivered his last speech to the Nauvoo Legion. Not all gathered are Mormon. Some are outspoken enemies.

Ford has one company with him and two companies still in service back in Carthage. He has told all other Illinois county militias to disband and go home. The Warsaw men pretended to leave Carthage but have regrouped in Warsaw as a murderous posse. Ford's arrival in Nauvoo is perfect timing for Joseph Smith's enemies. He is far enough way, about twenty miles. Before Ford gives his speech, he and his followers enjoy refreshments from the hand of Emma and her helpers. They pay for none of the services or the meals graciously given.

Notwithstanding the kindness of Emma and the Saints, Ford rails on the Saints. He tells them that the destruction of the *Expositor* was "an unwise action and the heavily armed Nauvoo Legions posed a threat to the peace of the region." Ford well understands the legion is operating under Nauvoo's legal charter. He also knows they have not been the aggressors. Nonetheless, he tells the Saints it was wise to have the Legion disarmed, concluding, "You ought to be praying Saints, not military Saints." A praying people still have the right to defend themselves. This is a fundamental principle of liberty Ford dismisses.

In his speech, Ford reflects the spirit of Lilburn W. Boggs. "Depend upon it, a little more misbehavior from the citizens, and the torch, which is already lighted, will be applied, and the city may be reduced to ashes, and extermination [will] inevitably follow."

Though desperately trying to portray innocence and civil judgment, Ford seals whose side he is on by telling the Saints, "If anything of a serious character should befall the lives or property of the persons who are prosecuting your leaders, you will be held responsible."—a warning he never voiced to the mob, which had already destroyed property, beat and killed some Mormons, and then bragged about it in Ford's hearing.

In coming days, Ford's haranguing of the Saints in Nauvoo will be recalled as "one of the most infamous and insulting speeches that ever fell from the lips of an executive."

Chapter 59
THURSDAY 4 P.M., JUNE 27, 1844
Carthage, Illinois

YOUNG BOY BY the name of William Hamilton is positioned on the roof of the courthouse. He is positioned at this lookout by the request of Captain Robert Smith, who still has command of the unruly Carthage Greys. The boy is attentive to his duty. About 4 p.m. he sees a large group of men coming from the west, from the direction of Warsaw. He leaves his position immediately to inform Captain Robert Smith. The boy is told "to tell no one." Captain Smith of the Greys tells the boy to watch their direction closely and inform him right way if the men coming are moving "directly toward the jail."

Positioned at the jail are seven men under the command of Franklin Worrell, Robert Smith's cohort. They have been anxiously awaiting the arrival of the men William Hamilton has seen approaching from the west. Both men know Thomas Sharp has prepared the men to make an attack on the jail. Before leaving Warsaw, Sharp delivers a speech on the "necessity of killing the Smiths to get rid of the Mormons." With the fiery speech and plenty to drink, the men approach Carthage ready for the assassination.

The path to the jail is unobstructed. Captain Robert Smith has stationed the main body of Carthage Greys a half mile away, not in the direction of the approaching mob. They are "in or near their tents on the southeast corner of the town square." The distance is needed because not all in the Carthage Greys agree with the events unfolding. Captain Smith knows this and has to keep those men and their soft hearts from interrupting the proceeding march of madness.

Many in the mob have blackened their faces with watered down gunpowder. Some report not only blackened faces but red and yellow as well. At least a hundred men are moving toward the jail. The prisoners' only view is to the south and east. They have no idea of the advancement.

Within four miles of Carthage, the main body of the mob leaves the road. They make their final approach passing through heavy timber, perhaps to deter locals and a few of the Carthage Greys from impeding their purpose.

But word has gotten out that a mob is approaching. Captain Robert Smith commands his men to come to order. But it is not in their nature to be in perfect order or "military formality." Some have to be awakened from their afternoon slumber. But Robert Smith isn't very eager to get the troops over to the jail. He needs to delay their arrival at the jail. The main contingency is camped on the southeast corner of the town square, a few blocks from the jail.

One of the Greys by the name of Tom becomes impatient. With concern for the men guarding the jail, thinking they will be butchered, he yells at his fellows, "Come on you cowards damn you, come on, those boys [the guards] will be killed." The cowards didn't move with the same anxiety as Tom. He runs to the jail solo, while Captain Smith—neglecting all justice and duty—slowly calls the Greys to ranks and an even slower "disciplined march" as if it were a "dress parade." With their guns and their flags in the air, their march of injustice begins.

Meanwhile, the men of murder cautiously make their way through the timber on their approach to town.

To this point, the prisoners still cannot see or hear their approach. They pass the late afternoon in various ways. John Taylor sings a hymn titled "A Poor Wayfaring Man of Grief," a song about a stranger in a dire situation and who is in want. His needs are met by the kindness of another man. The kind man is well rewarded for his deeds. The last verse reads:

Then in a moment to my view,
The stranger started from disguise:
The tokens in his hands I knew,
The Savior stood before mine eyes.
He spake—and my poor name he named—
"Of me thou hast not been asham'd;
These deeds shall thy memorial be;
Fear not, thou didst them unto me."

When John Taylor finishes, Joseph Smith asks him to sing it again. Taylor doesn't feel to do so. Hyrum, who is grinding out the somber moment by reading extracts from Josephus, urges him on. Taylor consents and sings the hymn again. It has a melancholy tone and a message that resonates with Joseph.

A changing of the guard occurs just after 4 p.m. Eight men bitter toward Joseph now guard the jail. It is the last changing of the guard. By 4:15, Joseph is conversing with the guards about his persecutors, particularly Joseph Jackson and William and Wilson Law. At least one, but most likely all of the guards, is familiar with the script as the mob from the west prepares to overrun the jail.

Willard Richards and Hyrum keep each other preoccupied in conversation. John Taylor leans through the south window and ponders their dismal situation. Joseph continues his conversation with the guards. The door to the bedroom is open. Joseph is most likely in the hall speaking with the guards who occupy the stairs and hall. Some of the guards are positioned at the front door of the jail. Joseph is not looking to escape. He knows an entirely different release is near.

Chapter 60

THURSDAY 5 P.M., JUNE 27, 1844

Carthage, Illinois

*A*T THE HOUR, George Stigall, the jailor whose bedroom the prisoners are occupying, comes to share his sentiments on the gloomy situation the prisoners are facing. Having been out on errands and watching closely the tenor of men in and around Carthage, Stigall tells Joseph that he and the other men would be "safer in the cell." His intentions seem to be neutral and his counsel honest. Joseph tells Stigall that after supper they will go into the cell.

Stigall leaves the men and the property for another errand.

Joseph turns to Willard Richards and says, "If we go into the cell, will you go in with us?"

Richard's answers, "Brother Joseph, you did not ask me to cross the river with you—you did not ask me to come to Carthage—you did not ask me to come to jail with you—and do you think I would forsake you now? But I will tell you what I will do; if you are condemned to be hung for treason, I will be hung in your stead, and you shall go free."

Joseph has no interest being hung. Upon leaving Nauvoo a few days before, he stated, "Well, if they don't hang me I don't care how they kill me." It isn't his preferred way to go out of this existence.

Nevertheless, Joseph says to Richards, "You cannot." Richards emphatically responds, "I will." Joseph knows he is willing, but that isn't going to happen. Joseph Smith's prophecy to Richards is about to be fulfilled. A year earlier he told Richards "the time [will] come that the balls would fly around [you] like hail, and [you] should see [your] friends fall on the right and on the left, but that there should not be a hole in [your] garment."

This is a remarkable prophecy, especially when considering the size of Richards, who is probably around three hundred pounds—and who is sitting in a room just over fifteen feet squared. He is a large target in tight confinement.

The firestorm is about to begin.

A few of the guards interrupt the exchange of Joseph and Willard Richards. They come to the room with some wine and pipes. The pipes are ignored. The bottle of wine is uncorked. Joseph Smith, John Taylor, and Willard Richards share a taste with the guards. The guards take the wine and the pipes and abruptly leave the room.

Odd silence pervades. John Taylor gravely looks out a south facing window one more time and then turns from the window sill. Joseph, Hyrum, and Willard Richards wait out the dull moment. They have no idea of the ambush coming. Their attackers have arrived undetected from the west.

Immediately there is a "rustling at the outer door of the jail, and a cry of surrender." The Carthage Greys fire three or four shots into the mob, most likely blanks never intended to harm those storming the jail. The mob returns the shots. The jailer's boy is descending the stairs with supper dishes and hears whizzing above and around him. His mother is in the kitchen when a bullet whizzes over her while she bends down to get a pie out of the oven. The bullet lodges in the wall. Henry Harmon, a twelve-year-old boy, witnesses the unfolding scene.

Willard Richards quickly takes a glance through the curtain of the window, the same window Taylor has just left. The shots fired at the door are followed by "many rapid footsteps." Taylor springs for a hickory cane that was left by one of their friends. Joseph and Hyrum slam the door to their room. Richards and Taylor join them at the door. All four men place themselves near and against the door. They match the men and the strength on the other side of the door. Their enemies tightly occupy the space at the top of the stairs.

The lock to the door is useless.

It doesn't matter.

The mob doesn't shrink this time.

After an initial struggle pushing at the door with Joseph and his fellow prisoners, one of the mob members discharges his rifle into the door near the lock. A second shot explodes through the upper door panel.

The second shot clear the men at the door, except Hyrum. His position is directly in the path of the second shot. He receives the bullet to the left side of face, just off the nose. Simultaneously, shots irrupt from outside the jail, blasting the windows. Another bullet is shot through one of the bedroom windows and enters Hyrum's right back side.

"Emphatically" he falls to the ground exclaiming, "I am a dead man."

Members of the Carthage Greys marching toward the jail hear the commotion from their position about sixty yards away. Men of the Carthage Greys who want to help with the assassination begin shooting from the ground, possibly from structures above the ground. The men in the hallway are slowed in their attack because loaded guns need to be passed up to the shooters or other men with loaded guns have to get into position. The guns are producing "a fog" in the hall and the prisoners' room. They are also producing a horrific noise.

The noise and smoke give Joseph and the two others some time to position themselves for better defense. During the madness, Joseph Smith springs from the wall and for a quick moment bends over his brother's motionless body. "Oh! my poor, dear brother Hyrum!" Hyrum has kept his promise that where his brother dies he would die.

Joseph promptly returns to the door, which Taylor and Richards are trying to keep from being swung completely open. He moves to the door with a "quick, firm step." He has taken from his pocket the pistol Cyrus Wheelock left earlier. With a "determined expression in his face," Joseph fires the pistol "six successful times; only three of the loads" express their vengeance. The others fail to discharge. This brings "no hope" for the prisoners. "Instant death" seems to be the cold reality.

Joseph's resistance causes the mob to cease firing for a moment. He steps back from the door. The mobbers again lift their guns. Taylor and Richards muscle their best effort to deflect the barrels either into the air or down to the ground. Another bullet grazes the chest of the lifeless body of Hyrum hauntingly stationary on the floor. The bullet goes through his neck and lodges into his head.

Taylor, using the hickory cane, keeps parrying off the barrage of rifle barrels, which seem to be increasing in the doorway as the scene unfolds. Joseph is standing right behind Taylor and says matter-of-factly, "That's right, Brother Taylor, parry them off as well as you can." Taylor will later confirm these were the last words he heard Joseph Smith speak in the flesh.

Angry mob members not having a play on the action keep pushing their way up the stairs to the landing. This pushes the "assailants further and further into the room." Hope of survival leaves the room. Taylor makes a rush to the east window, which is already open. He is an easy target for the men shooting from within and without the jail. Taylor can't get the push he needs to leap from the window. He is struck by a bullet in the thigh. The large window sill catches him and a bullet from outside strikes him in the chest. He is thrown back into the room on the floor.

During the madness, Taylor's watch is broken "leaving the hands to standing at 5 o'clock, 16 minutes and 26 seconds."

Taylor's instincts are still strong. He rolls himself under the bed, which is up against the east and south walls. During his attempt to roll under the bed, he is shot three more times: below his left knee, in his left hip, and in the left forearm. The last ball rolls down into his hand under the flesh and comes to a stop in his palm.

At this point, Hyrum is dead and John Taylor severely wounded—amazingly still breathing. Joseph Smith makes a surge for the same window Taylor tried to leap from. Joseph is shot at least three times, two in his back from the doorway and once by a bullet that hits his right breast from outside. At this heightened instant, Richards hears Joseph say, "O Lord my God!" Joseph Smith's impulse to get out of the room pushes his body head first through the window. Richards is right behind him, taking the position in the window sill as Joseph's feet cross out the window. Richards watches as Joseph's body falls about fifteen feet and lands on his left side next to a well. There is no struggle for life. He is dead.

A "fifer of the Warsaw Company" comes running into the jail yard directly for the lifeless body. He strikes Joseph with his fife several times on the head, shouting, "You were the ruination of my father. I will have revenge."

Richards, within hearing of those gathered around his dead friend, is spared another barrage of shooting. Someone in the mob shouts, "He's leaped the window." The declaration clears those in the jail. They retreat to the exterior. Richards withdraws from the window thinking it no use to leap from the same window on "a hundred bayonets." However, Richards returns to the window and exposes his large frame to the mob below him. He watches as more and more members of the mob run around the corner to where the body of Joseph Smith lies. He watches long enough to be "fully satisfied" that Joseph is dead.

Expecting another assault from the mob to kill him, Richards quickly makes his way to the cell room to see if the iron doors are open. Taylor calls out to him, "Stop, doctor, and take me along." Richards is a doctor and an Apostle in the Church. Finding all the doors open, he retreats back to Taylor. He wants to hide his body in the cell room in hopes that Taylor will live to tell the tale. He places Taylor under his arm and drags him to the cell lamenting, "Oh! Brother Taylor is it possible that they have killed Joseph and Hyrum? It cannot surely be, and yet I saw them shoot them! Oh Lord, my God, spare Thy servants." He adds, "Brother Taylor, this is a terrible event."

Chapter 61

EVENING OF JUNE 27, 1844

Carthage, Illinois

As the murderers stand around the body of Joseph Smith, one of them shouts, "The Mormons are coming." The assassins have enough strength in their knees to flea but not stand by their deed. They retrace their steps back to Warsaw, leaving two men, Taylor and Richards, who were eyewitnesses to the bloody evening.

A lonely and sickening feeling finds way to Taylor's mental faculties and overrides the immediate pain of his physical body. He languishes over the breathless bodies of his close friends. Strangely, Richards and Taylor are spared, a fulfillment of the law of witnesses. Richards and Taylor begin to sense the significance of their lives being spared. Their immortal words will occupy records beyond this world. Their escape from death balances the scale of eternal justice. The event will one day be weighed, and judgment will one day be rendered.

Though it may seem probable, the Mormons do not come. They are not yet aware of what has happened. They are still giving Ford their attention. He is prolonging his grandstanding and the posturing of authority. However, the signal—a cannon fire midway between Carthage and Nauvoo—that the murderous deed is accomplished is heard. Ford rejects the hospitality of Emma Smith and others to stay the night in Nauvoo. Instead he makes an abrupt exit. As the state's highest officer and those with him leave Nauvoo, Zina Huntington tells a friend the "trees and the grass are in mourning . . . fearful silence pervade[s] the city."

Ford and his entourage take the Carthage road, looking to stop any Mormon runners heading to Nauvoo with the news that Joseph and Hyrum are murdered. Ford needs a few hours to distance himself from the main body of Latter-day Saints.

Though the Saints have been told to stay home, Willard Richards does not fear retaliation. At 8 p.m. he sends an urgent note. John Taylor abruptly signs the letter in an attempt to hide his true physical condition and not give his family alarm. He begs Richards to say that he is only "slightly wounded." The note reads:

> Carthage Jail, 8:05 o'clock, P.M., June 27th, 1844.
>
> Joseph and Hyrum are dead. Taylor wounded, not very badly. I am well. Our guard was forced, as we believe, by a band of Missourians from 100 to 200. The job was done in an instant, and the party fled towards Nauvoo instantly. This is as I believe it. The citizens here are afraid of the Mormons attacking them. I promise them NO!
>
> W. Richards,
>
> N. B.—The citizens promise us protection. Alarm guns have been fired.
>
> John Taylor.

The note doesn't make it to Nauvoo. The messenger is intercepted by Governor Ford and his men. They will not allow him to proceed. He is ordered to return to Carthage with them. Ford doesn't feel like he has enough distance from the Mormons, and he hasn't had the time to tell Carthage residents to flee and to take all their personal and county records with them. He is sure the Mormons will come and burn the town; another misjudgment on his part.

Ford arrives at Carthage at midnight. He gives some orders and gathers some items. He warns that all should leave town and take as many belongings with them as possible. Ford is saying flee, and Mormon leaders are saying be still. The proverb rings true, "The wicked flee when no man pursueth."

Some Mormon men do arrive from nearby communities but have restrained any feelings of retaliation. They help Richards remove the bodies of Joseph and Hyrum to the Hamilton Hotel. It is unknown if Ford looks upon the bodies of Joseph and Hyrum. It is unknown if he looks into the faces of Willard Richards and John Taylor. Whether he sees them or not, Ford lives with the fact two have died and two have lived through the terrible event. The two who lived know his part firsthand.

Joseph Smith's enemies, after years of threatening, chasing, and imprisoning him, have finally ended his life. He is out of the hands of oppression and mobocracy. He is no longer on trial by judges, juries, politicians, or apostates who take advantage by operating under alarming injustices. The chase is over and the fleeing has begun. Ford flees Carthage in great haste at sunrise. The other citizens are not far behind him.

Chapter 62

FRIDAY, JUNE 28, 1844

Nauvoo and Carthage, Illinois

*A*T SUNRISE IN Nauvoo the first reports are arriving of the deaths. George Grant knocks on the door of Hyrum's home. His wife Mary Fielding Smith has been up all night with an unnerving feeling, and with a three-year-old suffering with measles. When Grant knocks on the door, she is reading the Bible. "They are both murdered," he tells her. "It cannot be possible, can it?" she exclaims. Grant conveys it is true. Mary Fielding falls back against the bureau. Grant helps her to a chair.

Joseph's and Hyrum's bodies are placed into wagons at 8 a.m. Samuel Smith, their younger brother, is present. Their bodies are covered with branches to shield them from the sun. They have been dead for over fifteen hours. The wagons pull out and reach Nauvoo by 3 p.m. Thousands eagerly gather on Mulholland Street to meet the procession. Their bodies are taken to the Mansion House, where their wives downheartedly await their arrival. A mass of people has gathered in front of the home on the corner of Main and Water Streets. Willard Richards addresses them and admonishes them to keep the peace and trust in the law, and when that fails, "call upon God to avenge them of their wrongs." In a united voice, the people agree.

Inside the home, Emma Smith views her lifeless husband. On first seeing him, she screams and falls back. Dimick Huntington, a loyal family friend, catches her. Emma then falls upon her husband's lifeless body and kisses his face, "calling him by name and [begging] him to speak to her once more."

The thirty-eight-year-old man who had spoken and compiled volumes of words, the man who had prophesied and performed miracles, the man who had boldly stood before his enemies and fervently taught modern revelations to eager listeners doesn't respond.

Joseph and Hyrum's mother, Lucy, is also present at the Mansion House. She views their bodies after they are washed and dressed in their burial clothes. Upon seeing her dead sons, she exclaims, "My God, my God, why has thou forsaken this family!"

Notwithstanding the scene of anguish, a reply comes to her mind. "I have taken them to myself, that they might have rest."

Lucy, in this indescribable experience, looks upon her sons' "peaceful, smiling countenances," which tribulation and mobocracy had for a short time stolen. Again a voice comes to her mind. "Mother, weep not for us, we have overcome the world by love; we carried them the gospel, that their souls might be saved; they slew us for our testimony, and thus placed us beyond their power; their ascendency is for a moment, ours is an eternal triumph." At this moment, Lucy's mind recalls her experience in Far West, Missouri, over five and half years earlier when her sons were being dragged off by enemies. It was at that time she had the impression come to her mind "that in five years Joseph should have power over all his enemies."

It was a strenuous five years. Lucy courageously yields to the promise and its fulfillment. Joseph Smith's body, as does his brother Hyrum's, lies in quiet slumber—beyond enemy power.

EPILOGUE

"When a man begins to be an enemy to this work, he hunts me, he seeks to kill me, and never ceases to thirst for my blood. He gets the spirit of the devil—the same spirit that they had who crucified the Lord of Life—the same spirit that sins against the Holy Ghost. You cannot save such persons; you cannot bring them to repentance; they make open war, like the devil, and awful is the consequence."

(Joseph Smith, *History of the Church*, 6:514–15)

OVER TEN THOUSAND people viewed Joseph's and Hyrum's bodies on Saturday, June 29, 1844. Their deaths were announced in many, if not all, of the leading newspapers of the day. An impartial account of the assassination appeared on the front page of a New York newspaper. But the writer's judgment on the result of the Joseph Smith's death missed the mark. The final line of the article reads: "Joseph Smith, the Mormon prophet, is dead—Thus ends Mormonism." Many probably felt that way. Even some Mormons must have speculated and worried about the fate of their religious movement that was only fourteen years old.

While the Latter-day Saints mourned the death of Joseph Smith, others welcomed it. The *New York Herald* printed: "The death of the modern mahomet will seal the fate of Mormonism. They cannot get another Joe Smith. The holy city must tumble into ruins, and the 'latter-day saints' have indeed come to the latter day." Clergymen from other parts of America condoned the assassins.

Alexander Campbell was ecstatic at the news. He had lost many talented members of his congregation to Mormonism in the 1830s. Upon hearing of the death of Joseph Smith, Campbell penned: "The money digger, the juggler, and the founder of the Golden Bible delusion, has been hurried away in the midst of his madness to his final account. . . . The hand of the Lord was heavy upon him. An outlaw himself, God cut him off by outlaws. . . . It was the outrages of the Mormons that brought upon the head of their leader the arm of justice. . . . Religion or religious opinions had nothing to do with it. It was neither more nor less than the assassination of one whose career was in open rebellion against God and man."

Another reverend chimed in: "Our deliberate judgment is, that he ought to have been dead ten years ago, and that those who at length have deprived him of his life, have done the cause of God, and of the country, good service. . . . Smith was killed, as he should have been. THREE CHEERS to the brave company who shot him to pieces!"

Willard Richards lived nearly ten years after the events unfolded in Carthage Jail. John Taylor lived over four decades. One of the four bullets that struck his body that day was never removed. His dying words in 1887 were, "I feel to thank the Lord." Both of these men wrote about and testified in public concerning the events at Carthage Jail. They declared that injustice had carried the day and that apostates, ruthless Missourians, and jealous Illinoisans were to blame, with Governor Ford largely to blame for not intervening in Joseph and Hyrum Smith's behalf.

A few months after Joseph's and Hyrum's deaths, Ford revoked the Nauvoo Charter. A few years later, he attempted to excuse himself and justify the occurrences. His writings were posthumously printed in 1854, titled *History of Illinois*. Ford had died in 1850. Like the Higbee, Foster, and Law brothers, along with Joseph Jackson, he died in obscurity. Encouraged by his acquittal, Thomas Sharp continued to oppose the Latter-day Saints by publishing his rhetoric justifying the murders in the *Warsaw Signal*. When the Saints went west, Sharp left the *Warsaw Signal* and served as a justice of the peace. He would also serve three terms as the mayor of Warsaw. He lived fifty years after the murders. He died in Carthage, Illinois.

Five men stood trial in May of 1845 for the murders of Joseph and Hyrum. All were acquitted. When the court had issued the verdict, enemies of the Church once again increased the persecution in and around Nauvoo.

In 1976, Missouri governor Christopher S. Bond overturned the executive order of Lilburn W. Boggs that called for the expelling and extermination of the Latter-day Saints. He expressed deep regret for the injustice and undue suffering imposed upon the Mormons by state officials and citizens one hundred and forty years earlier.

In 2004, the Illinois House of Representatives adopted a resolution expressing regret for the assassination of the Prophet Joseph Smith and his brother Hyrum at Carthage Jail. The legislature acknowledged in the resolution: "WHEREAS, The biases and prejudices of a less enlightened age in the history of the State of Illinois caused unmeasurable hardship and trauma for the community of Latter-day Saints by the distrust, violence, and inhospitable actions of a dark time in our past. . . . We acknowledge the disparity of those past actions and suspicions, regretting the expulsion of the community of Latter-day Saints."

Religious movements have, do, and will yet come and go. But Joseph Smith didn't feel he was starting a community religion. He declared that he was laying the foundation of the kingdom of God on earth—the same kingdom that the ancient prophet Daniel foresaw established in the last days and which he described to King Nebuchadnezzar of Babylon nearly six hundred years before Christ's birth. Daniel told Nebuchadnezzar that this kingdom in the last days "shall never be destroyed . . . and it shall stand forever" (see Daniel 2:36–49).

Wilford Woodruff, a contemporary of Joseph Smith and later President of the Church, said that in 1834 "the Prophet called on all [the leading men] to gather into the little log school house [in Kirtland, Ohio]. . . . It was a small house, perhaps 14 feet square. During the meeting the men . . . shared their vision of the work they were engaged in. When they finished sharing Joseph Smith said, 'Brethren, I have been very much edified and instructed . . . but I want to say to you before the Lord, that you know no more concerning the destinies of this Church and kingdom than a babe upon its mother's lap. You don't comprehend it. . . . This Church will fill North and South America—it will fill the world.' "

This assurance seems to have impelled Joseph Smith beyond the agitations and constant threats of his enemies. We sense that as Joseph Smith's ministry matured, he understood himself as a key player in the kingdom of God on earth and in heaven. Through all his troubles, Joseph Smith held together a substantial number of loyal followers who gave their means and industry to the establishment of what he termed the restored religion of Jesus Christ.

Joseph Smith believed and plainly stated that he had companionship among the ranks of a few choice prophets and seers in earth's history. He argued that the same God that called upon them called upon him. Their fate was his fate. He knew that the people of the earth haven't always treated those claiming revelation from Jesus Christ favorably. Often they have been killed for their testimony of Jesus Christ. John the Baptist and the Apostle Paul were beheaded. Some traditions hold that Peter was brutally crucified on a cross upside down. Phillip was scourged and crucified. Others were axed, clubbed to death, or burned at the hands of angry mobs. Arguably, Joseph Smith joins those ranks, and no earthly mob then and now can ever strip him from those ranks.

Initially following the death of Joseph Smith, the Latter-day Saints continued to gather in Nauvoo and, with great sacrifice, finished the temple. The first group of Latter-day Saints to go west crossed the Mississippi River on ice in February of 1846 under the leadership of Brigham Young. They began another city 1,300 miles later. Prior to the completion of the transcontinental railroad, over 70,000 Latter-day Saints would trek west by wagon and handcart. These Latter-day Saints came from far countries and all of the states in America. They would rendezvous, assimilate, and unite, not under the leadership of Brigham Young but under their own witness that God had spoken through Joseph Smith, a modern-day prophet.

These trekking Latter-day Saints built under a peak that Brigham Young had seen in vision while back in Nauvoo. In his vision, he declared Joseph Smith appeared and showed him the peak. As the peak came into view, a flag descended upon it. Joseph Smith then said to Young in the vision: "Build under the point where the colors fall and you will prosper and have peace." The peak that he saw is just north of downtown Salt Lake City.

Salt Lake City was surveyed and laid out from this peak. It is an indisputable fact that this Great Basin city, along with many other cities and towns in the West, have come to fruition under the legacy of thousands of Mormon pioneers and their descendants. In many ways, these cities and towns are extensions of Nauvoo and the legacy of Joseph Smith.

BIBLIOGRAPHY

Please contact Ryan at authorryanjenkins@gmail.com if you seek a specific source for a quotation in the narrative. Provide the chapter, page number, and a portion of the quote.

Adams, Charles Francis. *Diary of Charles Francis Adams (1807–1886)* For the Period May 14, 1844, to May 16, 1844. Transcription of diary available online; see Book of Abraham Project, http://www.boap.org/.

"A Foul Deed." *St. Louis Daily Missouri Republican.* May 14, 1842. Available online.

Allred, William M. *Biography and Journal of William Moore Allred.* Photocopy of holograph, Church History Department: Salt Lake City, Utah. Archives, 10.

Anderson, Richard Lloyd. "Atchison's Letters and the Causes of Mormon Expulsion from Missouri." *BYU Studies,* 26:3. Provo, Utah: Brigham Young University, 1986.

Baker, LeGrand L. *Murder of the Mormon Prophet: Political Prelude to the Death of Joseph Smith.* Salt Lake City, Utah: Eborn Books, 2006.

Ballard, Timothy. *The Lincoln Hypothesis.* Salt Lake City, Utah: Deseret Book, 2014.

Barnett, Steven G. "Wilson Law: A Sidelight on the Expositor Incident." *BYU Studies,* 1979, 19:2, 244–246.

Barney, Gwen M. *Anson Call and the Rocky Mountain Prophecy.* Salt Lake City: Call Publishing, Paragon Press, 2002.

Barney, Ronald O. "Joseph Smith Goes to Washington." In *Joseph Smith, the Prophet and Seer.* Edited by Richard Neitzel Holzapfel and Kent P. Jackson. Salt Lake City: Deseret Book, 2010, 391–420.

Barrett, Ivan J. "Joseph Smith: The Chosen of God and the Friend of Man." Brigham Young University Devotional, August 12, 1975. Available online.

Baugh, Alexander L. "A Call to Arms: The 1838 Mormon Defense of Northern Missouri." *BYU Studies.* Provo, Utah: Dissertation, 1996. Brigham Young University printed the dissertation in 2000.

Baugh, Alexander L. "Joseph Smith in Northern Missouri." In *Joseph Smith, the Prophet and Seer.* Edited by Richard Neitzel Holzapfel and Kent P. Jackson. Salt Lake City: Deseret Book, 2010, 291–346. Available online.

Bentley, Joseph I. *Legal Trials of the Prophet: Joseph Smith's Life in Court.* FAIR Conference, 2006. Available online.

BIBLIOGRAPHY

Berrett, LaMar C., general editor. *Sacred Places: Ohio and Illinois, A Comprehensive Guide to Early LDS Historical Sites, Vol. 3*. Salt Lake City: Deseret Book, 2002.

Black, Susan Easton. "James Adams of Springfield, Illinois: The Link between Abraham Lincoln and Joseph Smith." *Mormon Historical Studies,* March 2009, Vol. 10, Issue 1, 33–49.

Blake, Reed. "Martyrdom at Carthage." *Ensign*, June 1994, 30–39.

Blake, Reed. *24 Hours to Martyrdom*. Salt Lake City: Bookcraft, 1973.

Brewster, Hoyt W. *Martyrs of the Kingdom*. Salt Lake City: Bookcraft, 1990.

Brown, Benjamin. "Autobiography (1794–1853)." In *Testimonies For The Truth* by S. W. Richards. Liverpool: England, 1853.

Bruno, Cheryl L. "Keeping a Secret: Freemasonry, Polygamy, and the Nauvoo Relief Society, 1842–44." In *Journal of Mormon History*. Vol. 39, No. 4, fall 2013.

Bushman, Richard Lyman. "Joseph Smith and Abraham Lincoln." In *Joseph Smith and the Doctrinal Restoration*. Provo, Utah: Brigham Young University, Religious Studies Center, 2005, 89–108.

Bushman, Richard Lyman. *Joseph Smith: Rough Stone Rolling: A Cultural Biography of Mormonism's Founder*. New York: Vintage Books, 2005.

Call, Anson. *Autobiography of Anson Call, 1810–1890*. Typescript, Harold B. Lee Library: Brigham Young University. Available online.

Call, Duane D. *Anson Call and His Contributions Toward Latter-Day Saint Colonization*. A Master Thesis Submitted to the Faculty of the Division of Religion of Brigham Young University, 1956.

Cannon, Brian Q. "John C Calhoun Jr Meets the Prophet Joseph Smith Shortly Before the Departure for Carthage." *BYU Studies*, 33, No. 4, 1993.

Cannon, Donald Q. "The King Follett Discourse: Joseph Smith's Greatest Sermon in Historical Perspective." *BYU Studies*, 18, No. 2, 1975.

Cannon, Donald, Q. "Spokes on the Wheel: Early Latter-day Saint Settlements in Hancock County, Illinois." *Ensign*, February 1986, 62–68.

Cannon, George Q. *The Latter-Day Prophet: History of Joseph Smith Written for Young People*. Salt Lake City: Juvenile Instructor, 1990.

Church History in the Fulness of Times Student Manual. Salt Lake City, Utah: The Church of Jesus Christ of Latter-day Saints, 1989.

Clayton, William. *William Clayton Journals*. Published by the Clayton Family Association. Salt Lake City, Utah: Deseret News, 1921.

Coates, Lawrence G. "Refugees Meet: Mormons and Indians in Iowa." *BYU Studies*, 21, No. 4, 1981.

Cook, Lyndon W. "William Law Nauvoo Dissenter." *BYU Studies*, 22, No. 1.

Cook, Lyndon W. "James Arlington Bennett and the Mormons." *BYU Studies*, 19, No. 2.

Dahl, Larry E., and Donald Q. Cannon. *Encyclopedia of Joseph Smith's Teachings*. Salt Lake City: Bookcraft, 1997.

Davidson, Karen Lynn, David J. Whittaker, Richard L. Jensen, and Mark Ashurst-McGee, eds. Histories, *Volume 1: Joseph Smith Histories, 1832–1844*. Vol. 1 of the Histories series of *The Joseph Smith Papers,* edited by Dean C. Jessee, Ronald K. Esplin, and Richard Lyman Bushman. Salt Lake City: Church Historian's Press, 2012.

Davidson, Karen Lynn, Richard L. Jensen, and David J. Whittaker, eds. Histories, *Volume 2: Assigned Historical Writings, 1831–1847.* Vol. 2 of the Histories series of *The Joseph Smith Papers,* edited by Dean C. Jessee, Ronald K. Esplin, and Richard Lyman Bushman. Salt Lake City: Church Historian's Press, 2012.

Dennis, Ronald D. "The Martyrdom of Joseph Smith and His Brother Hyrum by Dan Jones." *BYU Studies*, 24, No. 1, 1984.

Dew, Sheri and Pearce, Virginia H. *The Beginning of Better Days: Divine Instruction to Women from the Prophet Joseph Smith.* Salt Lake City: Deseret Book, 2012.

Dibble, Philo. *Autobiography (1806–1843): Early Scenes in Church History.* Available online. See also *Four Faith Promoting Classics.* Salt Lake City: Bookcraft, 1968.

Dibble, Philo. "Recollections of the Prophet Joseph Smith." *Juvenile Instructor* 27, 1 June 1892, 345.

Durham, Reed C. Jr. "Nauvoo Expositor." In *Encyclopedia of Mormonism: The History, Scripture, Doctrine, and Procedure of the Church of Jesus Christ of Latter-day Saints,* Vol. 3: N–S. Edited by Daniel H. Ludlow. 4 vols. New York: Macmillan, 1992.

Enders, Donald L. "Carthage Jail." In *Encyclopedia of Mormonism.* Edited by Daniel H. Ludlow. 4 vols. New York: Macmillan, 1992.

Ellsworth, Paul D. "Mobocracy and the Rule of Law: American Press Reaction to the Murder of Joseph Smith." *BYU Studies*, 20, No. 1, 1979.

Ford, Thomas. *A History of Illinois: From Its Commencement as a State in 1818 to 1847.* Chicago: S. C. Griggs, 1854.

Foster, Robert D. "A Testimony of the Past: Loda, Illinois, February 14, 1874." *True Latter Day Saints' Herald*, April 15, 1875.

Garr, Arnold K. "Joseph Smith: Campaign for President of the United States." *Ensign*, February 2009, 49–52.

Garr, Arnold K. "Joseph Smith: Mayor of Nauvoo." In *Mormon Historical Studies*, Vol. 3, No. 1. Provo, Utah: Brigham Young University, 2002.

Givens, George W. *In Old Nauvoo: Everyday Life in the City of Joseph.* Salt Lake City: Deseret Book, 1990.

BIBLIOGRAPHY

Godfrey, Kenneth W. "Council of Fifty." In *Encyclopedia of Mormonism*, vol. 1. New York: Macmillan Publishing, 1992.

Godfrey, Kenneth W. "Crime and Punishment in Mormon Nauvoo, 1839–1846." *BYU Studies*, 1992, 32:1, 195–228.

Guhleman, Henry V., M.D. "Governors suicide calls attention to mental illness." Missouri Department of Mental Health website. 2011. Retrieved 4 October 2013.

Hales, Brian C. *Joseph Smith's Polygamy: Volume 2: History*. Salt Lake City: Greg Kofford Books, 2013.

Hancock, Mosiah Lyman. *Autobiography 1834–1907*. Typescript, Brigham Young University. Compiled by Amy E. Baird, Victoria H. Jackson, and Laura L. Wassell (daughters of Mosiah Hancock). Available online.

Harmon, Henry M. *Journal History*, June 28, 1844. This statement given in the Historian's Office in Salt Lake City, April 14, 1857, Robert L. Campbell, Clerk.

Harris, Dennison L. "Verbal Statement of Bishop Dennison L. Harris to President Joseph F. Smith in the Presence of Elder Franklin Spener, at the house of Bishop Dorius of Ephraim, San Pete County, Utah, on Sunday Afternoon, May 15, 1881, and reported by George F. Gibbs." LDS Church Archives. Salt Lake City, Utah.

Hartley, William G. Missouri's. "1838 Extermination Order and the Mormons' forced Removal to Illinois." *Mormon Historical Studies*. Available online.

Hartley, William G. "The Saints' Forced Exodus from Missouri." In *Joseph Smith, the Prophet and Seer*. Edited by Richard Neitzel Holzapfel and Kent P. Jackson. Provo, Utah: Religious Studies Center, Brigham Young University; Salt Lake City: Deseret Book, 2010, 347–90.

Hedges, Andrew H., and Alex D. Smith. "Joseph Smith, John C. Bennett, and the Extradition Attempt." In *Joseph Smith, the Prophet and Seer*. Edited by Richard Neitzel Holzapfel and Kent P. Jackson. Provo, Utah: Religious Studies Center, Brigham Young University; Salt Lake City: Deseret Book, 2010.

Hedges, Andrew H., Alex D. Smith, and Richard Lloyd Anderson, eds. *Journals, Volume 2: December 1841–April 1843*. Vol. 2 of the Journals series of *The Joseph Smith Papers*. Edited by Dean C. Jessee, Ronald K. Esplin, and Richard Lyman Bushman. Salt Lake City: Church Historian's Press, 2011.

Higbee, Elias. Letter to Hyrum Smith, December 5, 1839, Washington City, "Corner Missouri and 3d Street." Joseph Smith Collection, Letterbook, 2, Church History Library.

Holland, Jeffrey R. "The Only True God and Jesus Christ Whom He Hath Sent." *Ensign*, November 2007, 40–42.

Holland, Jeffrey R. "The Will of the Father in All Things." BYU Speeches, January 17, 1989.

"John C. Bennett." An editorial published in *Times and Seasons,* Aug. 1, 1842; punctuation and grammar modernized. Joseph Smith was the editor of the periodical at the time.

Jenkins, Ryan C. "Quiet Slumber: Revelation through Dreams." *The Religious Educator*, publication of Brigham Young University: Provo Utah, 2011, 73–89.

Jessee, Dean C., Mark Ashurst-McGee, and Richard L. Jensen, eds. *Journals, Volume 1: 1832–1839.* Vol. 1 of the Journals series of *The Joseph Smith Papers,* edited by Dean C. Jessee, Ronald K. Esplin, and Richard Lyman Bushman. Salt Lake City: Church Historian's Press, 2008.

Jolley, Jerry C. "The Sting of the Wasp: Early Nauvoo Newspaper—April 1842 to April 1843." BYU Studies, 22:4, Fall 1982, 487–496.

Jones, Gracia N. *Emma and Joseph: Their Divine Mission.* American Fork, Utah: Covenant Communications, 1999.

Jones, Gracia N. "My Great-Great-Grandmother, Emma Hale Smith." *Ensign*, August 1992, 30–39.

Joseph Smith Papers. See website: http://josephsmithpapers.org/.

Journal of Discourses. 26 vols. London: Latter-Saints' Book Depot, 1854–86.

Kimball, Heber C. *Journal of Heber C. Kimball.* Salt Lake City, Deseret Book Company, copyright 1840.

Kimball, James L. Jr. "The Nauvoo Charter: A Reinterpretation." *Journal of the Illinois State Historical Society*, 54, Spring 1971, 66–78.

Laub, George. "George Laub's Nauvoo Journal." *BYU Studies*, 18, No. 2, 1978.

Leany, Isaac. "Biography of Isaac Leany, 1815–1873: Struggles of an 1847 Pioneer." In *Autobiography of Willaim Leany*, typescript. Harold B. Lee Library, Brigham Young University.

Leonard, Glenn M. Nauvoo: *A Place of Peace, A People of Promise.* Salt Lake City: Deseret Book Company, 2002.

Lyon, Joseph L., and David W. Lyon. "Physical Evidence at Carthage Jail and What It Reveals about the Assassination of Joseph and Hyrum Smith." *BYU Studies*, 47, no. 48, 2008.

Mace, Wandle. Journal of Wandle Mace, 1809–1846. Autobiography of Wandle Mace (As told to his wife, Rebecca E. Howell Mace), typescript. Harold B. Lee Library, Brigham Young University.

Madsen, Truman G. *Joseph Smith the Prophet.* Salt Lake City: Bookcraft, 1989.

Manscill, Craig K. and Derek R. Mock. " 'That Thy Days May Be Prolonged': Attempts on the Life of Joseph Smith." In *Joseph Smith and the Doctrinal Restoration.* Provo: Brigham Young University, Religious Studies Center, 2005, 253–71.

BIBLIOGRAPHY

Markham, Stephen. Letter from Stephen Markham to Wilford Woodruff. The Church of Jesus Christ of Latter Day Saints, Historian's Office: Personal Letter, Document Number: 103. Online: http://freepages.genealogy. rootsweb.ancestry.com/~sjensen/jensen/references/ref103.htm.

McConkie, Mark L. *Remembering Joseph: Personal Recollections of Those Who Knew the Prophet Joseph Smith.* Salt Lake City: Deseret Book Company, 2003.

Meacham, Jon. *American Lion: Andrew Jackson in the White House.* New York, New York: Random House, 2009.

Oaks, Dallin H. "Priesthood Blessings." *Ensign*, May 1987.

Oaks, Dallin H. and Marvin S. Hill. *Carthage Conspiracy: The Trial of the Accused Assassins of Joseph Smith.* Chicago: University of Illinois Press, 1975.

O'Driscoll, Jeffrey S. *Hyrum Smith: A Life Of Integrity.* Salt Lake City: Deseret Book, 2003.

Peace and Violence among 19th-Century Latter-day Saints. From Gospel topics on LDS.org. The Church of Jesus Christ of Latter-day Saints. Retrieved June 2014.

Pratt, Parley P. *Autobiography of Parley P. Pratt.* Salt Lake City: Deseret Book Company, 1985.

Quincy, Josiah. "Joseph Smith at Nauvoo." *Figures of the Past From the Leaves of Old Journals*, 3, Boston, 1883, 376-400.

Rau, Allan and Susan. *Thomas Sharp and the Warsaw Signal.* May 21, 2013. Paper submitted for Seminaries and Institutes Midwestern Church History Workshop. The Allans presented the paper July 2013.

Rawson, Glenn and Lyman, Dennis. *The Mormon Wars.* American Fork, Utah: Covenant Communications, 2014.

Regional Studies in LDS History: Missouri. Various authors. Salt Lake City: Deseret Book Company, 1994.

Reynolds, John. *My Own Times: Embracing Also the History of My Life.* Chicago: Fergus Printing, 1879.

Rich, Mary A. Phelps. "The Life of Mary A. Rich" (Autobiography). Typescript available at Harold B. Lee Library, Brigham Young University, Provo, Utah.

Richards, Willard. "Two Minutes in Jail." *Times and Seasons*, Vol. 5, No. 14, 1 August 1844, 598–99. From the *Nauvoo Neighbor.*

Roberts, B. H. *The Life of John Taylor.* Salt Lake City: Deseret Book Company, 1963.

Robinson, Joseph Lee. *The Journal of Joseph Lee Robinson: Mormon Pioneer* (1811–1893). Published journal scanned by David and Joni Nielsen. Formatted as an ebook by Kevin Merrell.

Sainsbury, Derek. *The Cadre for the Kingdom: A collective biography of the electioneer missionaries of Joseph Smith's 1844 presidential campaign.* Doctoral Dissertation: University of Utah, 2011.

Schindler, Harold. *Orrin Porter Rockwell: Man of God, Son of Thunder.* Salt Lake City: University of Utah Press, 1966.

Shurtleff, Stella and Brent Farrington Cahoon, eds. "Autobiography William Farrington Cahoon." In *Reynolds Cahoon and His Stalwart Sons.* Salt Lake City, Utah: Paragon Press, 1960.

Skinner, Andrew C. "The Impact of the Doctrinal Restoration: How the World Was Different after Joseph Smith." In *Joseph Smith and the Doctrinal Restoration.* Provo: Brigham Young University, Religious Studies Center, 2005, 9–33.

Smith, Emma. "Virtue Will Triumph." *Nauvoo Neighbor*, March 20, 1844.

Smith, George D., ed. *An Intimate Chronicle: The Journals of William Clayton.* Salt Lake City: Signature Books, 1995.

Smith, Heman. *Journal of History; October 1916.* Publication of the Reorganized Church of Jesus Christ of Latter-day Saints: Lamoni, Iowa.

Smith, Henry A. *The Day They Martyred the Prophet.* Salt Lake City: Bookcraft Publishers, 1963.

Smith, Joseph. *History of the Church of Jesus Christ of Latter-day Saints.* Edited by B. H. Roberts. 2d ed. Rev. 7 vols. Salt Lake City: The Church of Jesus Christ of Latter-day Saints, 1932–51. Reprinted by Deseret Book, 1974.

Smith, Joseph. *Teachings of Presidents of the Church: Joseph Smith.* Salt Lake City: The Church of Jesus Christ of Latter-day Saints, 2007.

Smith, Joseph. *The Personal Writings of Joseph Smith.* Edited by Dean C. Jesse. Salt Lake City: Deseret Book, 1984. http://www.gospelink.com/library/contents/256.

Smith, Joseph. *The Words of Joseph Smith.* Edited by Andrew F. Ehat and Lyndon W. Cook. Provo, Utah: Religious Studies Center, Brigham Young University, 1980.

Smith, Joseph III. *The Memoirs of President Joseph Smith III (1832–1914).* Independence: Herald Publishing House, 1979.

Smith, Joseph Fielding. *Teachings of the Prophet Joseph Smith.* Salt Lake City: Deseret Book Company, 1976.

Smith, Lucy Mack. *History of the Prophet Joseph Smith by His Mother.* Edited by Preston Nibley. Salt Lake City: Deseret Book, 1958.

Snow, Lorenzo. *Teachings of Presidents of the Church: Lorenzo Snow.* Salt Lake City: The Church of Jesus Christ of Latter-day Saints, 2012.

Stoddard, Sarah. *Journal of Sarah Stoddard (1805–1846).* Diary in family possession. Online at "Book of Abraham Project." Brigham Young University, Provo Utah.

BIBLIOGRAPHY

Stuy, Brian H. *Joseph F. Smith.* In a compilation of Collected Discourses. Burbank, California: B. H. S. Publishing, 1987.

Swinton, Heidi S. *American Prophet: The Story of Joseph Smith.* PBS Documentary, 1999.

Talmage, James E. *The House of the Lord.* Salt Lake City: The Church of Jesus Christ of Latter-day Saints, original text 1912; republished for Church employee distribution, 2013.

Thiriot, Amy Tanner. "Cyrus Hubbard Wheelock: In Desert, On Mountain, On Land, or On Sea." *Keepapitchinin,* November 27, 2012. Retrieved January 18, 2014.

Thurston, Morris A. "The Boggs Shooting and Attempted Extradition." In *BYU Studies,* Vol. 48, Number 1, 2009.

Times and Season. November 1839–February 1846. A twice-monthly publication in Nauvoo. Available online, http://www.centerplace.org/history/ts/.

Turley Richard E Jr. and Brittany A. Chapman. *Women of Faith.* Vol 1. Salt Lake City: Deseret Book, 2011.

Vale, Van. "The Doctrinal Impact of the King Follet Discourse. In *BYU Studies,* Vol. 18, No 2, 1978.

Valletta, Thomas R., general editor. *Great American Documents for Latter-day Saint Families.* Salt Lake City: Deseret Book, 2011.

Valletta, Thomas R. Personal discussions and email correspondence in fall of 2013 concerning Joseph Smith's 2 Corinthians 11 discourse on May 26, 1844.

Van Wagoner, Richard S. *Mormon Polygamy: A History.* Salt Lake City: Signature Books, 1986), 48; citing Robinson, Journal, 23–24.

Van Wagoner, Richard S. (1986), "Sarah Pratt: The Shaping of an Apostate." *Dialogue: A Journal of Mormon Thought,* 1986, 19, 2.

Van Wagoner, Richard S. *Sidney Rigdon: A Portrait of Religious Excess.* Salt Lake City: Signature Books, 1994.

Walker, Jeffrey N. "Early Nineteenth-Century Mormonism: Joseph Smith's Legal Bulwark for Personal Freedom." BYU Education Week, 2013.

Walker, Jeffrey N. "Mormon Land Rights in Caldwell and Daviess Counties and the Mormon Conflict of 1838: New Findings and New Understandings." In *BYU Studies,* 47, no. 1, 2008. Available online.

Walker Jeffrey N. "A Change of Venue: Joseph Smith's Escape from Liberty Jail." *The Foundation for Apologetic Information and Research,* August 2007 Conference.

Sharp, Thomas C. *Warsaw Signal,* June 11, 1844. Transcript of papers can be found online at http://www.sidneyrigdon.com/dbroadhu/IL/sign1844.htm#0611.

Webster, Noah. *An American Dictionary of the English Language.* New York: S. Convers, 1828. Reprint, San Francisco: Foundation for American Christian Education, 1980.

Welch, John W. *A Chronology of the Life of Joseph Smith.* BYU Studies, Vol. 46, No. 4, 2007.

Whitney, Helen Mar. *Woman' View: Helen Mar Whitney's Reminiscences of Early Church History.* Salt Lake City: Deseret Book, 1997.

Winder, Michael K. *Presidents and Prophets: The Story of America's Presidents and the LDS Church.* American Fork, Utah: Covenants Communications, 2007.

Writing of Early Latter-Day Saints. Various Authors. Salt Lake City, Utah: Deseret Book, 2013.

ABOUT THE AUTHOR

RYAN C. JENKINS has been a student of the life and teachings of Joseph Smith for nearly twenty-five years. After obtaining his Master of Education from Weber State University in 2004, Ryan began writing opinion pieces for Northern Utah newspapers on family, freedom, politics, and religion. He was a blogger on the subject of faith for two years; many of his posts were featured on realclearreligion.org. He was also an associate editor for *Great American Documents for Latter-day Saint Families* (2012). Professionally, he has experience in business, public relations, and religious education. He has been teaching and writing for eighteen years. Ryan and his wife, Melissa, have six children. They reside in Columbia, Missouri. Find out more at ryancjenkins.com.

0 26575 16492 3